OECD Public Governance Reviews

Brazil's Federal Court of Accounts

INSIGHT AND FORESIGHT FOR BETTER GOVERNANCE

OECD

BETTER POLICIES FOR BETTER LIVES

This work is published under the responsibility of the Secretary-General of the OECD. The opinions expressed and arguments employed herein do not necessarily reflect the official views of OECD member countries.

This document and any map included herein are without prejudice to the status of or sovereignty over any territory, to the delimitation of international frontiers and boundaries and to the name of any territory, city or area.

Please cite this publication as:
OECD (2017), *Brazil's Federal Court of Accounts: Insight and Foresight for Better Governance*, OECD Public Governance Reviews, OECD Publishing, Paris.
http://dx.doi.org/10.1787/9789264279247-en

ISBN 978-92-64-27923-0 (print)
ISBN 978-92-64-27925-4 (PDF)
ISBN 978-92-64-27924-7 (epub)

Series: OECD Public Governance Reviews
ISSN 2219-0406 (print)
ISSN 2219-0414 (online)

The statistical data for Israel are supplied by and under the responsibility of the relevant Israeli authorities. The use of such data by the OECD is without prejudice to the status of the Golan Heights, East Jerusalem and Israeli settlements in the West Bank under the terms of international law.

Photo credits: Cover © Lisa Kolbasa/Shutterstock.com; © Castor & Pollux/thenounproject.com; © Jacob Melton/thenounproject.com; © Faisalovers/thenounproject.com; © Ed Gray/thenounproject.com.

Corrigenda to OECD publications may be found on line at: *www.oecd.org/publishing/corrigenda*.

Foreword

Brazil's supreme audit institution (SAI), the Tribunal de Contas da União (TCU), has a distinctive mandate to shape the underpinnings of good governance. TCU is responsible for examining public accounts to hold officials accountable, and its performance audits and evaluations have a direct bearing on the effectiveness, efficiency and economy of government. In this role, TCU is a critical inducer of change in the Brazilian government towards better governance in a complex and fluid policy environment.

The objective evidence, recommendations and advice that are a result of TCU's work are critical inputs for informed policy making, more effective programme implementation, and ultimately, better outcomes for citizens. This role is crucial given the governance challenges Brazil currently faces. Brazil's tax revenue and public expenditure are high amongst Latin American and Caribbean and OECD member countries. Nonetheless, low trust and satisfaction among citizens, fanned by corruption scandals and under-performing programmes, signals the need for a greater understanding about underlying problems and opportunities for improvement. TCU, as a purveyor of insight and foresight into the root of challenges and potential solutions, can play a vital role in improving how government works to restore citizens' trust.

This report advances the premise that successful policy outcomes depend on not only effective implementation, but also on the policy-making process itself to ensure the coherence, sustainability and long-term vision of the public sector. The report draws from OECD and TCU's collaboration on the role of SAIs in contributing to good governance, culminating in the flagship publication, "Supreme Audit Institutions and Good Governance: Oversight, Insight and Foresight," which demonstrates how SAIs can more effectively contribute to good governance across the policy cycle. This report assesses how TCU can leverage its unique and horizontal view to induce changes in how policies are designed, implemented and evaluated.

To do so effectively requires TCU to orient aspects of its work towards understanding how the Centre of Government (CoG) – central entities in the executive branch responsible for policy making – can more effectively foster coherence, efficiency and standardisation across government. For instance, TCU could identify areas of fragmentation, overlap and duplication of programmes that can lead to waste and inefficiency across government. It could also employ its horizontal perspective to strengthen long-term planning, sustainable budgeting and evaluation of national goals, including improved co-ordination of key actors.

Elaborating on this concept, the report focuses on four key governance functions that are critical to both the design and execution of policies that can improve the fiscal, economic, social and environmental conditions within Brazil, namely: 1) mechanisms for policy coherence, 2) strategic and sustainable budgeting, 3) effective internal control and risk management and 3) meaningful evaluation that leads to improvements in policies and programmes.

The Executive Branch takes the lead on these functions in both design and implementation. Yet, TCU can take steps to ensure that its audit and advisory work offer sound evidence and insights to strengthen governance processes.

Acknowledgements

This report was led and drafted by Gavin Ugale and Alison McMeekin, with the guidance and support of numerous individuals within OECD's Public Governance and Territorial Development Directorate, including Rolf Alter, Director, Luiz de Mello, Deputy Director, Janos Bertok, Head of the Public Sector Integrity Division and Julio Bacio Terracino, Deputy Head of the Public Sector Integrity Division, and Ronnie Downes, Deputy Head of the Budgeting and Public Expenditures Division. Valuable support was provided by William Begley, Thibaut Gigou, Meral Gedik and Laura McDonald (Public Sector Integrity Division). Erin McLaughlin Villas, an independent consultant, provided critical insights for the section on data analytics.

This report contributes to a 3-year collaboration with Brazil's Tribunal de Contas da União (TCU) to support supreme audit institutions (SAIs) and TCU to induce better governance through audits, evaluations and advisory work. The OECD thanks the Ministers, management, auditors and staff of TCU for their contributions to this report as well as the broader community of SAIs. In addition, the OECD extends its appreciation and gratitude to TCU President Raimundo Carreiro, as well as former TCU Presidents Minister Aroldo Cedraz (2015-2016) and Minister Augusto Nardes (2013-2014), for their insights and leadership throughout the various phases of this ongoing collaboration. The OECD would also like to thank the Ministers who provided input during interviews and consultations, ensuring that the OECD's consultative approach reached all levels of the TCU. This includes President Raimundo Carreio, Minister Aroldo Cedraz, Minister Augusto Nardes, Minister Benjamin Zymler, Minister José Múcio, Minister André Luis de Carvalho, substitute-Minister Marcos Bemquerer and substitute-Minister Weder de Oliveira.

This project would not have been possible without the unwavering efforts of TCU's core team, to whom the OECD expresses its deepest thanks. Claúdio Souza Castello Branco, Secretary-General of External Control; Rainério Rodrigues Leite Secretary-General of the Presidency; Felício Ribas Torres Joint Secretary-General of the Presidency; Marcelo Barros Gomes, Coordinator-General for Social Policies Issues; Luis Aktutsu, Coordinator-General for Public Efficiency ; Leonardo Rodrigues Albernaz, Head of the Department of Government Macro Analysis; Ana Paula Silva da Silva, Head of the Department of External Control - State Management; Dagomar Henriques Lima, Head of the Department of Methods and Support for External Control; and to the committed Federal Government Auditors of TCU, including Rodrigo Araujo Vieira, Leonardo Naves Sousa, Cristina Monken Mascarenhas and Maridel Piloto de Noronha.

The OECD also thanks over 80 TCU staff who offered insights during a week-long workshop in May 2016 in Brasilia. This report's analysis of the interaction between the TCU and key governance functions in Brazil also benefitted from the inputs of dozens of representatives of Brazil's Executive Office of the President of Brazil (*Casa Civil da Presidência da Republica*), Ministry of Finance (*Ministério da Fazenda, MF*), Ministry of Planning, Development and Management (*Ministério do Planejamento, Desenvolvimento e Gestão*) and the Ministry of

Transparency, Supervision and Comptroller General of the Union (*Ministério da Transparência, Fiscalização e Controladoria-Geral da União*). We thank them for their open participation in annual events with the TCU and OECD and insights provided between 2013 and 2016.

The enclosed recommendations made to TCU are rooted in good practices found in the comparative framework, "Supreme Audit Institutions and Good Governance: Oversight, Insight and Foresight" (OECD, 2016). Over a dozen leading SAIs supported this project throughout the last three years. For their invaluable contributions, the OECD expresses gratitude for colleagues at the SAIs of Canada, Chile, the European Union, France, Korea, Mexico, the Netherlands, Poland, Portugal, South Africa and the United States. We also thank our colleagues from Australia, Belgium, Costa Rica, Denmark, Sweden and the United Kingdom for their consultations. The OECD remains committed to supporting SAIs, and bringing together all branches of government, for improving governance through shared insights and mutual learning.

Table of contents

Tables

Figures

Boxes

Acronyms and abbreviations

ANAO	Australian National Audit Office
CBA	Central Budget Authority
CCCI	Internal Control Co-ordination Commission (*Comissão de Coordenação de Controle Interno*)
CGU	Ministry of Transparency, Supervision and Comptroller General of the Union (formerly known as *Controladoria-Geral da União*)
CMO	Joint Committee of Plans, Public Budgets and Auditing of the bicameral Congress (*Comissão Mista de Planos, Orçamentos Públicos e Fiscalização*)
COAG	Council of Australian Governments
CoG	Centre of Government
COSO	Committee of the Sponsoring Organisation of the Treadway Commission
CPR	TCU's audit of the fiscal year (*Contas do Presidente da República*)
FOD	Fragmentation, Overlap and Duplication
LRF	Fiscal Responsibility Law (*Lei de Responsabilidade Fiscal*)
GAO	US Government Accountability Office
IDB	Inter-American Development Bank
IFI	Independent Fiscal Institution
IIA	Institute of Internal Auditors
IMF	International Monetary Fund
INTOSAI	International Organisation of Supreme Audit Institutions
ISSAI	International Standards for Supreme Audit Institutions
LAC	Latin and Caribbean (region)
LDO	Budgetary Guidelines Law (*Lei de Diretrizes Orçamentárias*)
LOA	Annual Budget Law (*Lei Orçamentária Annual*)
LRF	Fiscal Responsibility Law (*Lei de Responsabilidade Fiscal*)
MF	Ministry of Finance (*Ministério da Fazenda, MF*)
MPF	Federal Public Ministry (*Ministério Público Federal*, MPF)
MP	Ministry of Planning, Development and Management (*Ministério do Planejamento, Desenvolvimento e Gestão*)
MTEF	Medium-term expenditure framework
MTFF	Medium Term Fiscal Framework
NAO	National Audit Office (UK)

OAG	Office of the Auditor General (Canada)
OECD	Organisation for Economic Co-operation and Development
OLACEFS	La Organización Latinoamericana y del Caribe de Entidades Fiscalizadoras Superiores (*Organisation of Latin American and Caribbean Supreme Audit Institutions*)
PAC	Growth Acceleration Plan (*Programa de Aceleração do Crescimento*)
PEFA	Public Expenditure and Financial Accountability (*Framework of*)
PET	TCU's Strategic Plan (*Plano Estratégico do Tribunal*)
PMIMF	Integrated modernisation plan (*Programa de Modernizacão Integrada do Ministério da Fazenda*)
PNE	National Education Plan (*Plano Nacional de Educação*)
PPA	Multi-annual plan (*Plano Pluriannual*)
RAP	Budgetary carry-over (*Restos a Pagar*)
SAG	Under-Secretary for Monitoring and Assessment of Government Policies (*Subchefia de Análise e Acompanhamento de Políticas Governamentais*, SAG).
SAGI	Secretariat of Evaluation and Information Management (*Secretaria de Avaliação e Gestão da Informação*)
SAI	Supreme Audit Institution
SDG	Sustainable Development Goals
SECCOR	Department of Institutional Relations on Fight Against Fraud and Corruption (*Secretaria de Relações Institucionais no Combate à Fraude e Corrupção*)
SEGECEX	Secretary General of External Control (*Secretária-Geral de Controle Externo*)
SEGEP	Secretary for Public Management (*Secretaria de Gestão Pública*)
SEMAG	Secretary of Governmental Macro-Evaluation (*Secretaria de Macroavaliação Governamental*)
SIGPLAN	Management and Planning Information System, (*Sistema de Informaçõoes Gerenciais e de Planejamento*)
SIMEC	Integrated Monitoring, Execution and Control System (*Sistema Integrado de Monitoramento, Execução e Controle*)
SIOP	Integrated Planning and Budget System (*Sistema Integrado de Planejamento e Orçamento*)
SOF	Federal Budget Secretariat (*Secretaria de Orçamento Federal*)
STCP	Secretariat of Transparency and Corruption Prevention (*Secretaria de Transparência e Prevenção da Corrupção*)
STLI	Logistics and Information Technology Secretariat (SLTI) of the Ministry of Planning, Development and Management (*Ministério do Planejamento, Desenvolvimento e Gestão*, MP)
STN	Secretariat of the National Treasury (*Secretaria do Tesouro Nacional*)
TCU	Tribunal de Contas da União (do Brasil) (*The Supreme Audit Institution of Brazil*)

Brazil's Federal Court of Accounts
Insight and Foresight for Better Governance

Executive summary

Supreme audit institutions (SAIs) have a unique mandate in government for ensuring that policies are well-informed, coherent and forward-looking. In the last decades, many SAIs have embraced a role that goes beyond traditional oversight and holding governments accountable for public expenditures. These SAIs have become critical purveyors of insight and foresight for policy makers through new approaches to audits and advisory work. Their evolution reflects a drive towards more informed policy making, particularly within the Centre of Government (CoG), as well as evidence-based programme delivery to ensure citizens' needs are met.

This report highlights opportunities for Brazil's Federal Court of Accounts, the Tribunal de Contas da União (TCU), to strengthen its capacity to support good governance through its audits, evaluations, supervisory proceedings and co-ordination across the public sector. TCU is well-advanced in this area, yet opportunities remain for it to further integrate principles and concepts of good governance into its audits and other areas of work. Chapter 1 describes over-arching institutional challenges and actions TCU can take to lead by example and improve its own governance, including the following:

1.1. TCU could ensure that the formulation of its strategic plans enable it to tackle systemic and emerging risks to society over the medium and long-term;

1.2. TCU could continue strengthening its capacity and internal co-ordination to improve its horizontal view on cross-cutting issues and remain responsive to emerging risks; and

1.3. TCU could enhance its monitoring and evaluation techniques in order to generate, measure and communicate financial and non-financial impacts of cross-cutting audit activities.

Chapters 2 through 5, described below, look to TCU's audit environment and illustrate how TCU could better support four governance areas that present some of the most pressing challenges for the Brazilian government, including: 1) creation of policy coherence, 2) strategic and sustainable budgeting, 3) internal control and risk management and 4) monitoring and evaluation.

Auditing for greater policy coherence and co-ordination across Brazil's federal government

The size and complexity of Brazil's government, which involves numerous entities with decision-making authority at the federal level, poses challenges to ensuring coherence and co-ordination in the formulation, implementation and evaluation of policies and programmes. The government has made some efforts to improve in this area, and TCU has looked at institutional mechanisms for promoting coherence and assessing the role of the

CoG to strengthen coherence in government. Building on these efforts, OECD recommends the following:

2.1. TCU could more systematically assess institutional mechanisms for coherence, including the capacities of audited entities to constructively communicate and co-ordinate with entities relevant to the achievement of interrelated policy goals; and

2.2. TCU could develop a body of audit work to assess policy interactions and policy effects across government, beginning with a pilot review of fragmentation, overlap and duplication of programmes in key sectors.

Auditing for a more strategic and sustainable budget

The budget is a critical policy document, as it lays out objectives, multi-year priorities and resource allocations. In Brazil, policy makers in charge of proposed budgetary reforms, which focus on greater fiscal responsibility and limiting expenditure, will require objective information about the effectiveness and efficiency of policies and programmes. TCU has been active in this space, including audits of Brazil's budget system. To help ensure a more sustainable and strategic budget in Brazil, the OECD recommends the following:

3.1. TCU could encourage more meaningful medium-term perspectives in the budget by (a) auditing overall performance of multi-year sectoral plans, and (b) highlighting key findings on the alignment of annual budgetary allocations with multi-annual priorities;

3.2. TCU could help to improve the reliability of evidence and information for making performance-based budgetary decisions through assessments of key areas, such as expenditure programmes funded by earmarks and the effectiveness of operational cost measurement;

3.3. TCU could enhance its contributions to the dialogue on fiscal discipline by periodically assessing in-year progress reports to discern how adjustments to fiscal targets and plans affect the achievement of goals; and

3.4. TCU could further assess whether adequate institutional procedures and safeguards are in place to ensure the quality, reliability and sustainability of budget forecasts and medium-term projections.

Auditing for a stronger internal control system and risk management function

A key function of good governance is an internal control system and risk management function that supports government in the achievement of its policy objectives. In Brazil, the internal control system is continually evolving, yet recent corruption scandals and places greater urgency for continued and lasting change towards a culture of integrity in the Brazilian government. To support a strong internal control system and risk management:

4.1. TCU could strengthen the effectiveness and consistency of internal control and risk management approaches across government by identifying and communicating systemic and high-risk areas for central entities to address;

4.2. TCU could induce managers to overcome implementation challenges for further institutionalising key risk management and control activities; and

4.3. TCU could strengthen the capacity of government to prevent fraud and corruption through audits and guidance that ensure the effectiveness of policies and use of tools, such as data analytics.

Auditing for more effective and efficient government-wide monitoring and evaluation

Monitoring and evaluation (M&E) is a management tool to create and use evidence for better policy making. M&E in Brazil is decentralised, and guidance has historically pertained to evaluations in the context of the multi-annual plan. The 2016 establishment of the Monitoring and Evaluation Committee of Federal Public Policies, is a step forward; however, there is still a need for more systematic and higher-quality information on the results of programmes. OECD recommends the following:

5.1. TCU could strengthen the effectiveness of M&E across government by further emphasising the role of the CoG and the need to further standardise results-based management;

5.2. TCU could induce improvements in institutional and programme evaluations by auditing entities' readiness, capacity and indicators to manage for results; and

5.3. TCU could assess the communication and coordination mechanisms, including interoperability of information and data systems, to improve M&E of cross-cutting government policies and programmes.

Brazil's Federal Court of Accounts
Insight and Foresight for Better Governance

Chapter 1

Strengthening the contributions of TCU to good governance in Brazil

Supreme audit institutions (SAIs) face a demanding auditing environment, where governance challenges persist and consistently present new risks. In this context, SAIs must remain flexible and responsive to changes and emerging risks in their own planning and auditing. This chapter explores opportunities for the Tribunal de Contas da União (TCU), Brazil's SAI, to make improvements to its own strategy and operations in order to more effectively contribute to good governance in Brazil. This includes a greater focus on the institutional characteristics that position TCU to better support the policy cycle – formulation, implementation and evaluation – with evidenced-based solutions and insights that focus on long-term policy outcomes. This chapter explores steps that TCU can take to ensure it systematically upholds the principles of good governance in its own work, including its strategies, audit programming and internal mechanisms for monitoring and evaluation.

1.1. Introduction

In recent years, Brazil has experienced high tax revenues and spending, yet citizen satisfaction and trust in government remains low. There are opportunities for entities across the federal government to be more accountable to citizens by creating policies and programmes that use public resources responsibly. In addition, addressing governance challenges requires evidenced-based solutions and an openness to improve approaches across the policy cycle. The Tribunal de Contas da União (TCU), as Brazil's SAI, plays a central role in this process, supporting policy makers and government managers to adopt policies that are effective, efficient and economical.

SAIs, regardless of their model, can contribute to more evidence-based policy making and improvements in governance. For instance, the United States Government Accountability Office (Westminster model) offers insights to reduce duplication, fragmentation and overlap in government. Portugal's Court of Accounts (Court model) reviewed the adequacy of internal audit and control in state-owned enterprises, leading to a more systematic establishment of audit boards. The Netherlands Court of Audit (Board model) compared the quality of underlying assumptions of budgetary decisions to point to the inability of a government merger to reap the expected financial gains. TCU makes its own unique contributions to good governance, as described in subsequent sections.

The International Standards for Supreme Audit Institutions (ISSAI) highlights how SAIs can be responsive to changing environments and emerging risks, including risk assessments of the audit environment and developing a work programme that is responsive to society's changing needs (ISSAI 12) (INTOSAI, 2013a). This chapter discusses how TCU can more closely align its work with ISSAI 12 and the selected international principles below, chosen for their pertinence to an SAI's contributions to better governance in a complex policy making environment with cross-cutting issues. Particularly relevant principles for this chapter include:

- Demonstrating ongoing relevance to citizens, Parliament and other stakeholders by being responsive to changing environments and emerging risks (Principle 5);
- Enabling those charged with public sector governance to discharge their responsibilities in responding to audit findings and recommendations and taking appropriate corrective action (principle 3);
- Being a credible source of independent and objective insight and guidance to support beneficial change in the public sector (4) and communicating effectively with stakeholders (6).

This chapter assesses TCU's current activities in relation to these principles, and suggests opportunities for maximising TCU's contributions to more efficient, effective and economic policy making in Brazil. In general, the chapter illustrates how TCU has a strategic planning process that is forward-looking and comprehensive, but opportunities remain for further operationalising concepts of good governance and ensuring that TCU operations are well aligned with the highest governance risks.

1.2. Overview: Good governance in Brazil and the role of TCU

Good governance through better policies, programmes and services in Brazil

To understand how TCU can better contribute to good governance, it is first necessary to define the term for purposes of this report. "Good governance" is the optimisation of the institutional arrangements and processes used to formulate, implement and deliver policies, programmes and services to benefit citizens and society. It is the determinant of policy outcomes that bear impact on economic growth, productivity, equality and environmental management, amongst other areas needed for overall well-bring. Good governance assures that the mechanisms driving the policy cycle in formulation, implementation, and monitoring and evaluation are operating effectively, efficiently and economically, and are underpinned by broader governance principles such as rule of law, transparency, integrity and accountability (OECD, 2016a).

Improving policy-making processes towards good governance, and thus outcomes, relies on a whole-of-government approach from actors across branches of power, as well as civil society. This refers to the institutional structures and networks that enable the state to achieve coherence in strategy, policy and purpose, without inefficiencies, fragmentation, redundancies and overlaps. It requires adequate systems of co-ordination and checks and balances. This includes a strategically agile Centre of Government (CoG), a functioning Legislature and independent external and internal control. Collectively, over time, entities that make up the CoG should articulate and implement a long term, big-picture strategic vision for the country aimed at sustaining prosperity and well-being for its citizens, the economy and society.

A spotlight on the Centre of Government and co-ordinated approaches to good governance

To ensure that public expenditure is used to drive improvements in economic and social outcomes, the CoG has a unique position and responsibility for co-ordinating government to this end. The CoG is the administrative structure that serves the Executive (President or Prime Minister, and the Cabinet collectively). Often the CoG is made up of more than one unit, fulfilling different functions. The CoG can include other core institutions at the "Centre" that directly support whole-of-government functioning, and usually exercise some oversight of ministries' activities.[1] CoGs in OECD member countries fell into the spotlight during fiscal and economic crises of the last decade. In a context of multidimensional policy issues, CoGs are increasingly responsible to ensure a more co-ordinated approach to governance (OECD, 2014a).

In Brazil, the institutions that generally constitute the CoG consist of the Presidency (*Casa Civil*), the Ministry of Finance (*Ministério da Fazenda*, MF) and the Ministry of Planning, Development and Management (*Ministério do Planejamento, Desenvolvimento e Gestão*, MP) (TCU, 2016a). Within the MF and MP, there are specialised secretariats and units that are responsible for steering and policy setting related to different governance functions. For instance, within the MP, the Federal Budget Secretariat formulates the annual budget proposal and in the MF, the National Treasury Secretariat takes the lead on the accounting and control of the budget execution. The role of the CoG in particular policy functions is explored in this report to understand how TCU can use audit and advisory work to strengthen the centre's effectiveness and efficiency (OECD, 2014a).

In 2014, Brazil's government effectiveness was rated the low score of 47/100, a trend that is worsening with political and economic crises (World Bank, 2014). Given the substantial sum of money dedicated to high priority areas like education and health, mentioned below, improving effectiveness and efficiency of government expenditure can have a significant impact on the overall development of the country and the quality of life for the average Brazilian. Particularly in the face of fiscal austerity and persistent economic recession, policy makers need to know what works and what does not in order to ensure quality delivery of services. For this, meaningful monitoring and evaluation should feed into policy formulation so that entities can adjust for improvements.

Interconnected policy challenges, and "wicked problems,"[2] require governments to ensure communication and co-ordination as well as budget sustainability to implement solutions over the medium and long-term. For example, Brazilian citizens indicated, in 2016, that protecting the environment is a priority social issue to be resolved (Edelman, 2016). Improvements have been made in environmental protection, but successes are impeded by a lack of coherence between key sectors for environmental protection, including water and agricultural sectors (OECD, 2015a; Sabogal et al, 2016). Cross-governmental, sustainable and inclusive action is needed for other complex issues, such as public safety, population ageing, climate change and continued eradication of poverty in Brazil. Moreover, the complexity of the Sustainable Development Goals (SDGs) will challenge governments to better understand the spill over effects of certain policies on others.

In Brazil, tax revenue is high but citizen satisfaction and trust in government is low

In recent years, policy making in Brazil has been characterised largely by high tax revenue and increases in public expenditure, particularly in social areas. Tax revenues constitute 33.4% of Brazil's GDP in 2014, the highest of all Latin American and Caribbean countries (OECD, 2016d). Brazil's public administration has had a high level of public expenditure in recent years, as exemplified by select sectors. For instance, Brazil's expenditure on educational institutions rose as a percentage of GDP by 4% between 2010 and 2012, while the average in OECD countries was a decrease of 3% (OECD 2016d). By 2016, Brazil's investments in educational institutions amounted to 5.6% of the GDP, with an OECD average of 5.3% (OECD 2016d).[3] Health spending and social security contributions have also claimed a large share of public expenditure, constituting 8.2% (World Bank, 2015) and 8.7% of GDP, in 2014 respectfully, while the latter average in the Latin American and Caribbean region was 3.7% (OECD, 2016d).

Nonetheless, increases in spending have not always led to perceived improvements in service delivery. Despite the increases in expenditure in particular areas citizen satisfaction has decreased with both education and health more than ten percentage points from 2007-2014, to 45% and 32% respectively (OECD, 2015b). Moreover, levels of education and skills are lower, on average, in Brazil than in OECD member countries, including Mexico and Chile, despite Brazil's higher investment in education (Figure 1.1). Brazil has higher than average 'life satisfaction'[4] and is at par with OECD member countries for civic engagement and governance (Figure 1.1).

A state that is responsive to citizens' needs ensures that its functions and supporting activities are working well. Effective governance arrangements can restore citizens' trust in their government's ability to develop and implement policies that lead to sustainable and inclusive growth. It can also position governments to address weaknesses, at the roots, that are uncovered during crisis moments. This means demonstrating value for money – or effectiveness, efficiency and economy – with limited public resources to deliver the best possible outcomes (OECD, 2016a).

Figure 1.1. **OECD Better Life Index in Brazil (2015)**

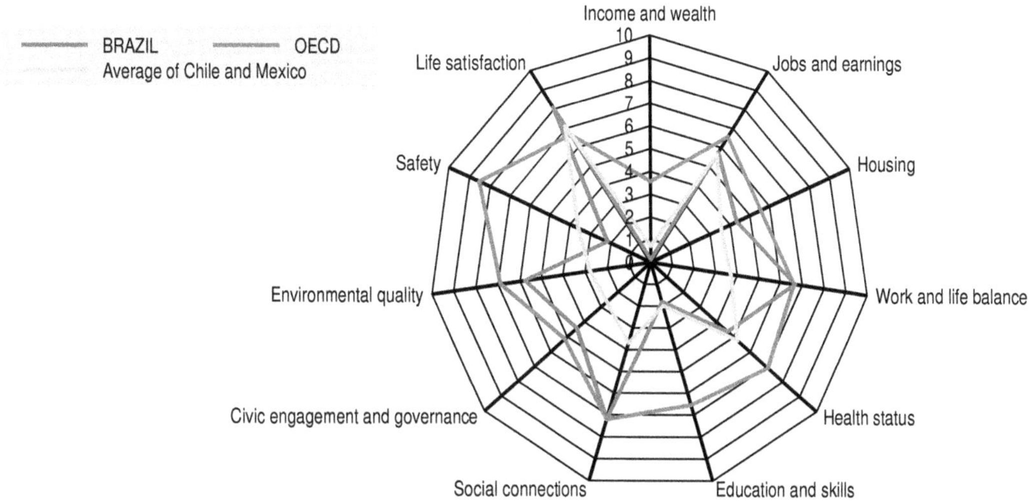

Source: OECD (2016d), «Better Life Index 2015», *OECD Social and Welfare Statistics* (database), OECD Publishing, Paris *http://dx.doi.org/10.1787/data-00823-en* as cited in OECD (2015c), *OECD Economic Surveys: Brazil 2015*, OECD Publishing, Paris *http://dx.doi.org/10.1787/eco_surveys-bra-2015-en*.

In addition, OECD experiences show that restoring trust in government is important for strengthening integrity in society, such as paying taxes, promoting adherence to regulations and fostering greater public security (OECD, 2015b). From 2014-2015, Brazil's rating in the Corruption Perception Index decreased from 43 to 38, which constituted the biggest deterioration in public trust on the index that year (TI, 2015). This decline in trust coincides with a fall in the legitimacy of the state from 5.1 in 2015 to 5.9 on the 2016 Fragile State Index (FFP, 2016). Trust in government also can affect investment opportunities that come with a more stable, transparent and productive public administration. Optimising government arrangements and processes is important in the face of mistrust in government.

Through their audits, evaluations and advisory work, of cross-cutting issues in particular, SAIs can play a critical role in restoring citizens' trust in government. Constitutionally independent from the executive branch, SAIs bring a unique horizontal view of the functioning of government. As demonstrated in OECD's report, "Supreme Audit Institutions and good governance: Oversight, Insight and Foresight" (2016) SAIs are using this vantage point to assess policy-making processes at every stage of the policy cycle: formulation, implementation and evaluation. To do so effectively requires high-level commitment, as well as strategic and operational changes within an SAI. This chapter focuses on recommendations (see Table 1.1) for TCU to ensure its relevance and responsiveness to a changing environment, and to remain a credible source of information for citizens, auditees and decision-makers.

Table 1.1. **Summary of recommendations: Strengthening TCU's contributions to good governance**

TCU could ensure that the formulation of its strategic plans enable it to tackle systemic and emerging risks to society over the medium and long-term.

- TCU could further and more systematically integrate medium and long-term policy issues into its new risk-based approach to audit programming to ensure that its activities are responsive to society's needs and aligned with TCU's strategic plans.
- TCU could ensure that audits integrate governance elements, and serve as a vehicle to collect information on broader governance issues and national goals that are systematic and cross-cutting.

TCU could continue strengthening its capacity and internal co-ordination to improve its horizontal view on cross-cutting issues and remain responsive to emerging risks.

- TCU could improve the coherence and effectiveness of its work on cross-cutting, high-risk governance issues by strengthening integration of audit teams and internal co-ordination mechanisms.
- TCU could build capacity and knowledge for improving the extent to which audits identify emerging risks and challenges facing government and society.

TCU could enhance its monitoring and evaluation techniques in order to generate, measure and communicate financial and non-financial impact of cross-cutting audit activities.

- TCU could further develop methods to generate and communicate a more aggregate measure of its financial and non-financial value and benefits to society.
- TCU could strengthen the coherence of its recommendations on governance-related issues, emphasising analyses of previous recommendations made to the Centre of Government.

1.3. Ensuring a systemic, long-term and citizen-oriented view

TCU could ensure that the formulation of its strategic plans enable it to tackle systemic and emerging risks to society over the medium and long-term.

SAIs that seek to improve their contributions to good governance – or more efficient, effective and economical public policies and programmes – should also ensure their own institutions are governed well. This begins at the strategic level. International standards relevant to SAIs can offer a framework for understanding how SAIs are strategically aligning themselves with principles of good governance. For instance, the United Nations Resolution 69/228, emphasises the need for strengthening SAIs to promote and foster the efficiency, accountability, effectiveness and transparency in government (United Nations, 2014). In addition, ISSAI 12 notes, "objectives and principles [that] are intended for SAIs to strive towards and to enable all SAIs to communicate and promote the value and benefits that they can bring to democracy and accountability in their respective jurisdictions" (INTOSAI, 2013a).

Table 1.2 elaborates on select principles of ISSAI 12, and shows linkages to the mission and priorities of TCU's current strategic plan for 2015 to 2021. TCU's strategic planning captures much of the spirit of ISSAI 12. This underscores the importance TCU places on activities that go beyond its judicial function, and include other mandates in service of the Congress and Brazilian citizens. For example, TCU conducts evaluations and offers recommendations for improvement in public administration (TCU, 2016b), and identifies vulnerabilities in the internal control systems related to public procurement, contracting and public-private partnerships (Santiso, 2009). Moreover, TCU's Systemic Reports (i.e. Fiscs), based on surveys that TCU carries out in a range of sectors, such as health, education, social welfare and information technology, offer an aggregated view of TCU's work in these areas, emphasising challenges, risks and potential solutions. Annex 1.A1 further demonstrates how TCU has incorporated good governance elements into its various strategic documents.

Table 1.2. **Elements of ISSAI 12 reflected in TCU's Strategic Plan (2015-2021)**

Select key ISSAI 12 Principles	TCU Strategic plan (2015-2021)
Enabling those charged with public sector governance to discharge their responsibilities in responding to audit findings and recommendations and taking appropriate corrective action (Principle 3)	TCU's mission is "to monitor the budgetary and financial implementation of the country and contribute to the improvement of public administration for the benefit of society"
• Demonstrating ongoing relevance to citizens, Parliament and other stakeholders by being responsive to changing environments and emerging risks (Principle 5); • Being a credible source of independent and objective insight and guidance to support beneficial change in the public sector (Principle 4) and Communicating effectively with stakeholders (Principle 6).	Strategic Plan (2015-2021) outlines three main priorities: 1) improve governance and management in public and political organisations, 2) curb mismanagement of public resources and 3) foster a transparent government.

Source: INTOSAI (2013a) 'ISSAI 12: The Value and benefits of Supreme Audit Institutions – Making a Difference to the Lives of Citizens', INTOSAI Professional Standards Committee, Copenhagen, Denmark, available at: *http://www.issai.org/data/files/D8/53/3D/6F/79CD65107FA83C65BA5818A8/issai-12-e.pdf* accessed 21 June 2017, and TCU (2015b) Strategic Plan of The Federal Court of Accounts for the period of 2015-2021 (Plano Estratégico do Tribunal de Contas da União para o período 2015-2021), PORTARIA-TCU N° 141, DE 1° DE ABRIL DE 2015, Brasilia, *http://portal.tcu.gov.br/tcu/paginas/planejamento/2021/index.html.*

As reflected in its strategic plan for 2011 to 2015, TCU has focused efforts in strengthening the 'effectiveness' component of its mission by promoting improvements in governance through use of performance audits, advice and consultations. The strategic plan includes concrete activities that are critical for SAIs to effectively contribute to good governance, including risk-based analyses, systemic diagnoses of government programmes, timely resolution of cases of wrongdoing and various actions to enhance management and innovation. For instance, TCU's strategic objective 5 focuses on conducting surveys in relevant areas in order to promote the assessment of the governance and management of public policies and contribute to the reduction of bureaucracy (TCU, 2015b). TCU has allocated 17% of external control resources to this objective, which is amongst the highest allocation for external control activities (TCU, 2015a).

In addition, TCU's strategic planning process is comprehensive and includes scenario planning in order to adopt a broader view of horizontal, medium and longer-term governance challenges. It seeks to reflect the insights of all stakeholders, including civil society in addition to the executive branch and the Congress. Further information about TCU's strategic planning process is provided in Box 1.1. The approaches adopted for the 2011-2015 Strategic Plan were carried forward for the planning process of the 2015-2021 Strategic Plan (*Plano Estratégico do Tribunal*, PET). The predominant steps of the current PET were (i) an institutional diagnosis of internal and external perceptions of TCU's work, as well as an assessment of the political, economic, social, technological, legal and administrative environment, (ii) identification of strategic drivers for TCU's work, and (iii) elaboration of a strategic mapping that appears in the PET (TCU, 2016a).

The 2011-2015 PET (as described in Box 1.1) gave thoughtful consideration to longer-term trends that would impact TCU's work, yet TCU could take additional steps to ensure that scenario planning is based on the highest risks for society. Principle 5 of ISSAI 12 suggests that to provide value and benefits for citizens, SAIs should remain responsive to a changing environment and emerging risks (INTOSAI, 2013a). To further align with this principle, TCU could ensure that medium and long-term risks for society also steer the

External Control and Guidelines (2-year basis), as well as the annual plans of the Secretary General of External Control (*Secretária-Geral de Controle Externo*, SEGECEX), described further below. More specifically:

- TCU could further and more systematically integrate medium and long-term policy issues into its new risk-based approach to audit programming to ensure that its activities are responsive to society's needs and aligned with TCU's strategic plans.
- TCU could ensure that audits integrate governance elements, and serve as a vehicle to collect information on broader governance issues and national goals that are systematic and cross-cutting.

Box 1.1. **TCU's strategic planning process: using the results of assessment of emerging trends affecting government**

TCU's strategic planning involves: *i)* clarifying the organisation's mission and values; *ii)* developing a vision for the future; *iii)* analysing external opportunities and risks; *iv)* assessing internal strengths and weaknesses; *v)* evaluating alternative strategies; and *vi)* developing monitorable action plans. Since the first TCU Strategic Plan (*Plano Estratégico do Tribunal*, PET) in 1994, seven strategic plans have been issued by TCU, each varying in their approach.

TCU's 2011-15 Strategic Plan was developed using a balanced scoreboard approach and scenario analysis, driven by an awareness of the growing complexity of audit environment. Seeking to align with other supreme audit institutions, TCU wanted a strategy that would be effective in the long term and that would not become obsolete quickly.

To formulate a strategy that incorporated potential changes in the environment that could impact TCU's work, TCU used a scenario analysis based on the "Grumbach method". The Grumbach method is used to support the formulation of strategies by organisations that find themselves in a competitive and turbulent environment, where traditional models of planning, forecasting and projections are not appropriate. This approach applies traditional tools of strategic planning together with scenarios planning methods, for example, Delphi, Cross-Impact and the Monte Carlo Simulation.

The Grumbach method closes the strategic management cycle by prioritising and planning the strategic initiatives and their monitoring. Among the issued examined in the scenario planning were:

- macro and micro-economic trends within the Brazilian economy
- take up of e-government and m-government
- participation of society in the oversight of public expenditure
- private participation in the delivery of public services
- increasing outsourcing in government service delivery
- ability of the public administration to attract and retain officials
- actions to prevent and detect corruption within the public sector.

TCU used a consultative process, informing the scenario analysis with a survey of 1,500 external experts on the economy, the environment and through direct citizen engagement, as well as surveys and consultations across TCU.

Source: Adapted from OECD (2014b), *Chile's Supreme Audit Institution: Enhancing Strategic Agility and Public Trust*, OECD Public Governance Reviews, OECD Publishing, Paris. *http://dx.doi.org/10.1787/9789264207561-en*

TCU could further and more systematically integrate medium and long-term policy issues into its new risk-based approach to audit programming to ensure that its activities are responsive to society's needs and aligned with TCU's strategic plans.

Ongoing social, political and economic changes in Brazil create a challenging auditing environment, which places high demands on TCU to ensure its continued relevance and impact. Process to understand this environment should ultimately help to TCU to concentrate limited resources on critical, high-risk areas. TCU's existing strategic documents provide a foundation for taking a longer-term, risk-based perspective in fulfilling its mission and objectives. As mentioned above, TCU's strategic planning process includes scenario planning to ensure that the Strategic Plan, usually covering a 5 or 6 year period, enables TCU to remain relevant to society's issues. However, TCU staff indicated that the implementation of the Strategic Plan is difficult in practice, and that annual plans are not always reflective of aims set out in either the Strategic Plan (6 year) or the External Control Plan (2 year).

According to TCU officials, one factor that complicates this issue is the increasing number of Congressional requests[5] for supervisory activities made in-year in addition to, or in place of, those laid out in the 2-year External Control Plan or in the annual plans of SEGECEX secretariats. Such requests may come from Minister rapporteurs or Congress, the latter of which have been on the rise as a percentage of total activities in recent years (TCU, 2016c,d; 2015a; 2014a). Some SAIs face similar challenges. For instance, at the U.S. Government Accountability Office (GAO), required and requested audits comprise approximately 90% of its work (OECD 2016a). Ensuring impact and relevance for tackling key policy challenges meant effectively prioritising within its audit portfolio, in part, through discussions and consultation with Congressional requesters, while still maintaining autonomy in its audit programming and selection of auditees. Engaging requesters in advance, like the GAO, could help TCU to balance immediate priorities with medium and long-term goals.

Interviews with TCU staff suggest room for improvement in addressing challenges and emerging risks on an annual basis. The External Control Plan and Guidelines ("Diretrizes") at the operational level inform the preparation of annual plans of each unit at the tactical level (TCU, 2016a). The annual plans are prepared at the secretariat level and include proposals for audits and initiatives, aligned with the Strategic Plan. According to TCU staff, approximately 90% of audits are proposed by the secretariats with the technical knowledge on the audit subject and the other 10% comes from requests, namely from Congress for supervisory proceedings. Secretariats make these proposals to TCU's Ministers, who have an overarching view of all TCU's activities and can consult rapporteurs formerly assigned to the sector or audit subject.

In interviews and workshops, TCU officials expressed concern that there is too much flexibility for annual plans of individual units to direct resources to areas without consulting internally or comparing to the work of other units. This can lead to overextension or lack of coherence between TCU units, which can ultimately undermine broader strategic objectives. In 2015, more resources were channelled towards certain objectives (e.g. objectives 4, 8 and 10, as described in Annex 1.A1) than had been originally anticipated, and would require readjustment in coming years if annual plans are to meet the objectives by 2021.

TCU is exploring the integration of a more rigorous risk-based approach to audit programming on an annual basis. TCU resolution (Res 269/2015, art 19) requires that audit programming involves the selection of audit topics to be based on risk criteria, materiality, relevance and opportunity, but this is not yet fully in practice (TCU, 2015c). TCU has launched an initiative to develop a methodology to comply with this regulation called Method for

Selection of Objects and Control Actions (*Método de Seleção de Objetos e Ações de Controle*). In 2015, TCU began this by assessing whether it is addressing the most relevant issues through its audits.

TCU can build on these efforts to adopt risk-based approaches to make planning of programmes and resource allocation more systemically focused upon emerging risks and medium to long-term policy issues. Basing audit programmes on a risk-analysis will help to ensure (i) that TCU's activities are based on cross-cutting policy issues and priorities for society; and (ii) resources are allocated in accordance with identified institutional priorities articulated in various plans. TCU has a broad scope of engagement across a wide variety of subject matter and governance functions, but it cannot provide complete assurance on government performance or compliance. A strategic, risk-based approach helps TCU to optimise the allocation of finite audit resources. Adopting more rigorous risk-based audit programming that focuses on risks to government and to society at an aggregate level could enable TCU to more closely align resource allocation to the most pressing needs.

In addition, a systematic risk-based approach to audit programming can help ensure that short-term initiatives do not detract from TCU's efforts to induce change in governance functions over the medium and long-term. Integrating a risk-based approach into individual audit programmes of units would serve to align TCU's efforts across Secretariats, and would provide SEGECEX with a more robust and consistent framework to assess proposed annual plans of SEGECEX units. Moreover, the annual plans themselves would be geared more towards the most pressing, cross-cutting needs and highest risks in government. A risk-based audit programme would act as a guide when developing such plans and during internal deliberations on the scope and focus of the portfolio and individual audits.

TCU could also apply this more rigorous risk-based approach to the 2-year External Control Plans. Such systematic risk-based audit programming can contribute to the evidence-based use of resources and prioritisation of policy objectives that are forward looking. Risk-based programming provides a framework of analysis that TCU officials can refer to for internal agreement of audit priorities. Moreover, in addition to facilitating the selection of audits and allocation of resources, a risk-based approach to audit programming can aid SAIs in communicating its decision making internally and externally in order to ensure that salient issues are brought to the attention of managers and relevant stakeholders. This also helps to strengthen the transparency of the SAI and support its justification for any actions its takes. For practical implementation of a risk-based approach that integrates emerging and medium to long-term risks to society, TCU could first look to the general steps for developing a risk-based audit programme, as illustrated in Figure 1.2.

Figure 1.2 highlights the importance of "data and information" as inputs (stage 2.1) to risk-based audit programming, which can involve considerations of the national government agenda and priorities. Considering such information as inputs into its process can help to ensure that risks are reflective of emerging challenges and long-term policy goals. This would help TCU to be proactive in it is audit programming, going beyond auditing and oversight that is reactive to short-term challenges. To inform its risk-based programming, TCU can draw from its audits and evaluations for information about broader governance issues, as well as the obstacles for improving policies and programmes. Box 1.2 illustrates further the sources and activities for improving inputs into its risk-based audit programming for strengthening the insight and foresight offered by TCU's audits.

Figure 1.2. **Steps for developing risk-based audit programming**

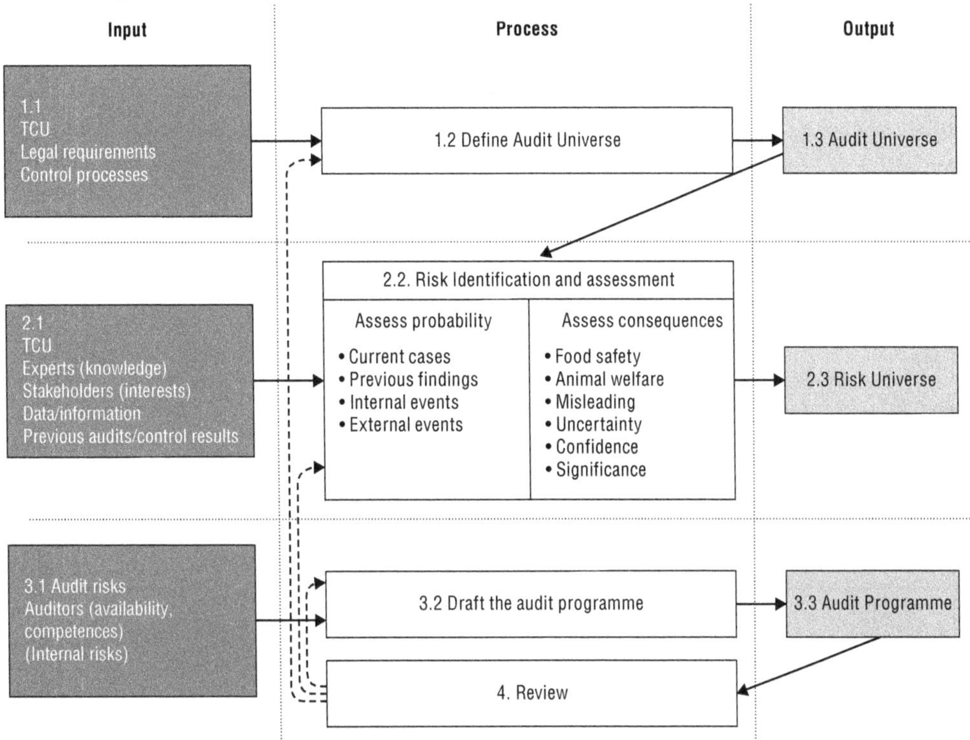

Source: National Audit Systems Network (2014) 'Planning for Audits of Official Control Systems' Version 1, February 2014, *http://www.livsmedelsverket.se/globalassets/produktion-handel-kontroll/vagledningar-ontrollhandbocker/vagledningar-och-information-fran-eukommissionen/risk-based-planning-for-audits-of-official-control-systems-february-2014*

Box 1.2. **Techniques to evaluate changing and emerging risks in the audit environment**

TCU would benefit from having a deeper understanding of medium and long-term challenges to improving the governance and management of public administration, such that its audit work can promote lasting improvements in public administration. This approach is important to ensure that TCU can continue looking ahead, while government is more focused on short-term responses to crisis matters. To anticipate medium and long-term risks, which can then be integrated into its audit programming, TCU could generate insight and foresight activities to better understand the current and future audit environment. Table 1.3 provides examples of SAIs activities in this respect. Such foresight is particularly important where Executive Branch entities may be more limited in perspective by political cycles.

For deepening TCU's understanding of medium and longer-term challenges to governance and thus to society it can integrate and build from the work that TCU has done previously. For instance, TCU surveyed public officials in 2014 on their capacity for leadership, for strategy and for control. These elements are in line with international indicators on Executive Branch Effectiveness from the *World Governance Indicators Project* (WGI, 2017). Such information provides TCU with a baseline understanding of the maturity of public official's capacity, and where risks may appear.

TCU can also look to internationally comparative data, such as OECD's Better Life Index, the Social Progress Imperative and the World Happiness Report, where indicators provide a commentary on a range of social and economic outcomes. More consistent reference to TCU's own General Governance Index (IGG) can also be useful in diagnosing challenges in the audit environment (TCU, 2016e). Other sources could include the World Governance Indicators, the

Box 1.2. **Techniques to evaluate changing and emerging risks in the audit environment** *(cont.)*

Social Progress Index and eventual progress measurement of Brazil against the SDGs. Such indices can offer a snapshot for TCU to better understand its future environment. To strategically align itself with ISSAI 12, such data sources and indicators can be incorporated into its risk-based audit programming to complement their use during individual audit engagements.

Table 1.3. **Oversight, insight and foresight: Capabilities and activities**

Role	Purpose	Examples of SAI activities
Oversight	Strengthening accountability by ensuring government funds are spent as intended and in compliance with applicable laws and regulations.	Assessing the compliance, as well as effectiveness and efficiency of, internal audit in supporting a more robust system of internal control and risk management.
Insight	Improving short-term policy outcomes by pinpointing systemic issues, cross-cutting challenges and trends in order to determine success factor and avoid pitfalls.	Ranking high-risk institutions in public administration to encourage improvements in management before risks materialise.
Foresight	Contributing to medium and long-term policy outcomes by forecasting policy implications and predicting risks.	Assessing government's preparedness to address population ageing and workforce management, or assessing progress against international commitments to project whether goals would be reached.

Scanning such material annually, and anticipating risks of the future, would provide TCU with a more systematic analysis of short, medium and long term challenges that the country currently, or could, face in the future. There is an opportunity to make this understanding consistent and systematic, by integrating elements into TCU's new risk-based approach to audit programming. TCU officials noted that TCU has been working for two years on developing these approaches, with principles of risk being widely adopted for the 2017 planning cycle.

Source: OECD (2016a), *Supreme Audit Institutions and Good Governance: Oversight, Insight and Foresight*, OECD Public Governance Reviews, OECD Publishing, Paris. *http://dx.doi.org/10.1787/9789264263871-en*; Social Progress Imperative, *http://www.socialprogressimperative.org/*; World Bank World Governance Indicators Project, *http://info.worldbank.org/governance/wgi/index.aspx#home*; World Happiness Report, *http://worldhappiness.report/*

Criteria for risks can be drawn from different sources and can change depending on the type of audit. For example, material errors in the accounts of the programme can be a main criterion for prioritising risks related to financial audits. For performance audits, criteria can focus more on elements of effectiveness, efficiency and economy, and the extent to which the policy or programme is achieving its goals. Time elapsed since the last audit, or the occurrence of major changes in the audited entity, are other examples of criterion. Use of criteria for assessing risks facilitates ranking of audit priorities, according to the perceived impact and probability of the risk posed by a particular audit subject. Box 1.3 provides examples from countries with risk-based audit programming.

TCU could ensure that audits integrate governance elements, and serve as a vehicle to collect information on broader governance issues and national goals that are systematic and cross-cutting.

In the last few years, TCU has invested resources into developing a more holistic view of governance, both horizontally across ministries and vertically between levels of government together with state audit institutions (Tribunals de Contas dos Estados, TCEs). For instance, SEGECEX has developed products that take a more holistic look at the functioning of a particular sector (e.g. Fiscobras and FiscSaude), and Secretary of Government Macro-Evaluation (*Secretaria de Macroavaliação Governamental*, SEMAG) co-ordinates inputs of different units for the drafting of the year-end opinion on the President's consolidated accounts. In addition, TCU has conducted cross-cutting audits that assess the maturity of particular governance functions, such as the maturity of risk management across government (see Chapter 4), or the IT audit on integration of information technology across government. The latter was praised by Executive representatives consulted for this study for its usefulness in highlighting areas for improvement.

Box 1.3. **Risk-Based Audit Programming in Supreme Audit Institutions for Directing Resources to the Highest Risks**

The approach of supreme audit institutions (SAIs) to audit programming depends, in part, on their mandate and their level of discretionary authority and independence. Nonetheless, audit institutions can take different approaches to audit programming. One example is the "cycle-based" approach, whereby all entities in an audit universe (i.e. the range of organisations and activities that can be audited) are audited in year-based cycles, such as every 3 to 5 years. This approach ensures a total coverage of the audit universe within a certain timeframe, yet some audits may have limited or no value. Another approach is the "audit-on-demand" or "incident-based" audit programming. This approach involves responding to the demands or requests related to specific matters or incidents. For instance, in some countries, SAIs respond to specific requests of the Parliament, and they reserve resources for this purpose.

The "risk-based" approach focuses audit capacity and efforts on key risk areas of the audit universe. For SAIs facing an expanded audit mandate, like Mexico's SAI (the Auditoría Superior de la Federación, or ASF), a risk-based approach facilitates prioritisation of audits and targets resource allocation based on a qualitative or quantitative (or both) assessment of the audits' added value. This approach can be borne from necessity in a complex, resource-constrained environment, where it may not be realistic for SAIs to audit all entities, programmes or policies. Moreover, international standards for auditing call for SAIs to take a risk-based approach when selecting audits. For instance, International Standard for Supreme Audit Institutions (ISSAI) 300 on Fundamental Principles of Performance Auditing notes:

Auditors should select audit topics through the SAI's strategic planning process by analysing potential topics and conducting research to identify risks and problems…The topic selection process should aim to maximise the expected impact of the audit while taking account audit capacities (e.g. human resources and professional skills). Formal techniques to prepare the strategic planning process, such as risk analysis or problem assessments, can help structure the process but need to be complemented by professional judgement to avoid one-sided assessments.

Risk-based audit programming and planning in SAIs can vary, but it generally involves a process of criteria development, risk identification, analysis, scoring and mapping, prioritisation and selection of audits in relation to strategic objectives, capacity and resources. Criteria selection can be drawn from different sources, as illustrated in the examples below. For instance, criteria can change depending on different type of audits. For financial audits, material errors in the accounts of the programme can be a main criterion. For performance audits, criterion can focus more on elements of effectiveness, efficiency and economy, and the extent to which the policy or programme is achieving its goals. The risk map and result of the assessment provides an overview of risks, and the ranking reflects criteria linked to the perceived impact and probability of the risk, such as the length of time since the last audit or the occurrence of major changes in the audited entity. The following are examples from countries with risk-based audit programming.

Belgium

The Belgian Court of Accounts uses a 'Financial Operational Risk Model' (FORM), which is an integrated risk-based planning model. The prioritization of audits is based on three criteria, one of which is the financial-budgetary significance for evaluating the budgetary relevance of the institution on a consolidated level. Budget thresholds are determined taken into account the total federal budget. The second criterion relates to budget priorities and controls. As part of this, the Court considers policies as well as horizontal issues affecting different public entities. The third criterion involves general considerations based on the professional judgement of the Court's management. This criterion receives less weight for programmes with smaller budgets.

Box 1.3. **Risk-Based Audit Programming in Supreme Audit Institutions for Directing Resources to the Highest Risks** *(cont.)*

Denmark

The Danish Rigsrevisionen uses a risk-based approach at the audit-planning level. The purpose of the analysis is to obtain insights into the department's situation and to uncover potential risk areas. Initially, Rigsrevisionen carries out a strategic analysis of each ministerial area and department. The strategic analyses of the departments also include reviews of the underlying agencies and public bodies and their management. Subsequently, a similar strategic analysis is carried out on in the public body. Before the audit is launched, Rigsrevisionen discusses the strategic analysis with the management of the department and the relevant public body to reduce the risk of overlooking significant areas in the audit. The strategic analysis provides the basis for planning the audit, which is focused on the identified risk areas to ensure that required audits are carried out and audit opinions on the accounts can be issued.

The European Court of Auditors (ECA)

The ECA has a yearly policy and risk review to take into account issues like developments in policy areas, stakeholders' priorities, results of recent audits, the work of other audit institutions and media coverage. This review is done in the form of 'policy scans' for each major policy area and helps ECA to define priorities and align them with strategic objectives. The 'policy scans' inform various audit chambers to prepare lists of proposed audit tasks and information on their relative priority. After consideration and approval of the tasks, ECA's annual work programme sets out the audit tasks to be implemented during the year and the resources allocated to them. The programme is reviewed and updated during the year to take into account any changes to priorities. Performance and compliance audit topics are selected at the ECA's discretion on the basis of criteria like such as risk of irregularities, poor performance, potential for improvement and public interest.

Source: Lonsdale, J. et al (2011), *Performance Auditing: Contributing to Accountability in Democratic Government*, Edward Elgar Publishing, Cheltenham, United Kingdom; Rigsrevisionen (Danish SAI) (2016), "The strategic analysis", 17 August, *http://uk.rigsrevisionen.dk/how-we-audit/annual-audit/strategic-analysis/*; European Court of Auditors (2015), "Work programme", *www.eca.europa.eu/Lists/ECADocuments/WP2015/WP2015_EN.pdf*; INTOSAI (2004), "ISSAI 300: Fundamental Principles of Performance Auditing", *http://www.issai.org/data/files/33/45/70/E6/F93E7510D33F2E75CA5818A8/issai-300-english.pdf*.

This work illustrates concrete steps TCU has taken to integrate governance elements into its audit and evaluation work; however, TCU has yet to consistently apply criteria that would facilitate comparability on systematic issues across audits over time. When audits are more intentionally geared towards identifying challenges and solutions for cross-cutting policy issues, it allows for easier tracking of improvements and it facilitate coherence among policies and programmes. Moreover, a systematic approach can provide better inputs to inform TCU's risk-based audit programming. One step TCU can take is to synthesise issues raised across its work streams, products and services, such as audit reports, contract assessments, asset declaration analysis and fielding of citizen complaints. As part of this effort to address systemic, cross-cutting issues, TCU could further define what should be considered of "systemic importance" to ensure coherence between assessments on this issue, and communicate effectively across the organisation. TCU could make such audits cyclical, reviewing on a systematic basis that is pre-determined and planned for in TCU's annual audit plans.

In addition, TCU could strengthen its approach to supporting good governance by more systematically looking upstream to policy formulation, implementation and evaluation of policies and programmes being audited – not simply to the results of policies and programmes. For instance, audits could further integrate criteria that hold government to account for improved governance and policy making (discussed further in chapter 2 through 5 for specific governance functions). Moreover, opportunities remain for TCU to leverage findings from its variety of accounting and supervisory proceedings in order to highlight areas of importance to the CoG in the execution of their duties.

TCU's own *Framework to Assess Governance in Public Policies* (2014) and *Framework for Evaluation of the Centre of Government* (2016) offers a starting point for further institutionalising its audits and evaluations of systemic issues. As a supplement to these frameworks, audit teams can look to the international principles promoted in subsequent chapters of this review. Further, OECD's (2016) comparative review entitled "Supreme Audit Institutions and Good Governance: Oversight, Insight and Foresight", maps international governance principles around key stages of policy making, which can serve as a reference tool for audit teams in developing audits that will better inform the maturity of governance (OECD, 2016a).

1.4. Improving TCU's capacity and co-ordination to remain strategically agile in a changing audit environment

TCU could continue strengthening its capacity and internal co-ordination to improve its horizontal view on cross-cutting issues and remain responsive to emerging risks.

ISSAI 12 calls for SAIs to lead by example in their work, which includes ensuring good governance of the SAI itself by adopting and complying with good governance principles (ISSAI 12, principle 9.1) (INTOSAI, 2013a). To achieve this, SAIs faced constant demand for greater efficiency, effectiveness and economy in a changing audit environment. Not only do the policy issues of the audit environment change, but so do the processes through which policies and processes are developed. In turn, this can require upskilling of those who are required to audit such policies. Indeed, INTOSAI's General Standards in Government Auditing (ISSAI, 200) require SAIs to: develop and train SAI employees to enable them to perform their tasks effectively, and to define the basis for the advancement of auditors and other staff (INTOSAI, 2013b).

TCU has taken steps to adapt its strategy and modernise its operations in order to better support good governance and drive improvements in the performance of public administration. These actions include, amongst others, (i) internal reorganisation and specialisation of units, (ii) a decrease in the number of supervisory proceedings, with a greater emphasis on going into greater depth in the audit subject; (iii) improving the balance between compliance and performance audits, including shifting the allocation of resources to the latter (see Figure 1.3); and (iv) an evolved vision and elaborate strategic planning process, as discussed above (TCU, 2016d; 2015a). As noted in Figure 1.3, despite the relatively equal provision of HD to both compliance and performance audits, the output of compliance audits remained higher in 2015. The 104 performance audits undertaken in 2015 required 45.5% of HD, whereas the 242 compliance audits required 52.5% (TCU, 2015a).

Overall, fewer audits are being undertaken at TCU than previously. Yet emphasis is shifting towards performance audits that are more labour-intensive. As TCU continues this shift, and as it considers strengthening its contributions to good governance, it could consider how it will "support the skills and experience available within the SAI and identify the skills which are absent; provide a good distribution of skills to auditing tasks and assign a sufficient number of persons for the audit," as promoted by ISSAI 200 (INTOSAI, 2013b).

Figure 1.3. **Allocation of TCU's human resources, by audit type: 2011-2015**

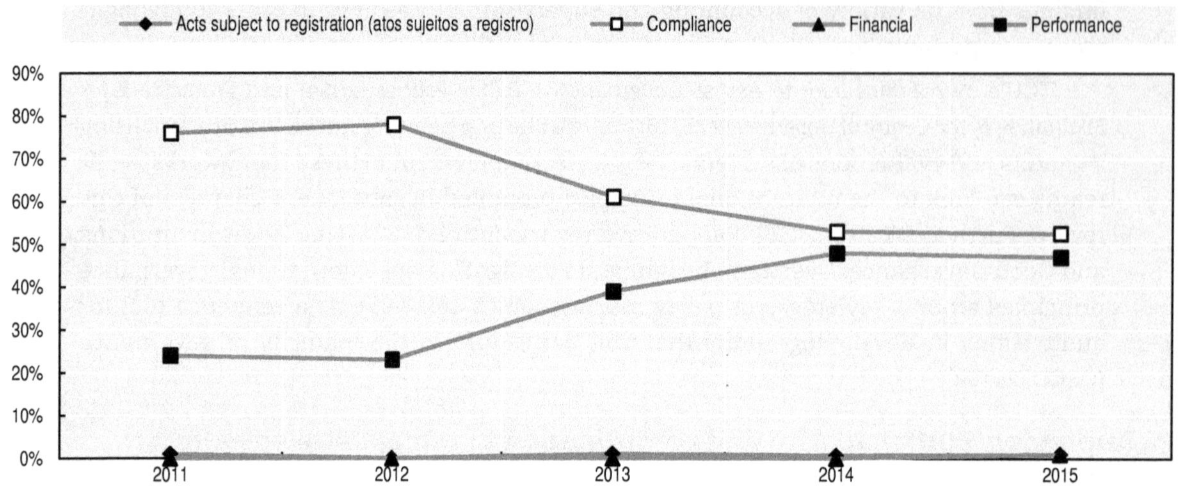

Source: TCU (2015d), Report of the Secretary General of External Control (Relatório da Secretaria-Geral de Controle Externo), Brasilia, accessed July 2017. *http://portal.tcu.gov.br/lumis/portal/file/fileDownload.jsp?fileId=8A8182A2572667DE0157298FA4C94D16&inline=1*

To provide value and benefits to society, TCU could continue to build the capacity and co-ordination needed to take a more horizontal view on cross-cutting issues and to remain responsive to emerging risks to society. To this end, TCU could consider the following actions:

- TCU could improve the coherence and effectiveness of its work on cross-cutting, high-risk governance issues by strengthening integration of audit teams and internal co-ordination mechanisms; and
- TCU could build capacity and knowledge for conducting audits to identify emerging risks and challenges facing government and society.

TCU could improve the coherence and effectiveness of its work on cross-cutting, high-risk governance issues by strengthening integration of audit teams and internal co-ordination mechanisms.

To better position itself for addressing cross-cutting issues that affect multiple government programs and policies, TCU could take steps to further integrate its work internally that touch on such issues. This could include: (i) reducing the level of fragmentation or siloes between audit units and (ii) optimising information-sharing and resources across audit activities. TCU officials highlighted the need for reducing siloes or fragmentation between department in order to avoid duplication and to ensure coherence of findings on similar topics.

TCU reorganised internally by relevant sectoral areas as part of the 2011-2015 PET. It created four thematic co-ordination offices in SEGECEX (social issues, infrastructure, development and essential public services). The reorganisation was aimed at greater specialisation of audit staff, enabling each new secretariat to better identify its own risks and relevant situations, as well as to better understand the models and tools of governance that are required for success in those domains (OECD, 2014b). According to TCU officials, the reorganisation is still a work in progress, and they highlighted siloes that still exist between staff.

To reduce siloes and strengthen coherence of work on cross-cutting issues, TCU could consider structural changes that focus on select whole-of-government challenges. These departments or teams can help to provide a horizontal view of cross-cutting governance and policy issues. For instance, TCU recently established, in early 2017, a new department of Institutional Relations on Fight Against Fraud and Corruption (*Secretaria de Relações Institucionais no Combate à Fraude e Corrupção* - SECCOR). The purpose of SECCOR is to develop, encourage, monitor, support and co-ordinate control actions to combat fraud and corruption, by strengthening the relationship between TCU and the other control and inspection bodies and entities, as well as capacity building for obtaining, analysing and processing information (Article 14) (TCU, 2017).

SECCOR provides a level of centralisation around a specific theme that arises across all SEGECEX secretariats. TCU could dedicate additional resources, or simply assign working groups with appropriate authority, to provide a centralised repository for other systemic issues (e.g. monitoring and evaluation across government with regards to the Sustainable Development Goals). This would also help to preserve institutional memory and build expertise related to long-term, systemic problems.

In addition, finding greater synergies across TCU requires effective mechanisms to stimulate information sharing and ensure consistency of findings. For example, TCU could consider integrating units' annual work plans to facilitate information sharing between actors who have previously worked on different audits or themes, and have transferable expertise relevant to audit subject. Moreover, pooling the wealth of expertise in a more systematic way would help to build a broader view of policy challenges and solutions. For example, greater information sharing during the design of audit engagements between different specialists in TCU, such as those working on audits and investigators of public contracts, may enable TCU to flag worrisome trends or issues that can then help to shape the scope of a review. Similarly, for example, strategic interaction between those working on governance of health policies with governance of education policies could increase the likelihood that cross-cutting or systemic issues or vulnerabilities in government are more readily detected.

One way to formalise such interactions is to employ «matrixed» audit engagements in a more strategic, systematic way. Matrixed engagements are where staff from different units work on the same audit. These audits often address cross-cutting or diverse issues that require a range of subject matter and technical expertise. Officials said TCU uses this approach, but in an ad-hoc manner. TCU could apply this methodology more systematically, as matrixed engagements allow joint development of criteria and indicators. This is also meant to ensure that work is not duplicated and that messages of TCU are consistent and coherent. More consistent use of matrixed engagements would help to overcome the challenges that teams often have in building a broad view of the audit objective, particularly on complex and cross-cutting audit subjects.

TCU could build capacity and knowledge for improving the extent to which audits identify emerging risks and challenges facing government and society.

The General Standards in Government Auditing (ISSAI 200) require that SAIs should develop and train their employees to enable them to perform their tasks effectively, and to define the basis for the advancement of auditors and other staff (INTOSAI, 2013b). How an SAI defines whether an auditor can do its work effectively can change. As discussed above, having a keen awareness of the emerging risks to governance and society should also necessitate a changing evaluation of the skill sets required to tackle such risks. ISSAI 200 further suggests that SAIs prepare manuals and other written guidance and instructions concerning the conduct of audits (INTOSAI, 2013b).

In addition to auditing manuals, such as TCU's Performance Audit Manual (2010), TCU has recently developed frameworks for audit teams on cross-cutting subjects including assessment of public policies, IT, and Centre of Government, for audit teams to consider in conducting an audit. The frameworks have been welcomed for their promotion and dissemination of good practices and international principles, but there is uneven use of the contents across TCU. TCU could build on these efforts by strengthening their dissemination through trainings, and emphasising how to integrate key elements into individual audits. To the extent applicable, TCU could incorporate further guidance in various manuals (e.g. performance audit manual) and internal documents that are meant to aid auditors during the audit planning phase. The guidance could help auditors in a practical manner when evaluating issues that are potentially systemic, such as questions related to specific governance topics to consider when interviewing executive branch entities.

TCU provides its staff with ongoing training and development opportunities in line with international standards. Much of the course work is online. TCU staff pointed to the benefits of also having in person and more practical trainings on auditing methodologies. Finally, TCU has been promoting more active engagement by the academic community. There may be greater opportunities to tap into academic expertise, to better prepare future auditors and to establish agreements for the co-development of tools (surveys, research, apps, etc). Engaging the academic community can also bring different perspectives on cross-cutting governance issues.

1.5. Enhancing TCU's monitoring and evaluation techniques to better assess its impact on governance

TCU could enhance its monitoring and evaluation techniques in order to generate, measure and communicate financial and non-financial impact of cross-cutting audit activities.

To encourage the monitoring and evaluation (M&E) of performance by the Public Administration," TCU's External Control plan (2015-2017) established an objective "to assess compliance with the decisions issued by TCU" (TCU, 2015b). TCU has a process for monitoring auditees' compliance with TCU's determinations and recommendations. For instance, when issuing 'determinations' in cases of non-compliance, TCU monitors the implementation according to an established deadline through analysis of documentation, or making inspections, which involves visiting the audited entity to collect data and information. In such cases, determinations are binding and there can be consequences for non-compliance. Unlike determinations, recommendations that focus on improvements to governance (i.e. efficiency effectiveness, economy) or transparency are not mandatory and are non-binding.

Communicating TCU's M&E of its own work and results of its recommendations is largely posited in financial terms. TCU officials expressed the need to revisit the metrics used for calculating impact, given that relying on financial impacts has traditionally dominated discussions about TCU's value-add. TCU is searching for ways to better quantify contributions to good governance through its audits and evaluations, recognising the results can be more qualitative and less tangible than other areas of work (e.g. judicial rulings and financial audits). Moreover, TCU has reduced in recent years the number of control activities, and subsequently the number of resulting recommendations. This has been an intentional effort of TCU, whose officials note that the current number of recommendations is unmanageable and does not facilitate easy tracking of the impact of audit recommendations.

To understand its impact and the results of its recommendations, particularly those meant to improve government performance, TCU could take actions to improve how it measures results. This could include efforts to more strategically asses and communicate qualitative, non-financial benefits that TCU provides to government and society. In addition, this could involve taking further development of ways for using M&E to generate, measure and communicate impact of cross-cutting audit activities. Specifically, TCU could consider the following:

- TCU could further develop methods to generate and communicate a more aggregate measure of its value and benefits to society - both financial and non-financial; and
- TCU could strengthen the coherence of its recommendations on governance-related issues, emphasising analyses of previous recommendations made to the Centre of Government.

TCU could further develop methods to generate and communicate a more aggregate measure of its financial and non-financial value and benefits to society.

To measure its own impact, TCU uses indicators and targets mapped out in the External Control Plan and Guidelines, and aggregates statistics based on individual activities. In 2015, TCU calculated its total potential benefit of its audit activities to be nearly 24 billion Brazilian Reais (BRL). TCU's rate of return to the public was calculated at 13.4 BRL for every 1 BRL spent on TCU (TCU, 2015a). Such benefits are determined through the valuation of select activities, such as improvements in the economy, efficiency, efficacy or effectiveness of public entities (valued at approximately 235 million BRL in 2014), or the value of condemnations in 2015 (6.6 Billion BRL) (TCU, 2015a). These figures are made public in TCU's annual report, along with others relevant to its performance and productivity, including the number of individuals convicted in debt or fraud, the value of condemnations, companies barred from public biddings and sentences pronounced.

While such indicators of TCU's performance are beneficial for understanding the return on investment for taxpayers, TCU officials expressed concern that the discussion about TCU's impact relies heavily on financial impacts. Indeed, TCU's current processes for tracking recommendations and measuring a broader notion of impact faces many challenges, given the high volume of recommendations and the lack of a systematic process for measuring certain types of benefits. These benefits include the results of recommendations that focus more on governance issues and are elaborated on in performance audits. The benefits of SAIs can be generally categorised as follows:

- Quantified financial benefits, such as TCU's return on investment measure of financial benefits divided by financial costs. Only a handful of SAIs are in practice of calculating such a figure, such as Costa Rica, the United Kingdom and the United States.
- Quantifiable non-financial benefits, such as the results that are deduced from perceptions surveys of auditees about the impact of SAIs' work on their institution.
- Qualitative benefits that cannot be quantified, which capture broader outcomes such as improving accountability or accuracy of performance indicators in government.

As part of nuancing its external control activities to longer-term impact on society, TCU could review its current monitoring approaches to assess its usefulness in providing a more aggregate picture of its overall benefits to society. Adopting a broader view of TCU's impact, which includes quantifiable non-financial benefits and qualitative data, could offer a more realistic picture of TCU's contributions to good governance and areas for improvement. TCU could expand beyond reporting on individual interventions, outcomes of its monitoring (*monitoramento*) and financial benefits, in order to better measure and communicate the value of governance related activities. Measuring and communicating benefits can be difficult and costly. It requires the capacity to make reliable, credible, complete, and accurate estimations. It also requires careful liaison with audited entities to ensure that benefits are not overstated. TCU can improve its chances of effective impact measurement and communication by considering its approach to this early in the audit planning process.

TCU could strengthen the coherence of its recommendations on governance-related issues, emphasising analyses of previous recommendations made to the Centre of Government.

ISSAI 12 stipulates that SAIs should enable those charged with public sector governance to discharge their responsibilities in responding to audit findings and recommendations and taking appropriate corrective action (principle 3) (INTOSAI, 2013a). The ability of an SAI to ensure take-up of its recommendations depends largely on the quality and clarity of recommendations. Equally important is the coherence between recommendations made to the same entity or on the same thematic topic or programme. Further, ISSAI 12 calls for SAIs to be a model organisation through leading by example. If TCU is to encourage coherence, communication and co-ordination in the Executive (chapter 2), it too should be applying the same principles in the execution of its duties.

As mentioned, TCU has a system to track and manage recommendations. According to TCU officials, TCU could improve its mechanisms to ensure that recommendations are coherent with one another. The coherence has been challenged by the previously high number of recommendations. Since 2012, TCU has decreased the number of supervisory proceedings (*fiscalizações*) including audits and, as a result, reduced the number of associated non-binding recommendations to auditees (TCU, 2015a). This progression is welcomed by some TCU staff, who noted that even the current number of recommendations is unmanageable and does not facilitate easy tracking of their impact. As coherence between policies and programmes of government are important to avoid waste, duplication, fragmentation and overlap, so too is it important that SAIs are issuing messages to auditees that are, at least, non-conflicting.

One way TCU could promote greater coherence in its recommendations is to assess previous recommendations made to the Centre of Government (CoG), and then clarify any inconsistencies internally and externally. The CoG has a critical role to play in co-ordinating and overseeing the implementation of government-wide initiatives. As such, it is equally critical that TCU's messages to the CoG, about the performance of the Brazilian government, are coherent and non-conflicting. Guidance to the CoG from TCU should be clear and support the CoG in discharging its critical functions. Such an analysis could discern the degrees of synergies, overlaps or contradiction between recommendations made in previous years. Enabling entities to discharge their responsibilities and take-up TCU's recommendations relies on their clear understanding of those recommendations.

The analysis of coherence of recommendations could be replicated in particular thematic areas or for specific institutions, for particular laws, against which new recommendations could be checked in real-time. This would help to pacify TCU concerns, expressed by some officials, about the quality of outcomes and recommendations of governance-related work, which is a newer area of work relative to TCU's other supervisory and accounts proceedings. For instance, an independent study of the implementation of the U.S. Government Accountability Office's (GAO) recommendations analysed over 40,000 GAO recommendations from 1984 to 2014 using text analytics. Such a longitudinal analysis was facilitated by the

GAO's consistent and persistent approach to quantifying agency compliance. The study hypothesised that audits related to the GPRA and Modernization Act of 2010 (GPRAMA), which establishes a framework for taking a crosscutting and integrated approach to improve government performance, would result in recommendations that were more difficult for agencies to implement than others. The findings showed that recommendations related to GPRAMA had, in fact, a 2% higher success rate [in terms of agencies' implementation] than recommendations unrelated to the GPRAMA (Deloitte, 2015).

Notes

1. This definition does not cover other units, offices, and commissions (e.g. offices for sport or culture) that may report directly to the President or Prime Minister but are, effectively, carrying out line functions that could be carried out equally well by line ministries. COG can include ministries of finance and treasuries, and government-wide planning and management ministries. TCU's definition of Centre of Government is the: Administrative structure of central institutions serving the Executive, representing the strategic core of the federal government for strategic planning, policy and technical co-ordination of government actions, monitoring the performance and communication of decisions and government achievements. It consists of state actors with great potential interference in the public policy cycle, which play cross central and government functions, even if they are not within the Chief Executive's Office and does not serve him only (TCU, 2016a).
2. Wicked problems are policy issues that are dynamic, poorly structured, persistent and social in nature, and highly intertwined with other social issues, such as climate change, immigration, poverty, nutrition, education, or homelessness (OECD, 2016a).
3. This expenditure is for all levels of education combined.
4. OECD's Better Life Index measures life satisfaction by how people evaluate their life as a whole rather than their current feelings. General satisfaction with life is rated on a scale from 0 to 10.
5. The number of activities requested by Congress in quarter 1 of 2016 was 19.1%, whereas 80.9% were undertaken at TCU's discretion. The number of Congressional requests was much higher in quarter 2 at 48.8% (51.2% at TCU's initiative). This substantial increase marks the highest proportion of supervisory proceedings (fiscalizações) resulting from Congressional requests in the last 2 years in any given quarter. Among the control activities completed in the first semester of 2016, 33.25% were requested by Congress and the remaining 65.75% were at the Court's own initiative. This information is summarised from TCU annual activity reports, that can be found online (TCU, 2016c,d; 2015a, 2014a).

References

Deloitte (2015), Accountability Quantified, Deloitte University Press, *https://dupress.deloitte.com/dup-us-en/topics/analytics/text-analytics-and-gao-reports.html*

Edelman (2016), Global Report, 2016 Edelman Trust Barometer, *http://www.edelman.com/insights/intellectual-property/2016-edelman-trust-barometer/global-results/*

European Court of Auditors (2015), "Work programme", *www.eca.europa.eu/Lists/ECADocuments/WP2015/WP2015_EN.pdf*; INTOSAI (2004), "ISSAI 300: Fundamental Principles of Performance Auditing", *http://www.issai.org/data/files/33/45/70/E6/F93E7510D33F2E75CA5818A8/issai-300-english.pdf*.

FFP (Fund for Peace) (2016), The Fragile State Index 2016, available at *http://fsi.fundforpeace.org/*, accessed 14 September 2016

INTOSAI (International Organisation of Supreme Audit Institutions) (2013a), 'ISSAI 12: The Value and benefits of Supreme Audit Institutions – Making a Difference to the Lives of Citizens', INTOSAI Professional Standards Committee, Copenhagen, Denmark, available at: *http://www.issai.org/data/files/D8/53/3D/6F/79CD65107FA83C65BA5818A8/issai-12-e.pdf* accessed 21 June 2017.

INTOSAI (2013b), ISSAI 200 – General Standards in Government Auditing, INTOSAI Professional Standards Committee, Copenhagen, Denmark, available at: *http://www.issai.org/en_us/site-issai/issai-framework/3-fundamental-auditing-priciples.htm*

Lonsdale, J. et al (2011), Performance Auditing: Contributing to Accountability in Democratic Government, Edward Elgar Publishing, Cheltenham, United Kingdom

National Audit Systems Network (2014) 'Planning for Audits of Official Control Systems' Version 1, February 2014, accessed October 2016, *http://www.livsmedelsverket.se/globalassets/produktion-handel-kontroll/vagledningar-kontrollhandbocker/vagledningar-och-information-fran-eukommissionen/risk-based-planning-for-audits-of-official-control-systems-february-2014*

OECD (2016a), *Supreme Audit Institution and Good Governance: Oversight, Insight and Foresight*, OECD Public Governance Reviews, OECD Publishing, Paris. *http://dx.doi.org/10.1787/9789264263871-en*

OECD (2016b), 'Navigating Wicked Problems', OECD Insights Blog, *http://oecdinsights.org/2016/10/04/navigating-wicked-problems/*

OECD (2016c), *Revenue Statistics in Latin America and the Caribbean 2016*, OECD Publishing, Paris. *http://dx.doi.org/10.1787/rev_lat_car-2016-en-fr*

OECD (2016d), «Better Life Index 2015», *OECD Social and Welfare Statistics* (database). *http://dx.doi.org/10.1787/data-00823-en* as cited in OECD (2015c), *OECD Economic Surveys: Brazil 2015*, OECD Publishing, Paris. *http://dx.doi.org/10.1787/eco_surveys-bra-2015-en*

OECD (2015a), *Water Resources Governance in Brazil*, OECD Studies on Water, OECD Publishing, Paris. *http://dx.doi.org/10.1787/9789264238121-en*

OECD (2015b), "Citizen satisfaction with public services", in *Government at a Glance 2015*, OECD Publishing, Paris. *http://dx.doi.org/10.1787/gov_glance-2015-56-en*, with data available at: *http://stats.oecd.org//Index.aspx?QueryId=66864*

OECD (2015c), 'Education Policy Outlook: Brazil' OECD Publishing, Paris. *http://www.oecd.org/edu/Brazil-country-profile.pdf*

OECD (2014a) 'Centre Stage: Driving Better Policies from the Centre of Government' OECD Publishing, Paris. *https://www.oecd.org/gov/Centre-Stage-Report.pdf*

OECD (2014b), *Chile's Supreme Audit Institution: Enhancing Strategic Agility and Public Trust*, OECD Public Governance Reviews, OECD Publishing, Paris. *http://dx.doi.org/10.1787/9789264207561-en*

Rigsrevisionen (Danish SAI) (2016), "The strategic analysis", 17 August, *http://uk.rigsrevisionen.dk/how-we-audit/annual-audit/strategic-analysis/*

Sabogal, David, Helen Bellfield and Simone Bauch, "Amazonia Security Agenda: Assessing policy coherence in Brazil, Colombia and Peru, the Water-Energy-Food Nexus approach", Policy brief, the Climate and Development Knowledge Network (CDKN), accessed online, September 2016, *http://globalcanopy.org/sites/default/files/documents/resources/Regional%20Policy%20Brief%20English%20FINAL.pdf*

Santiso, C. (2009), Political Economy of Government Auditing, Taylor and Francis Publishing, Abington UK, *http://www.routledge.com/books/details/9780415477734/*.

Social Progress Imperative, accessed online 20 February 2017, *http://www.socialprogressimperative.org/*

TCU (Tribunal de Contas da União) (2017), PORTARIA-SEGECEX N° 5 DE 7 DE MARÇO DE 2017 [Department of Institutional Relations for Control on Fight Against Fraud and Corruption], Brasilia.

TCU (2016a), Framework for Evaluation of the Centre of Government, TCU Publishing, Brasilia, *http://portal.tcu.gov.br/lumis/portal/file/fileDownload.jsp?fileId=8A8182A25454C5A801545DC1433145ED*

TCU (2016b), 'Gestão de pessoas' *http://portal.tcu.gov.br/transparencia/gestao-de-pessoas/*, accessed Oct 2016.

TCU (2016c), Trimestral activity report – Trimester 1 (Relatório Trimestral 2016 - 1° trimestre), *http://portal.tcu.gov.br/lumis/portal/file/fileDownload.jsp?fileId=8A8182A1550E2AD30155129EACD506FE*

TCU (2016d), Trimestral activity report – Trimester 2 (Relatório Trimestral 2016 - 2° trimestre), *http://portal.tcu.gov.br/lumis/portal/file/fileDownload.jsp?fileId=8A8182A256ED46890156FC6A8C537FC0*

TCU (2016e), General Governance Index, accessed 20 February 2017, *http://portal.tcu.gov.br/lumis/portal/file/fileDownload.jsp?fileId=8A8182A14F613FB5014F6B5206735279*

TCU (2015a), 2015 Annual Report (Relatório Anual - 2015), *http://portal.tcu.gov.br/lumis/portal/file/fileDownload.jsp?fileId=8A8182A153D422DA0153E2950D8064E1*

TCU (2015b), Strategic Plan of Brazil's Federal Court of Accounts, 2015-2021 (Plano Estratégico do Tribunal de Contas da União para o período 2015-2021) PORTARIA-TCU N° 141, DE 1° DE ABRIL DE 2015, Brasilia, *http://portal.tcu.gov.br/tcu/paginas/planejamento/2021/index.html*.

TCU (2015c), TCU Resolution 269/2015, ACÓRDÃO TCU 269/2015, *http://www.lexml.gov.br/urn/urn:lex:br:tribunal.contas.uniao;plenario:acordao:2015-02-11;269*, accessed 21 June 2017.

TCU (2015d), Report of the Secretary General of External Control (Relatório da Secretaria-Geral de Controle Externo), Brasilia , accessed July 2017. *http://portal.tcu.gov.br/lumis/portal/file/fileDownload.jsp?fileId=8A8182A2572667DE0157298FA4C94D16&inline=1*

TCU (2015e), External Control Plan of Brazil's Federal Court of Accounts (Plano de Contrôle Externo do Tribunal de Contas da União) April, 2015, Brasilia, *http://portal.tcu.gov.br/lumis/portal/file/fileDownload.jsp?fileId=8A8182A153234E0A01535D1006D60567.*

TCU (2014a) Annual activities report (Relatório de Atividades 2014), Brasilia, *http://portal.tcu.gov.br/transparencia/relatorios/relatorios-de-atividades/*, accessed 20 February 2017

TCU (2010) Performance Audit Manual, TCU: Brazilian Court of Audit, Brasilia, *http://psc-intosai.org/data/files/21/60/D0/A0/81B07510C0EA0E65CA5818A8/tcu_performance_audit_manual.pdf*

TCU (2007), 'Supreme Audit Institutions and Financial Sustainability in the Modern State' presented at EUROSAI/ OLACEFS Lisbon, 2007, *http://www.tcontas.pt/eventos/EurosaiOlacefs/Docs/3ST/Brasil-TCU/WS3BR-engl.pdf*, Accessed 30 Sep 2016

United Nations (2014), General Assembly resolution 69/228, Promoting and fostering the efficiency, accountability, effectiveness and transparency of public administration by strengthening supreme audit institutions, A/RES/69/228 (19 December 2014), available at *http://www.un.org/en/ga/search/view_doc.asp?symbol=A/RES/69/228*

World Bank (2014), Worldwide Governance Indicators 2014, *http://info.worldbank.org/governance/wgi/index.aspx*

World Bank, World Governance Indicators Project, *http://info.worldbank.org/governance/wgi/index.aspx#home;*

World Happiness Report, accessed online, 20 February 2017, *http://worldhappiness.report/*

ANNEX 1.A1

Incorporation of good governance concepts into TCU's strategies and plans

	Strategic level	Tactical level		Operational level	
	Strategic Plan	External Control Plan	Guidelines	Annual Plans of Units	Human resources dedicated
Description	Communicates the planning process, and provides common objectives for all of TCU, identifying responsibilities and means to achieve the institutional goals.1	Provides tactical guidance for the work to be carried out, including performance indicators, Units goals, Actions, and products to be developed.	An institutional alignment tool to guide implementation of strategic objectives, performance indicators, and communicating initiatives	Prioritises strategic objectives further and details initiatives.	Estimation of % of human resources to be allocated to each strategic objective, versus the actual allocation in 2015
Frequency	Every 6 years	Biannual	Biannual	Annual or Biannual	Biannual
Current	Select strategic objectives (2015-2021)	Select related external control actions (2015-2017)	Select related guidelines (2015-2017)	Select examples of external control activities	Estimated vs. actual human resource allocation 2015
	4. Intensifying activities based on risk analysis	4.2 Identify high-risk areas subject to TCU	Guideline 1 covering objectives 4 and 5: 1.4. Strengthen financial audits of TCU (by December 2016); 1.5. Improve and use analysis methodology risk to support the selection of control objects (by December 2016);		Estimate: 13% **Actual: 32.9%**
	5. Conduct surveys in relevant areas	5.1 Characterize and evaluate policy formulation, implementation and results through systemic diagnosis. 5.2 To assess governance and management of public policies and prioritized public organizations.		Survey to employ the Framework on Centre of Government (SecexFazenda, 2015)	**Estimate: 17%** actual: 11%
Select objectives related to governance	6. Improving the availability and reliability information Public Administration	6.1 Evaluate availability and quality of information offered by the Administration Federal Public Services and e-Gov, to promote the use of open format data, quality electronic services, social control, combating fraud and corruption and public credibility.	Guideline 2 covers objectives 6 and 8: 3.1. Propose a regular and periodic monitoring strategy for auditing the National Education Plan (2014- 2024), to systematize the data record and greater transparency to society (due by June 2015);	Audit of the financial statements of Ministry of Finance (SecexFazenda, 2016) Monitoring of yearly carry over (restos a pagar) (SEMAG, 2016)	**Estimate: 8%** Actual: 7.9%

	Strategic level	Tactical level		Operational level	
	Strategic Plan	External Control Plan	Guidelines	Annual Plans of Units	Human resources dedicated
	8. Encourage the monitoring and evaluation of performance by the Public Administration	8.1 To assess compliance with the decisions issued by TCU. 8.3 To assess government action with regard to fiscal responsibility and macroeconomic stability and the national financial system. 8.4 To assess the effectiveness and sustainability of financing of public policies	3.2. Designing integrated IT solution for the management of TCU's deliberations (due by December 2016); 3.3. Elaborate opening program and dissemination of data TCU (due by October 2015)	Operational/Performance audit to evaluate aspects of Governance of Policies Strengthening public Frontier	estimate: 5% **Actual: 13.6%** (may be higher in 2016 because of 8.7 To monitor and supervise actions related to the Olympics 2016 and the strengthening of high performance sport.)
	7. Induce improvement of risk management and internal controls of public administration	7.1 Assess co-ordination capacity, supervision and control of entities transferring resources, 7.2 Assess the environment and internal control mechanisms and the system risk management of public administration. 7.5 Evaluate the incentive to improve governance 7.9 To assess the effectiveness, efficiency and effectiveness of public plans and budgets.	Guideline 3 covers objective 7: 5.1. Improve governance assessments the Federal Public Administration (due by December 2016); 5.2. Develop and implement management model organizational risk to TCU (due by December 2016);	Monitoring to analyze the legality and legitimacy of the acquisition of a stake by Participações S/A Cash (Caixapar), a wholly owned subsidiary of Caixa Econômica Federal, the company CPM Braxis S/A (Rapporteur: Minister Bruno Dantas). Projected value of benefits: 321.660.000,00 BRL;	**estimate: 12%** actual: 9.5%

1. The strategy is represented in a Strategy Map, a graphic representation that reflects the mission, vision and the organization's strategy into a comprehensive set of objectives that guide the behaviour and institutional performance.

Sources: TCU (2015a), 2015 Annual Report (Relatório Anual - 2015), *http://portal.tcu.gov.br/lumis/portal/file/fileDownload.jsp?fileId=8A8182A153D422DA0153E2950D8064E1*; TCU (2015b), TCU Strategic Plan, 2015-2021 (Plano Estratégico do Tribunal de Contas da União para o período 2015-2021) PORTARIA-TCU N° 141, DE 1° DE ABRIL DE 2015, Brasilia, *http://portal.tcu.gov.br/tcu/paginas/planejamento/2021/index.html* .

Brazil's Federal Court of Accounts
Insight and Foresight for Better Governance

Chapter 2

Auditing for greater policy coherence in Brazil

Government-wide policy coherence is the quality of having unified and consistent public policies and programmes. It requires an overarching view of the functioning of government, and often falls under the remit of central institutions. Supreme Audit Institutions too can leverage audits across public sector entities, sectors and programmes to deepen the understanding of policy coherence in government. At Brazil's federal level, there are numerous entities with decision-making power but with little incentive or requirement to co-ordinate. A siloed approach does not work in an era marked by cross-cutting policy challenges, and intertwined commitments to sustainable development, that require co-ordinated action. This chapter explores how Brazil's supreme audit institution, the Tribunal de Contas da União (TCU), can promote (i) strengthening of institutional mechanisms for coherence and (ii) an understanding of policy interactions and policy effects. It is informed by activities of other supreme audit institutions seeking to reduce waste and inefficiency across government that is borne by a lack of coherence.

2.1. Introduction

Government-wide policy coherence is the quality of having unified and consistent public policies and programmes. Establishing government-wide coherence relies on effective management of conflicting objectives and trade-offs, reducing waste and avoiding unnecessary redundancies in expenditure of public funds across and between levels of government. Policy coherence is critical for tackling "wicked problems," which are policy issues that are dynamic, poorly structured, persistent and social in nature and highly intertwined with other social issues, such as climate change, immigration, poverty, nutrition, education, or homelessness (OECD, 2016a). An absence of coherence can limit the impact of intra-sectoral policies that are critical for citizens' well-being, such as water, land use and education (OECD, 2016b; 2015b; TCU, 2015).

In Brazil, the size and complexity of the government and the existence of multiple actors with decision-making power at the federal level create challenges for maintaining policy coherence. Brazil would benefit from improved inter-ministerial co-ordination, with the Centre of Government (CoG) taking a leading role and providing necessary guidance for synergies between federal entities. Brazil could also benefit from a comprehensive mapping of policies and programmes and their interactions. Supreme audit institutions (SAIs) can play a key role in assessing the capacity and effectiveness of CoG institutions and the bodies responsible for co-ordinating individual policies or programmes.

Many SAIs have developed work streams that go beyond traditional oversight, and they have begun to assess interactions between policies and actions of multiple government entities (OECD, 2016b). In the United States, for instance, the Congress required the SAI to assess the fragmentation, overlap and duplication of policies and programmes related to high-level cross-cutting priorities of the federal government. Drawing from such practices and international principles, the OECD recommends that Brazil's SAI, the Tribunal de Contas da União (TCU), strengthen its efforts to contribute to policy coherence by assessing institutional mechanisms that enable communication and co-ordination, as well as the policy interactions and effects that facilitate or hinder achievement of broader goals.

2.2. Overview: policy coherence at the federal level

Coherence has become increasingly important as governments respond to interconnected challenges and advance national goals that involve multiple entities. Since 2008, more than half of OECD member countries increased the number of cross-governmental initiatives. Governments are establishing teams of experts meant to tackle particularly complex goals, such as climate change, that come in addition to inter-ministerial committees (OECD, 2014a). OECD member countries have established specific units to co-ordinate whole-of-government approaches in order to deliver services and results (OECD, 2014a).

There are three main obstacles to bringing greater coherence to Brazil's policy making process highlighted here. The first is the nature of the decentralised policy-making environment, whereby policy implementation is carried out predominantly by its 26 diverse states and Federal District. With expectations for rapid implementation of policy reforms through the tiered Federal system, Brazil has relied heavily on testing of new approaches at the municipal level where delivery of services in rendered and where interaction with citizens occurs (Rio+ Centre, 2014). Successful programmes may then be rolled out horizontally (to other municipalities and states) and vertically (to the federal level). The inception and testing of ideas at the local level, and the range in capacity of service delivery across states and municipalities, makes it challenging to acquire a clear idea of the variety of programmes in Brazil, and their implications on one another (Rio+ Centre, 2014).

Secondly, the federal level works through its own brand of complexity that makes it challenging to bring coherence between policy initiatives. Political diversity in the Congress and in Ministries has a tendency to produce juxtaposing priorities across the national level. Thirdly, a high administrative burden may impact co-ordination across the government. The Index for Public Integrity (2016) rated Brazil's administrative burden as the second worst in all 105 countries ranked[1]. OECD work on regulatory policy shows that excessively burdensome controls can lead to a greater risk of circumvention of control processes, inefficiencies or unnecessary delays in delivering public services.[2] Cutting "red tape" can improve productivity, and was increasingly sought following financial crises in the 2000's (OECD, 2010). In Brazil, a high administrative burden is coupled with a shorter-term policy focus, denoted by the absence of long-term plans and goals in the Brazilian federal public administration, and existing siloes between ministries.

Governments may see mechanisms for policy coherence, and facilitating co-ordination, as time consuming or as an additional administrative burden. Yet, coherence is a worthwhile endeavour, particularly in times of fiscal consolidation and cutbacks, as it is a way of "doing more with less" and avoiding waste in expenditure. Coherence helps to ensure that duplication of entities' efforts are justified according to the broader policy objectives. It helps to determine when redundancy can lead to cost savings. In many cases, seeking policy coherence requires only modifications to existing structures or processes.

Through their audit work, supreme audit institutions (SAIs) can support the achievement of international principles related to policy coherence (OECD, 2016c). For instance, some SAIs incorporate, as a focus of their audits, mechanisms for effective co-ordination or elements that aim to build the capacity of leaders to manage increasingly cross-cutting policy interventions (OECD, 2016c). Moreover, audits and evaluations that look across sectors and ministries, particularly those with shared goals, can help to improve governance and reduce redundant, incoherent or competing efforts, as described below (see recommendation 2.2.). SAIs can also carry out such assessments of governance functions, like internal control and risk management, in order to address challenges and solutions for systemic issues (see Chapter 4).

TCU's focus on good governance in recent years includes the development of Frameworks that are relevant for assessing policy coherence. In particular, the introduction of the *Framework for Evaluation of the Centre of Government* (TCU, 2016a) should enable more systematic assessment of institutional mechanisms for policy coherence, as the criteria is mostly geared towards institutional mechanisms for communication and co-ordination. Most of TCU's work that comments on communication and co-ordination in recent years has focused on the legal framework and the effectiveness and consistency in practice. Recommendations are made below as to how TCU can leverage this existing work that touches upon institutional mechanisms needed for coherence.

Like its SAI peers around the world, TCU has begun exploring mechanisms for assessing policy coherence by tapping in to its "bird's eye view" of functioning across government. TCU's 2011-2015 strategic plan (PET) ushered in a restructuring of "secretariats" (units), aimed to enhance co-ordination between units and to focus each unit on public governance (OECD, 2014b; 2013a). The 2013 restructuring grouped staff together by sectors to enable specialisation and communication around thematic topics. For instance, social policies are captured under one co-ordinated and specialised Secretariat (OECD, 2013a). The success of the reorganisation in giving auditors a more holistic view of governance and improving communication was disputed in discussions with a range of TCU staff across levels. Recommendations are made in chapter 1 for TCU to further seek improvements in communication and co-ordination within TCU itself.

Between 2014 and 2016, TCU developed two key frameworks that provide criteria for the assessment of mechanisms that are critical to policy coherence. TCU's *Framework to Assess Governance in Public Policies* (2014) provides potential audit questions to enable auditors to consider how policies or programmes are governed. In doing so, it establishes guiding principles around co-ordination and coherence, as well as questions and criteria to analyse during an audit. This Framework is complemented by the new *Framework for Evaluation of the Centre of Government* (TCU, 2016a), which provides questions and concepts pertaining to the strategy, co-ordination, supervision and transparency of CoG institutions.[3]

OECD's recommendations related to policy coherence aim to support TCU's current strategic objectives 1 and 5 in particular. Objective 1 is to improve the governance and management in public and political organisations. Objective 5 is to conduct evaluations in relevant areas to promote the assessment of the governance and management of public policies (5.2) (TCU, 2015b). There is more yet that TCU can do to help support coherence through assessment of policy interactions and policy effects in the short, medium and long-term. These approaches aim to support reduction of waste and use of non-conflicting policies and programmes. TCU can move towards assessment of policy interactions and policy effects, as recommended in Table 2.1.

Table 2.1. **Recommendations: Auditing for greater policy coherence in Brazil**

TCU could more systematically assess institutional mechanisms for coherence, including the capacities of audited entities to constructively communicate and co-ordinate with entities relevant to the achievement of interrelated policy goals.

- TCU could conduct periodic assessments of the existence, capacity and effectiveness of entities (e.g. the Centre of Government, intergovernmental co-ordination bodies or decentralised entities) to communicate and co-ordinate around cross-cutting initiatives and "wicked" problems, including incorporating its frameworks into audits of year-end accounts.

TCU could develop a body of audit work to assess policy interactions and policy effects across government, beginning with a pilot review of fragmentation, overlap and duplication of programmes in key sectors.

- TCU could conduct periodic evaluations of the synergies and trade-offs between sectoral or national plans, in the short, medium or long-term, as well as between cross-cutting programmes that appear in the government's multi-annual plan.
- TCU could pilot a review of fragmentation, overlap and duplication in intra-sectoral policies or programmes, such as those geared towards poverty eradication, raising productivity and regional development, for instance.
- TCU could assess congruence of actions, trend indicators and the results of public policies related to the achievement of the Sustainable Development Goals.

2.3. Systematically assessing institutional mechanisms for coherence

TCU could more systematically assess institutional mechanisms for coherence, including the capacities of audited entities to constructively communicate and co-ordinate with entities relevant to the achievement of interrelated policy goals.

Adapting institutional mechanisms to bring greater coherence refers to enabling the capacity of entities, and particularly Centre of Government (CoG) institutions, to co-ordinate and communicate with each other on shared goals. Coherence supports the formulation of policies that are aligned, or at least not detrimental, to the success of others. It supports smooth implementation when those responsible for implementation are aware of the impact of their actions vis-à-vis others'. It further supports more consistent policy evaluation, when policy objectives are coherent, consistent and shared.

OECD experience shows that policy co-ordination is primarily a CoG responsibility. Over three-quarters of OECD member countries restructured the CoG between 2008 and 2012, reinforcing capacities and budgets.[4] These changes reflect government attempts to take a more coherent approach to cross-cutting issues that require a collective response (OECD, 2014a). Discussions with TCU highlight a need for a greater understanding of the importance and relevance of the role of the CoG in Brazil as a response to cross-cutting and complex issues. TCU's 2016 *Framework for Evaluation of the Centre of Government* seeks to promote a greater role for the CoG.

Policy co-ordination between entities in Brazil remains a challenge with 24 Ministries and 15 organisations with Ministerial status. Brazil's bureaucratic nature of public administration, and diffused power, promotes siloes and provides little incentives for entities to co-ordinate with one another. In addition, Brazil's cabinet has a hierarchic-bureaucratic nature, with the chief of staff playing a significant role in centralising decision making (Bertelsmann Stiftung, 2016). Yet, the CoG has been hesitant to accept a co-ordinating role according to TCU testimonials. Moreover, decades of coalition presidentialism have limited success in efforts for co-ordination and communication (Bertelsmann Stiftung, 2016). Twenty-six political parties are represented in the Congress, 10 of which are represented at the Minister level.

One example of efforts for cross-governmental co-ordination is the National Education Plan (*Plano Nacional de Educacão*, or PNE) (2014-2024). The PNE is one of few sectoral plans that take a long-term perspective. The PNE requires that the fulfilment of goals are subject to continuous monitoring and periodic evaluations performed by a group of actors that include the Ministry of education, the Education committee of the House of Deputies and the Committee of Education, Culture and Sport of the Senate, the National Education Council and the National Education Forum (Article 5). Brazil's states, Federal District and municipalities are meant to create mechanisms for achievement monitoring at the local level, as well as for co-operation arrangements that include permanent negotiation, co-operation and agreement processes in each state (article 7). The success of the PNE will depend largely on the collaboration between the Union, the Federal District, states and municipalities, recognized in the PNE for collaborative role in implementing the Plan (Brazil, 2014).

In other areas, attempts for co-ordination have not led to practical or effective application. For instance, the Internal Control Co-ordination Commission (*Comissão de Coordenação de Controle Interno*, CCCI), of which TCU is a part, was founded in 2001. This group has only met 4 times in 15 years, the last being in August 2015. The CCCI has a number of high level officials, and is chaired by the Chief Minister of the Comptroller General (CGU, 2016). Given the importance of internal control and accountability, co-ordination around the topic would be beneficial for Brazil. This is discussed further in chapter 4.

As part of its strategic plans, TCU has increasingly focused on policy coherence as a subject of its work, particularly performance audits, according to TCU Ministers and staff. The assessment of co-ordination and coherence has become more common as a result of the *Framework to Assess Governance in Public Policies*, a TCU framework meant to strengthen analysis of governance issues (TCU, 2014a). However, TCU has incorporated coherence issues, including communication and co-ordination, as part of its performance audits for years, including the following examples:

- Audit of the governance structure of the Federal Executive planning system - this analysis of the federal executive planning system demonstrates regulatory gaps which pose limitations on the operational system (Judgement 3580/2014) (TCU, 2014b).
- Assessment of governance aspects related to the Logistics Investment - the assessment included the Ministry of Transport, the National Land Transportation Agency; Valec Engineering, Construction and Railroads SA (Valec) and Enterprise Planning and Logistics S.A. (Judgement 1.205/2015) (TCU, 2014c).
- Audit of regional development policy - this focused on the national policy for regional development and aimed to understand and identify structural features that may be responsible for any successes and performance gaps. (Judgement 2919/2009) (TCU, 2009).

OECD's "Supreme Audit Institutions and Good Governance: Oversight, Insight and Foresight" (2016c) shows that the majority of 10 leading SAIs are assessing governments against international principles with regard to policy coherence. For instance, in a survey of 10 SAIs:

- 8 of 10 SAIs assessed mechanisms for effective co-ordination for implementation between levels of government, within entities and across entities.
- 6 of 10 SAIs assessed the capacity and/or efficacy of central government units (ex. CoG), including ensuring the long-term vision is harmonised with other key documents (fiscal plans), and the long-term vision is reflected in ministries work plans.
- 6 of 10 SAIs assessed the separation of roles functions/roles of relevant actors, in terms of co-ordination and/or overlap of functions in regulatory management, budgetary management and internal control.
- 6 of 10 SAIs assessed the effectiveness of central co-ordination bodies in communicating and co-ordinating, such as ensuring senior management of ministries are aware of trends and risks, as well as providing guidance to departments and line ministries.

TCU could build from the dissemination of comprehensive work already undertaken in developing the Frameworks, and in the lessons learned from audits that have looked at communication and co-ordination and central entities, to allow for a more systematic approach in this governance area. A more systematic approach means that audit questions (provided for in relevant frameworks and the performance manual) are applied and enable comparison between co-ordination mechanisms of entities and within different programmes. This also enables TCU to pull out good practices in this domain, which can inspire others. TCU could more systematically assess institutional mechanisms for coherence by taking the following actions:

TCU could conduct periodic assessments of the existence, capacity and effectiveness of entities (e.g. the Centre of Government, intergovernmental co-ordination bodies or decentralised entities) to communicate and co-ordinate around cross-cutting initiatives and "wicked" problems, including incorporating its frameworks into audits of year-end accounts.

TCU's work in this area could build on previous audits which already offer insights on communication and co-ordination. These audits could be guided by TCU's governance frameworks, which suggest questions that audit teams may consider in their performance audits. Table 2.2 provides those, along with others that the OECD's new *Framework for Policy Coherence* (2016d) identified as useful to better understand institutional mechanisms in country.

The aforementioned audits included communication and co-ordination as one element of a broader analysis. Yet, TCU has not made the CoG's institutional mechanisms for communication and co-ordination a specific audit subject. For instance, TCU has not conducted specific audits on the functioning of the Under-Secretary for Monitoring and Assessment of Government Policies (*Subchefia de Análise e Acompanhamento de Políticas Governamentais*, SAG). TCU could draw inspiration from the example of the United Kingdom's National Audit Office (NAO), which explicitly assessed institutional mechanisms for establishing coherence, or institutions' capacities to do so, as an audit subject.

The UK's NAO synthesised years of work on CoG institutions to create a report (NAO, 2014). Recognising its critical role, the NAO examined the CoG (HM Treasury and Cabinet Office), focusing on the effectiveness of the CoG's strategic planning, leadership and co-ordination functions. Additional sources for assessing the maturity of CoG functions include the *Centre of government institutional development matrix*, as developed by the IADB (IADB, 2014). TCU may also complement the questions provided for it its own Frameworks, with OECD's questions for establishing institutional mechanisms for coherence (Table 2.2).

Table 2.2. **Audit questions for assessing institutional mechanisms for coherence**

TCU's Framework for Evaluation of the Centre of Government
Has co-ordination effectively stimulated or been conducive to co-operation between line ministries?
How is the co-ordination role of the Centre of Government exercised for policy design and implementation?
How is the government communication strategy co-ordinated and aligned?
TCU's Framework to Assess Governance in Public Policies
To what extent do various government actors, involved in public policy making, work in a coherent and co-ordinated manner with each other?
How is it that the relationship between the levels of government allow for public policy to be developed in a cohesive and co-ordinated way?
Other suggested questions to integrate
What mechanisms are in place to help increase the informal flow of information across ministries, institutions and sectors?
How are sustained collaborative relationships promoted among senior-level officials across the government?
Have formal mechanisms been established for inter-ministerial collaboration, co-ordination and policy arbitration around national plans or strategies, policies or programmes? Do those mechanisms provide opportunities to inform ex ante on future policy making?

Sources: OECD (2016c), Better Policies for Sustainable Development 2016: A New Framework for Policy Coherence, OECD Publishing, Paris. *http://dx.doi.org/10.1787/9789264256996-en*; TCU (2016a), Framework for Evaluation of the Centre of Government, TCU Publishing, Brasilia, *http://portal.tcu.gov.br/lumis/portal/file/fileDownload.jsp?fileId=8A8182A25454C5A801545DC1433145ED*; TCU (2014a), Framework to Assess Governance in Public Policies, TCU Publishing, Brasilia, *http://portal2.tcu.gov.br/portal/pls/portal/docs/2686056.PDF*

As another example, the Australian National Audit Office audited government wide cross-cutting collaboration by reviewing current arrangements and the breadth of agency interdependencies. Cross-agency collaboration was audited by examining 200 cross agency agreements from twenty one public sector agencies. The audit found that there was inconsistency in overall clarity, quality and completeness of agreements across agencies. TCU could draw from this example, including consideration of the key elements for cross-agency collaboration elaborated in the Australian context, as illustrated in Box 2.1 below.

Box 2.1. **Mechanisms for greater coherence and co-ordination in Australia**

In 1992, the Council of Australian Governments was established to improve the effectiveness and efficiency of service delivery between the federal and state governments (Jones 2008). Since its inception, the COAG has developed numerous initiatives designed to prevent duplication, fragmentation and overlap in government, and promote policy coherence. Commitments of the COAG can be outlined in intergovernmental agreements or statements of cooperation (Jones 2008).

In addition, collaboration agreements can also be effective for enhancing policy coherence between agencies and departments at the same level of government. In Australia, formal bilateral or multilateral memoranda of understanding establish a foundation for the working relationship, which sets out roles and responsibilities as well as performance expectations and reporting arrangements. These agreements can also include specifications for particular deliverables, as well as quality measures and timeframes.

Cross agency agreements are diverse in their form and content, because each is tailored to a specific situation and set of agreements. Agreements can come in the form of exchange of letter, a detailed Memorandum of Understanding, or a high level collaborative agreement. These agreements can range from simple data sharing to establishing specific responsibilities when agencies can be interdependent. Almost all of these arrangements, however, are not legally binding because often they are between parts of the same legal entity. The inconsistencies in the agreements reflect the limited availability of guidance for developing non-legally binding agreements. In an audit report on effective cross-agency agreements, the ANAO outlined principles for agencies to create their own guidelines. These principles can help agencies improve a common understanding of cross-agency agreements, as well as establish internal scrutiny to ensure the agreements are functioning effectively and are tailored to their particular situation. In order to maximise policy coherence, all cross-agency agreements should contain:

- Objectives of the arrangement
- Desired outcomes and timeframes
- Roles and responsibilities of each party
- The goods or services to be provided
- Performance indicators
- Revenue and budgetary issues
- Implementing suitable governance and communication arrangements
- Considering risks and incorporating reporting and review provisions: Shared risk management mechanisms, such as dispute resolution mechanisms, can help agencies in planning for the management and early resolution of any problems.
- Development of guidance material and agency controls

Up to date registers can also enhance effectiveness of cross cutting agreements through internal monitoring and improving the quality and consistency of arrangements. The registers can easily inform an agency of poor performance under an arrangement and also ensure that deliverables and accountability requirements are met. These registers are particularly effective in agencies which have many agreements which need regular review.

Source: OECD (2016b), *Supreme Audit Institution and Good Governance: Oversight, Insight and Foresight*, OECD Public Governance Reviews, OECD Publishing, Paris. *http://dx.doi.org/10.1787/9789264263871-en*; Australian National Audit Office 'Effective Cross Agency Agreements,' Audit Report No. 41 2009-10, available at: *https://www.anao.gov.au/sites/g/files/net2766/f/ANAO_Report_2009-2010_41.pdf*; ANAO (2009); Jones, S. (2008), "Cooperative Federalism?" The Case of the Ministerial Council on Education, Employment, Training and Youth Affairs the Australian Journal of Public Administration 67 (2): 161–172, available at: *http://onlinelibrary.wiley.com/doi/10.1111/j.1467-8500.2008.00579.x/full*

It is critical for TCU to not only disseminate its frameworks internally, but also to further integrate them into existing audit work in order to institutionalise key governance concepts and promote consistency. This could include further incorporation of the frameworks into analysis of audits related to year-end accounts of line ministries. Such integration could help TCU to develop a birds-eye, holistic view of policy challenges and solutions related to specific sectors. Currently, audits related to the year-end accounts emphasise financial performance. There are opportunities for orienting some of the content of this fundamental aspect of TCU's work towards governance concepts, like measuring impact, assessing the quality of indicators and strategic planning. This would offer a comparative view of ministries working in different sectors, and when aggregated, can help to draw a picture about how government is functioning in a number of areas.

2.4. Strengthening assessments of policy interactions and policy effects across government

TCU could develop a body of audit work to assess policy interactions and policy effects across government, beginning with a pilot review of fragmentation, overlap and duplication of programmes in key sectors.

Mapping policy interactions in Brazil

Coherence requires a common understanding of the policy interactions across sectors that can facilitate or hamper the realisation of other policy goals. Brazil's government struggles to manage and co-ordinate conflicting objectives because of significant "intra-governmental friction" and difficulties in establishing transversal and co-ordinated policies across key ministries (Bertelsmann Stiftung, 2016). As mentioned above, siloes between a large number of Federal entities limits a shared understanding of the implications of policy interactions.

Deepening the understanding of policy interactions is particularly important at the current juncture in Brazil, where financial decisions are being made about citizen-sensitive policy areas, such as human security, health and environment. Trade-offs that will be made in the name of fiscal austerity and efficiency in social spending should be based on evidence about the pros and cons of each policy and programme individually, as well as on their interaction with others.

Medium and long-term policy commitments of governments put further pressure on countries to deepen the understanding of policy effects on a long-term horizon. In the context of Brazil, medium-term commitments are found in the latest Multi-annual plan (*Plano Pluriannual*, PPA), spanning from 2016-2019, as well as in entity and sector-level plans, such as the National Education Plan (2014-2024). Long-term commitment is made by default through adherence to the Sustainable Development Goals (SDGs) that are to be met by 2030.

Mapping and managing policy interactions in Brazil is a means of mitigating negative impacts of fragmentation, overlap and duplication. For instance, OECD's 2015 "Water Resources Governance in Brazil" discusses the need for a deeper understanding of the effects between Brazil's sectors of water management, agricultural development, waste management and health. Solutions for droughts (in the northeast) may simultaneously compete with demands for irrigation in Central Brazil, and for management of polluted water in large cities (OECD, 2015b).

Brazil would benefit from assessing existing efforts to understand policy interactions – in order to roll out good practices and build on the lessons learned. One such example is in the context of Brazil's national disaster risk management (DDR). The responsibility for Disaster and Risk Management co-ordination usually lies with an OECD member country's CoG, and particularly in a central planning or co-ordinating unit. Along with many OECD countries, Brazil has recognised the importance of linking DDR to other key sectors. Brazil has integrated its DDR planning into public investment and planning decisions, the national development plan, the civil defence policy planning, in land zoning and real estate development. Brazil could go further to integrate national risk planning into sector strategies and plans to ensure that efforts to co-ordinate the approach an enacted in individual plans for implementation (OECD, 2015c).

A second initiative that works to promote government-wide coherence is the Programme for the Strengthening of Institutional Capacity for Regulatory Management (PRO-REG) (PRO-REG, 2012). Established in 2007, PRO-REG provides a good example of information sharing to strengthen institutional capacity for regulatory management. One objective of the PRO-REG initiative is to "improve co-ordination and strategic views between sectoral policies and the regulatory process". The Management Committee and Consultative Committee were required to mobilise different institutions inside administration that are involved in the regulatory process. The programme is responsible for co-ordinating the formulation of concrete proposals to be implemented by regulatory bodies (OECD, 2008). With similar intentions, the Brazilian Foreign Trade Board (CAMEX) created an inter-ministerial technical group to gather streamline domestic legislation about foreign trade, by harmonising, rationalising and simplifying it[5]. The expected benefit of regulatory coherence is to bring about more effective, efficient and comprehensive regulations that result in cost savings.

Understanding policy effects in the short, medium and long term in Brazil

Policy coherence can be fostered with a better understanding of policy effects (both positive and negative consequences) in the short, medium and long-term. Governments need to have an understanding of the intended and potential effects of the policy in the policy design phase to ensure that the policy will be implemented and evaluated in a way that allows for accurate assessment and adjustment. Appropriate monitoring and evaluation, during and after implementation, is also important for gathering information on what has worked and what has not, and for making adjustments as needed. The role of monitoring and evaluation is discussed in detail in chapter 5.

Brazil's commitment to the SDGs will test the government's ability to make simultaneous progress in tackling "wicked" policy issues – those issues that are interrelated, involve many actors, and have unintended and often opaque consequences on other policy areas, such as poverty, health, education, climate and the economy (OECD, 2016a). Meeting the SDGs will require appropriate foresight of whether policies will achieve intended outcomes by 2020, 2025 and by 2030. The potential to use policy coherence as an opportunity to spur sustainable development, including meeting the SDGs, is discussed further in Box 2.2.

Acquiring a sense of policy effects over the short, medium and long term is no small task. Brazil could benefit from mechanisms to compare entity-level assessments of policy effects during the policy formulation process. Annual policy objectives for public sector entities could be established, where appropriate, in line with the guidelines and government targets in the PPA, the Budgetary Guidelines Law (LDO) and the Annual Budget Law (LOA) (Article 144 I, Law 11,784). When entities establish goals in accordance with the PPA, entities could be considering the contributions of different policy objectives, and programmes, to the country's medium-term framework. When priorities are established outside of the PPA however, and without a long-term vision in the country with which entities can align objectives, there is room for entity-level managers to develop goals that may be conflicting with those of other entities' or that may be on a different time horizon than those of other entities.

Box 2.2. **Policy Coherence for Sustainable development**

The United Nation's seventeen Sustainable Development Goals (SDGs) are ambitious objectives to achieve fair, long-term development globally. The development goals are by nature interconnected and overlapping and, as such, they demand a certain level of coherence in government policy and approach. Accordingly, the 2030 Agenda for Sustainable Development and the Addis Ababa Action Agenda call on countries to 'pursue policy coherence and an enabling environment for sustainable development at all levels and by all actors' (OECD, 2016d).

SAIs can contribute towards the achievement of SDGs in a number of ways, particularly in regard to SDG 16 to 'promote peaceful and inclusive societies for sustainable development, and provide access to justice for all and build effective, accountable and inclusive institutions at all levels'. For instance, increasing transparency in national budgets and ensuring all expenditure is accounted for (SDG 16.6.1) is linked to the core role of the SAI. In doing so, SAIs may play a role in the fight against illicit financial flows (SGD 16.4) and in reducing "corruption and bribery in all their forms" (SDG 16.5) (de Vries, 2016).

In regard to other SDGs, SAIs can monitor and report on the efficiency and effectiveness of national systems, as well as sectorial policies, to implement goals and targets. The Auditor General of South Africa, for example, did this with the country's Kha Ri Gude Campaign. The Kha Ri Gude Campaign sought to achieve a number of Millennium Development Goals and enable 4.7 million functionally illiterate and semi-illiterate adults to become literate and numerate in one of the eleven official languages of South Africa by 2015. A great deal of resources were invested in the campaign, however only 47% of the targeted 4.7 million unschooled adults had completed or passed the related tests (OECD, 2016c). The AGSA audited the campaign to answer the question: 'Was the Kha Ri Gude campaign economically, efficiently, and effectively implemented to ensure the reduction of adult illiteracy in South Africa?" Emulating the approach of AGSA, SAIs can help countries leverage lessons learned from the Millennium Development Goal strategies and evaluate the existing SDG strategies at the sectorial and national level to contribute to sustainable development.

Given the importance of policy coherence in achieving SDGs, countries are forced to consider the value of policy co-ordination for development. In Germany, for example, the Federal Ministry for Economic Cooperation and Development is responsible for promoting policy coherence for development across the German government and the EU. Having a seat in the cabinet allows the Federal Ministry for Economic Cooperation and Development to scrutinise all policies from a development perspective. Additionally, in recent years, Portugal's Inter-Ministerial Commission for Co-operation has broadened its mandate to include addressing policy coherence for development as well as co-ordinating the national development programme (OECD, 2016d).

Subsequently, monitoring and reporting on the effectiveness and efficiency of national and sectorial development strategies with a particular focus on policy coherence can be one of the most important ways SAIs contribute towards sustainable development. The Swedish National Audit Office (NAO), for instance, audited the government's gender equality initiative. From 2007-2014, the Government set aside SEK 2.6 billion to instruct fifty government agencies in gender mainstreaming as well as allocate funds directly to municipalities, county councils, and non-profit organisations. The audit showed that changes which had been made in the governance of agencies through the new Government Agencies Ordinance directed governance through instructions and dialogues with agencies and removed the focus on gender. Traditional sectorial thinking has been amplified with the new organisation-adapted governance through informal dialogue between agencies and ministries, which has in turn

Box 2.2. **Policy Coherence for Sustainable development** *(cont.)*

affected the possibilities of gender equality having an impact. The NAO saw a risk that there was a risk of losing gender as an element of governance across entities. The NAO thus recommended development of an institutional structure to strengthen the government's gender mainstreaming strategy, as they found it to be inadequately aimed at developing and integrating gender mainstreaming work in the ordinary structures and operations of the agencies. Ultimately, as the audit of the gender equality initiative illustrated the complexity of many SDG initiatives that must be met with improved policy coherence. As such, SAIs can focus on policy coherence when evaluating national and sectorial development strategies linked to SDGs (NAO, 2015).

Source: OECD (2016b), *Supreme Audit Institutions and Good Governance: Oversight, Insight and Foresight*, OECD Public Governance Reviews, OECD Publishing, Paris. *http://dx.doi.org/10.1787/9789264263871-en*; OECD (2016c), *Better Policies for Sustainable Development 2016: A New Framework for Policy Coherence*, OECD Publishing, Paris. *http://dx.doi.org/10.1787/9789264256996-en*; de Vries (2016) 'How National Audit Offices Can Support Implementation of the SDGs' Public Financial Management Blog, 28 June 2016, *http://blog-pfm.imf.org/pfmblog/2016/06/national-audit-offices-should-support-implementation-of-the-sdgs.html?utm_source=feedburner&utm_medium=email&utm_campaign=Feed%3A+pfmblog+%28PFM+blog%29*; National Audit Office of Sweden (NAO) (2015), 'Summary: The Government's gender equality initiative- temporary or permanent improvements?' Report no, RIR 2015: 13, 11 June 2015, Stockholm, *http://www.riksrevisionen.se/PageFiles/22905/Summary_2015_13.pdf*.

There is no requirement in Brazilian laws for consideration of policy effects in the short, medium or long-term, or interactions with other policies or programmes. Public entities are meant to widely disseminate institutional goals and results in each period, including through the Integrated Planning and Budget System (SIOP). However, the extent to which entities consider other goals and results, or policy effects, when developing their own, is unclear.[6] In previous audits, TCU has found that certain policies have been developed with no consideration of the potential effects and implications with other policies.

At current, the CoG does not have a mechanism for assessing the positive and negative impacts of policies and programmes on one another, across government, on a consistent basis. Brazil could benefit from a unit, whether within existing structures or new, specifically dedicated to understanding policy effects and policy interactions, as done in the United Kingdom, for instance.[7]

Medium and long-term commitments of put pressure on countries to deepen the understanding of policy effects on a long-term horizon. In the context of Brazil, these commitments include the latest PPA, spanning from 2016-2019, entity and sector-level plans, such as the National Education Plan (2014-2024), and commitment to the SDGs that are to be met by 2030.

The difficulty in understanding policy effects stems from inconsistent application of evaluation guidelines at the sector and entity level. Further, it is difficult for CoG officials to get into the technical details of the programmes or policies at hand. Thus it is critical that they provide guidance for the smooth and consistent application of guidelines in evaluation and in practitioner's consideration of evidence in future formulation stages of policy making.

OECD's 2015 "Water Resources Governance in Brazil" discusses the need for a deeper understanding of the effects between Brazil's sectors of water management, agricultural development, waste management and health. Solutions for droughts (in the northeast) may simultaneously compete with demands for irrigation in Central Brazil, and for management of polluted water in large cities. While maintaining flexibility at the state and municipal level,

Brazil would benefit from central level co-ordination that could work with relevant entities to mitigate counterproductive effects of varying goals of relevant sectors (OECD, 2015b).

TCU's audit work can help to fill this void in knowledge and evidence. To date, TCU's work and frameworks have focused on the existence of co-ordination bodies and their efficacy. TCU could strengthen its support to enabling policy coherence in Brazil, by expanding beyond effective interaction of entities to the interactions of cross-cutting policies themselves. To date, TCU's work and frameworks have focused on the existence of co-ordination bodies and their efficacy. TCU has looked across sectors, policies and programmes to understand the linkages, such as in the series of audits around the Regional Development Policy. However, these policy interactions could feature well a specific subject of an audit.

In seeking to inform policies with a deeper understanding of policy interactions and policy effects, TCU could develop a body of audit work to assess policy interactions and policy effects across government. Specifically:

- TCU could conduct periodic evaluation of the synergies and trade-offs: between sectoral or national plans, in the short, medium or long-term; and between cross-cutting programmes that appear in the PPA;
- TCU could pilot a review of fragmentation, overlap and duplication in intra-sectoral policies or programmes, such as those geared towards poverty eradication, raising productivity and regional development, for instance; and
- TCU could assess congruence of actions, trend indicators and the results of public policies related to the achievement of the Sustainable Development Goals.

TCU could conduct periodic evaluations of the synergies and trade-offs between sectoral or national plans, in the short, medium or long-term, as well as between cross-cutting programmes that appear in the government's multi-annual plan.

TCU could conduct periodic evaluation of the synergies and trade-offs: between sectoral or national plans, in the short, medium or long-term; and between cross-cutting programmes that appear in the PPA. With the Adoption of the Growth Acceleration plan (PAC), TCU's control task was to be carried out "in co-ordination with ministries, agencies and other governmental entities with the aim of ensuring a systemic and integration vision of the PAC". While the PAC has since been discontinued, TCU did conduct such audits (TCU, 2010; 2008; 2007). Other future audit subjects could include the National Education Plan, National Plan of Logistics and Transport, National Energy Plan and the Sustainable Amazon Plan, among others.

TCU can assess how plans, policies and programmes interact, through assessing key strategic documents of government. To this end, below (Table 2.3) are potential criteria for TCU to consider integrating into audits, based on international principles and good practices. TCU could use these to supplement existing governance frameworks of analysis to reflect these criteria.

TCU can gain further inspiration from the SAI of Korea – the Korean Board of Audit and Inspection (BAI) – which assessed a number of policies meant to stabilise housing of lower and middle-income families. BAI found that the incongruence between the medium and long-term housing supply plans was a determinant of excess housing that was not appropriately matched to population and ageing trends and projections for the long-term (see Box 2.3).

Table 2.3. **Suggested questions and criteria for assessing policy coherence**

Mapping policy interactions
• Have economic, social and environmental policy inter-linkages (synergies and trade-offs) been considered in the development of plans and priorities?
• Do existing inter-linkages (synergies and trade-offs) pose risk to the achievement of policy goals, or risk waste in public expenditure?
• How do the planned policy outputs of plans and priorities contribute to broader long-term goals, including commitments to the SDGs?
• How do the actions to attain one policy or programme support or hinder the actions of another?
Understanding policy effects in the short, medium and long-term
• In the formulation of policies and programmes, were enabling and disabling factors (e.g. trends, projections of growth, stability of the financial system, assessments of environmental risk) taken into account?
• Has the government identified and assessed contextual factors (corruption, barriers to trade, knowledge) which may impact the achievement of goals?
• Does the policy produce unintended effects, positive or negative, that could affect the well-being of citizens in other states, or in other countries?
• Which groups would be affected and how? How can the unintended negative effects be mitigated?
• Have the potential direct or indirect long-term effects on well-bring of future generations been identified?
• Are the economic, social and environmental costs of policy decisions considered?

Sources: Adapted from: OECD (2016c) *Better Policies for Sustainable Development 2016: A New Framework for Policy Coherence, OECD Publishing, Paris. http://dx.doi.org/10.1787/9789264256996-en* ; IDB (2014) 'Governing to Deliver: Reinventing the Center of Government in Latin America and the Caribbean' Inter-American Development Bank, Washington DC, *https://publications.iadb.org/bitstream/handle/11319/6674/Governing-to-Deliver-Reinventing-the-Center-of-Government-in-Latin-America-and-the-Caribbean.pdf?sequence=1*; NAO (2014) 'The centre of government' HC 171, Session 2014-15, 19 June 2014, *https://www.nao.org.uk/wp-content/uploads/2014/06/The-centre-of-government.pdf*; OECD (2014) 'Centre Stage: Driving Better Policies from the Centre of Government' OECD Publishing, Paris. *https://www.oecd.org/gov/Centre-Stage-Report.pdf*

Box 2.3. **The SAI of Korea – assessing policy interactions and effects in medium and long-term housing supply plans**

Objective of performance audit

The Korean government has formulated and implemented various policies to tackle the housing shortage and to stabilise the housing of the middle and lower income families. However, according to BAI, these policies and programmes did not seem to produce the desired effects and may have caused various side effects, including: the privatisation of public development interests; destruction of comparatively favourable residences for middle and lower income families; and waste from suspension or delay of some programmes.

BAI reviewed the appropriateness of the planning, implementation, and feedback stages, as well as institutional and programme performance. In *The housing stabilisation policy and key programmes for the middle and lower income families*, BAI provides alternative policy options that can contribute to housing stabilisation of middle and lower income families.

The main target institutions for the audit were the housing policy-formulating government agency, housing policy-delivery public institutions, and local agencies. Country laws/regulations (Framework Act on National Land); key national indicators on housing (housing supply rate, long-term rental rate). The audit required approximately 90 staff days for the preliminary study and 60 staff days for the field audit, which included 12 professional experts.

Outcomes/benefits

The audit pointed to an inconsistency between long- and medium-term housing supply plans. It found that an excess housing supply was caused by an inadequate supply plan that did not fully reflect the recent trends of low fertility and population aging. The following recommendations were made: 1) ensure consistency between medium and long term plans through efficient co-ordination; 2) take action to remedy the supply gap according to area and size; and 3) update the long-term housing policy by incorporating the changes in household type. The audit aimed to enhance the effectiveness of the government's housing policy by making housing supply plans more demand-oriented, and by specially responding to the needs of low-income families.

Source: BAI (2013), The housing stabilization policy of the middle and lower income families (서민주거안정시책 추진실태 공개문), Board of Audit and Inspection of Korea, *www.bai.go.kr/bai/cop/bbs/detailBoardArticle.do?bbsId=BBSMSTR_100000000009&nttId=1489&mdex=bai20&searchCnd=all_NTT_SJ_CN&searchWrd=%EC%84%9C%EB%AF%BC%EC%A3%BC%EA%B1%B0%EC%95%88%EC%A0%95&searchBgnDe=&searchEndDe=&searchYear=&pageIndex=1&recordCountPerPage=10*, (available in Korean only).

TCU could pilot a review of fragmentation, overlap and duplication in intra-sectoral policies or programmes, such as those geared towards poverty eradication, raising productivity and regional development, for instance.

Drawing from the work of the U.S. Government Accountability Office (GAO), TCU could pilot an assessment of fragmentation, overlap and duplication (FOD) in a specific national plan, or intra-sectoral initiative (GAO, 2015). The GAO's body of work focuses on addressing FOD and spurring cost savings. Box 2.4 provides further detail on how the GAO carries out this work on an annual basis. Required to support the identification, reduction or elimination of duplication in government, the GAO began its FOD work in 2011.

Box 2.4. **The U.S. Government Accountability Office: general process for assessing fragmentation, duplication and overlap in government**

Since 2011, the U.S. Government Accountability Office is required to conduct investigations to identify federal programmes, agencies, offices and initiatives with duplicative goals and activities within departments and nationwide. Accordingly, GAO releases an annual report suggesting opportunities to address fragmentation, overlap and duplication (FOD), and to achieve other financial benefits. This report is presented annually to Congress to aid in decision making. In addition, GAO conducts audits linked to the implementation of GPRA Modernization Act of 2010 (GPRAMA). GAO reported that full and effective implementation of GPRAMA was one way for the government to improve management of FOD across government (GAO, 2015b). In order to carry out its FOD reviews, the GAO generally uses a four step process:

1. Identify an approach for selecting programs for a FOD review. This involves establishing the goals and outcomes, the beneficiaries or other target population, key benefits or services, the administering agencies and the appropriations or budget structure. Using this approach, auditors can then identify programs to examine. Qualitative and quantitative methods can be used for assessing fragmentation, overlap and duplication as well as how the programmes are related. For example, compiling detailed descriptions of similarities and differences as well as scoring and rating are effective methods of analysis.
2. Identify potential effects, both positive and negative, of FOD in the selected programmes.
3. Evaluate the performance of each programme concerned to validate the effects of FOD and compare the performance of the programs.
4. Identify options to increase efficiency and reduce or better manage FOD. Specific management approaches may be necessary in order to increase efficiency, such as restructuring out-modelled government organisations and operations, implementing process or technology improvement methods, or implementing a strategic approach to spending.

Source: GAO (2011) 'Opportunities to Reduce Potential Duplication in Government Programs, Save Tax Dollars, and Enhance Revenue: Report to Congressional Addressees (GAO-11—318SP)', March 2011, available at: *http://www.gao.gov/assets/320/315920.pdf*; GAO (2015) 'Fragmentation, Overlap and Duplication: An Evaluation and Management Guide (GAO-15-49SP)', April 2015, available at: *https://www.gao.gov/assets/670/669612.pdf*.

Notes: 'Duplication' occurs when two or more agencies or programs are engaged in the same activities or provide the same services. 'Overlap' is when multiple agencies or programmes have similar goals, engaging in similar activities to achieve them or target similar beneficiaries. 'Fragmentation' refers to circumstances where more than one federal agency is involved in the same area of national need (GAO 2011). Examples of recent GAO reports include GAO (2016) '2016 Annual Report: Additional Opportunities to Reduce Fragmentation, Overlap and Duplication and Achieve Other Financial Benefits (GAO-16-375SP)', available at *https://www.gao.gov/assets/680/676473.pdf* and GAO (2015) '2015 Annual Report: Additional Opportunities to Reduce Fragmentation, Overlap and Duplication and Achieve Other Financial Benefits (GAO-15-404SP)' available at *https://www.gao.gov/assets/670/669613.pdf*.

The GAO's FOD work attempts to tackle the challenge of policy coherence in government. It asks, amongst a range of questions:

- How are programmes related to each other?
- Which programmes are unnecessarily duplicating others?
- Where can efficiencies be found between programmes with shared goals?
- What relations do these programmes have with others?
- Are there legitimate reasons for competition among or redundancies between programmes?[8]

The resulting annual reports shed light on what to enhance and mitigate, as shown in Table 2.4 As is done by GAO, these elements can guide TCU in interpreting the information that would be integrated into a FOD pilot.

Table 2.4. **Assessment of fragmentation, overlap and duplication in government: what to enhance and mitigate?**

Enhance	Mitigate
Relevant expertise	Difficulty in understanding programmes (citizens should not have too much red tape)
Shared resources	Programmes that waste efforts or resources
Shared information	Redundant administrative efforts
Overaching goals	Conflicting or contradictory programmes

Source: GAO (2016), Fragmentation, Overlap, and Duplication in Government Programs, Presentation in Brasilia, May 2016.

A first step for TCU would be to aggregate any existing work that touches on FOD in particular thematic or sectoral areas, and then begin to consider how the questions and criteria for enhancement and mitigation could apply to the Brazilian context. In considering previous audits, TCU can identify particular cross-cutting strategies or initiatives that may suffer from severe overlap or fragmentation and that would thus be a good audit subject of a pilot audit. The pilot approach is best accompanied by an intense communication strategy both internally and externally, that requires TCU to plan ahead for the greatest impact of resulting findings and recommendations to key stakeholders.

TCU could assess congruence of actions, trend indicators and the results of public policies related to the achievement of the Sustainable Development Goals.

As discussed above, Brazil is a signatory to the SDGs which will test the Government's ability to make simultaneous progress in tackling wicked problems such as poverty, health, education, climate and the economy, while adjusting as needed to be on track to meet those commitments. The OECD's *Policy Coherence for Sustainable Development* screening tool offers an integrated checklist of elements that governments could consider, much of which can be applied by governments in the preparation, implementation and evaluation of SDG approaches. Some of these questions are provided in Box 2.5, as suggested criteria for TCU to consider in governance audits geared towards assessments of SDGs.

Box 2.5. **Suggested questions for assessing policy coherence of SDGs**

- Are the current sustainable development priorities of government aligned to the vision of the SDGs?
- Are implementation responsibilities clearly divided among different levels of government, taking into account the distinct competences and comparative advantage of each level?
- What mechanisms are in place to ensure co-ordination and joint action of agencies from different government levels involved in international initiatives?
- Are formal mechanism established for inter-ministerial collaboration, co-ordination and policy arbitration for the SDGs? Is it located strategically within the central government structure?
- Are there mechanisms for transparent reporting to Congress and the public about progress on SDG goals?
- Are resources and capacity adequate to monitor and evaluate progress?
- Have specific indicators been established at the national level to measure progress against SDGs?
- Have critical interactions across SDGs and targets been mapped out? Have potential synergies and trade-offs been identified?
- Can existing indicators at national and subnational level be sued to capture policy interlinkages and examine co-relations across sectors (e.g. rate of deforestation due to agricultural expansion?)
- Have all the potential sources of finance been identified (public, private, domestic, international) for the SDGs?
- Are there specific mechanisms to avoid fragmentation of international, regional, and national funding instruments?

Source: Adapted from OECD (2016c), *Better Policies for Sustainable Development 2016: A New Framework for Policy Coherence*, OECD Publishing, Paris. *http://dx.doi.org/10.1787/9789264256996-en*

The Framework for Policy Coherence for Sustainable Development (OECD, 2016d) offers an example of a mapping of policy interactions in the areas of water, energy and food that pertain to the SDGs. Brazil would benefit from this type of mapping, as a way of highlighting potential synergies and trade-offs that may exist between the SDGs. A similar mapping to that in Figure 2.1 could be done for existing goals in sectoral, national, state-level and regional strategies, or in the broad aims of the current PPA. Naturally, the degree of success of policies and programmes laid out in these documents, such as the PPA (2016-2020) or the PNE (2014-2024) will impact related SDG goals by 2030.

A further example is one to score the degree of interaction between policy goals, as a method for understanding where efforts towards communication and co-ordination are of a higher priority, as shown in Table 2.5.

Figure 2.1. **Some examples of the interactions between water, energy and food in the SDG framework**

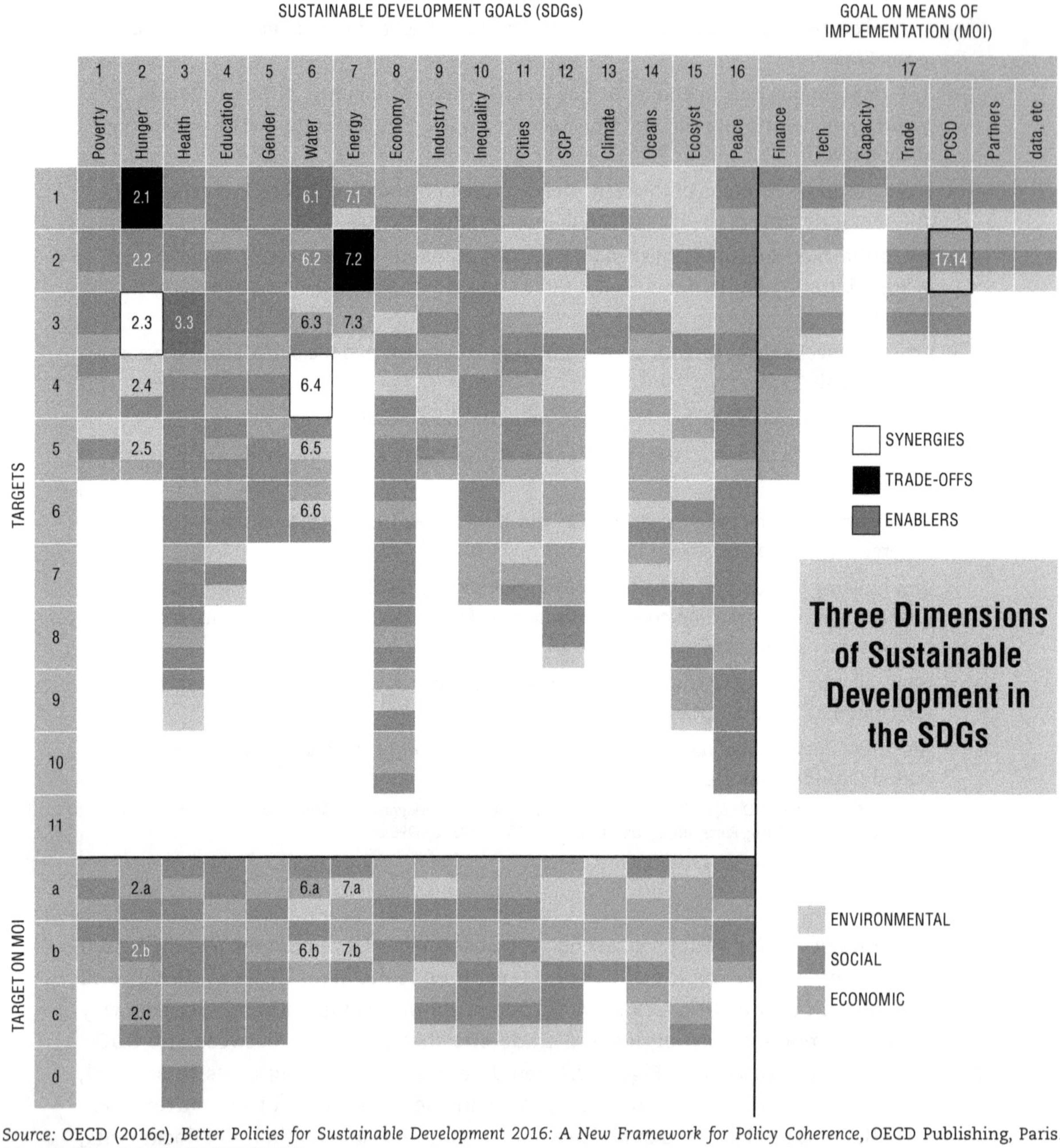

Source: OECD (2016c), *Better Policies for Sustainable Development 2016: A New Framework for Policy Coherence*, OECD Publishing, Paris. *http://dx.doi.org/10.1787/9789264256996-en*

Table 2.5. **Mapping the interactions between SDGs through goals scoring**

Goals Scoring
The influence of one Sustainable Development Goal or target on another can be summarised with this simple scale.

Interaction	Name	Explanation	Example
+3	Indivisible	Inextricably linked to the achievement of another goal.	Ending all forms of discrimination against women and girls is indivisible from ensuring women's full and effective participation and equal opportunities for leadership.
+2	Reinforcing	Aids the achievement of another goal.	Providing access to electricity reinforces water-pumping and irrigation systems. Strengthening the capacity to adapt to climate-related hazards reduces losses caused by disasters.
+1	Enabling	Creates conditions that further another goal.	Providing electricity access in rural homes enables education, because it makes it possible to do homework as night with electric lighting.
0	Consistent	No significant positive or negative interactions.	Ensuring education for all does not interact significantly with infrastructure development or conservation of ocean ecosystems.
-1	Constraining	Limits options on another goal.	Improved water efficiency can constrain agricultural irrigation. Reducing climate change can constrain the options for energy access.
-2	Counteracting	Clashes with another goal.	Boosting consumption for growth can counteract waste reduction and climate mitigation.
-3	Cancelling	Makes it impossible to reach another goal.	Fully ensuring public transparency and democratic accountability cannot be combined with national-security goals. Full protection of natural reserves excludes public access for recreation.

Source: Nature (2016), International weekly journal of science, *http://www.nature.com/news/policy-map-the-interactions-between-sustainable-development-goals-1.20075*

Notes

1. The Index for Public Integrity considers administrative burden a measures of the extent of domestic bureaucratic regulations. The component is constructed based on the average numbers of procedures and time it takes to start a business and pay corporate taxes. Brazil's public administration was ranked 104 out of 105 countries for administrative burden. While it is the second highest of the sample of 105, the index is inversed meaning that the lower the score, the higher the burden. Brazil received a score of 1.94.
2. More information on OECD's work on regulatory burden or "cutting red tape" can be found on the OECD's website: *http://www.oecd-ilibrary.org/governance/cutting-red-tape_19976674*.
3. As noted in chapter 1, TCU defines the Centre of Government as including the Office of the Presidency (Presidência da República), Ministry of Finance (Ministério da Fazenda) and Ministry of Planning, Development and Management (Ministério do Planejamento, Desenvolvimento e Gestão (TCU, 2016a).

4. Between 2008-2012, the size and structure of the Centre of Government changed in three-quarters of OECD countries between 2008 and 2012. The number of cross-ministerial policy initiatives grew after 2008 in 59% of OECD countries (OECD, 2014a).
5. CAMEX formed the inter-ministerial board with the Executive Ordinance 6062/2007 (Brazil-U.S. Business Council, 2013).
6. Pursuant to Chapter II (Capitulo II) on Performance Evaluation (Da avaliacao de desempenho) in Law 11,784, Article 144.2.3.
7. The United Kingdom's "What Works Network" was an initiative of the Cabinet, aiming to improve the way government and other entities create, share and use evidence for decision making. The network supports policy makers in making decisions based on evidence about what has been working and which initiatives are providing cost-efficient services. More information is available at: *https://www.gov.uk/guidance/what-works-network*.
8. According to GAO officials, the review of intelligence information by multiple entities is one example of beneficial competition, since multi-entity reviews can result in richer findings and insights. In addition, complex policy problems can benefit from competition between different, simultaneous solutions and approaches, particularly when a solution is unknown (i.e. the "letting a thousand flowers bloom" approach).

References

ANAO (2009), Effective Cross-Agency Agreements, Audit Report No. 41 2009-10, Commonwealth of Australia 2010, available at: *https://www.anao.gov.au/sites/g/files/net3201/f/ANAO_Report_2009-2010_41.pdf*

BAI (The Board of Audit and Inspection) (2013), 'The housing stabilization policy of the middle and lower income families' (서민주거안정시책 추진실태 공개문), *www.bai.go.kr/bai/cop/bbs/detailBoardArticle.do?bbsId=BBSMSTR_100000000009&nttId=1489&mdex=bai20&searchCnd=all_NTT_SJ_CN&searchWrd=%EC%84%9C%EB%AF%BC%EC%A3%BC%EA%B1%B0%EC%95%88%EC%A0%95&-searchBgnDe=&searchEndDe=&searchYear=&pageIndex=1&recordCountPerPage=10*

Bertelsmann Stiftung (2016a), Brazil: country report, Transformation Index 2016, *https://www.bti-project.org/fileadmin/files/BTI/Downloads/Reports/2016/pdf/BTI_2016_Brazil.pdf*

Brazilian Government National Education Plan (2014), (Plano Nacional de Educacão 2014-2024), House of Deputies (Cámara dos Deputados), Brasilia, *http://www.observatoriodopne.org.br/uploads/reference/file/439/documento-referencia.pdf*

Brazil-U.S. Business Council (2013) 'Advancing the Regulatory Coherence Agenda in Brazil,' Washington D.C., *http://www.brazilcouncil.org/wp-content/uploads/2015/11/021933_Brazil_RegCoherence_IN_final.pdf*

Cámara dos Deputados (2014) Plano Nacional de Educacão 2014-2024 Brasilia, *http://www.observatoriodopne.org.br/uploads/reference/file/439/documento-referencia.pdf*

CGU (Ministero da Transparência, Fiscalizacão e Controladoria-Geral da União) (2016) 'Composicão da CCCI' 20 June 2016, *http://www.cgu.gov.br/assuntos/auditoria-e-fiscalizacao/comissao-de-coordenacao-de-controle-interno-ccci/composicao* Accessed 30 Sep 2016

De Vries, G. (2016) 'How National Audit Offices Can Support Implementation of the SDGs' Public Financial Management Blog, 28 June 2016, *http://blog-pfm.imf.org/pfmblog/2016/06/national-audit-offices-should-support-implementation-of-the-sdgs.html?utm_source=feedburner&utm_medium=email&utm_campaign=Feed%3A+pfmblog+%28PFM+blog%29*

GAO (2016), Fragmentation, Overlap, and Duplication in Government Programs, Presentation in Brasilia, May 2016.

GAO (2015) 'Evaluating and Managing Fragmentation, Overlap and Duplication' available at: *http://www.gao.gov/assets/670/669612.pdf*

GAO (2011) 'Opportunities to Reduce Potential Duplication in Government Programs, Save Tax Dollars, and Enhance Revenue: Report to Congressional Addressees' March 2011, available at: *http://www.gao.gov/assets/320/315920.pdf*

Index of Public Integrity (2016), Index of Public Integrity 2015, available at: *http://integrity-index.org/* accessed 14 September 2016

IADB (2014), 'Governing to Deliver: Reinventing the Center of Gvoernment in Latin America and the Caribbean' Inter-American Development Bank, Washington DC, *https://publications.iadb.org/bitstream/handle/11319/6674/Governing-to-Deliver-Reinventing-the-Center-of-Government-in-Latin-America-and-the-Caribbean.pdf?sequence=1*

Jones, S. (2008), "Cooperative Federalism?" The Case of the Ministerial Council on Education, Employment, Training and Youth Affairs the Australian Journal of Public Administration 67 (2): 161–172, available at: *http://onlinelibrary.wiley.com/doi/10.1111/j.1467-8500.2008.00579.x/full*

NAO (National Audit Office of Sweden) (2015), 'Summary: The Government's gender equality initiative-temporary or permanent improvements?' Report no, RIR 2015: 13, 11 June 2015, Stockholm, *http://www.riksrevisionen.se/PageFiles/22905/Summary_2015_13.pdf.*

NAO (National Audit Office of the United Kingdom) (2014), 'The centre of government' HC 171, Session 2014-15, 19 June 2014, *https://www.nao.org.uk/wp-content/uploads/2014/06/The-centre-of-government.pdf*

Nature (2016), International weekly journal of science, *http://www.nature.com/news/policy-map-the-interactions-between-sustainable-development-goals-1.20075*

OECD (2016a), 'Navigating Wicked Problems', OECD Insights Blog, *http://oecdinsights.org/2016/10/04/navigating-wicked-problems/*

OECD (2016b), *Supreme Audit Institutions and Good Governance: Oversight, Insight and Foresight*, OECD Public Governance Reviews, OECD Publishing, Paris. *http://dx.doi.org/10.1787/9789264263871-en*

OECD (2016c), *Better Policies for Sustainable Development 2016: A New Framework for Policy Coherence*, OECD Publishing, Paris. *http://dx.doi.org/10.1787/9789264256996-en*

OECD (2015a), *Achieving Public Sector Agility at Times of Fiscal Consolidation*, OECD Public Governance Reviews, OECD Publishing, Paris. *http://dx.doi.org/10.1787/9789264206267-en*

OECD (2015b), *Water Resources Governance in Brazil*, OECD Studies on Water, OECD Publishing, Paris. *http://dx.doi.org/10.1787/9789264238121-en*

OECD (2015c), "Citizen satisfaction with public services", in *Government at a Glance 2015*, OECD Publishing, Paris. *http://dx.doi.org/10.1787/gov_glance-2015-56-en*, with data available at: *http://stats.oecd.org//Index.aspx?QueryId=66864*

OECD (2015d), 'Education Policy Outlook: Brazil' OECD Publishing, Paris. *http://www.oecd.org/edu/Brazil-country-profile.pdf*

OECD (2014a) 'Centre Stage: Driving Better Policies from the Centre of Government' OECD Publishing, Paris. *https://www.oecd.org/gov/Centre-Stage-Report.pdf*

OECD (2014b), *Chile's Supreme Audit Institution: Enhancing Strategic Agility and Public Trust*, OECD Public Governance Reviews, OECD Publishing, Paris. *http://dx.doi.org/10.1787/9789264207561-en*

OECD (2013a), *Brazil's Supreme Audit Institution: The Audit of the Consolidated Year-end Government Report*, OECD Public Governance Reviews, OECD Publishing. *http://dx.doi.org/10.1787/9789264188112-en*

OECD (2010), *Why Is Administrative Simplification So Complicated?: Looking beyond 2010*, Cutting Red Tape, OECD Publishing, Paris. *http://dx.doi.org/10.1787/9789264089754-en*

OECD (2008), 'Brazil: Strengthening governance for growth' OECD Reviews of Regulatory Reform, OECD Publishing, Paris, *http://www.oecd.org/brazil/oecdreviewsofregulatoryreform-brazilstrengtheninggovernanceforgrowth.htm*

Pro-Reg (2012), Pro-Reg Newletter, March 2012, *http://www.oecd.org/gov/regulatory-policy/50172881.pdf*

Rio+ Centre (2014) 'Policy Coherence for Development Challenges at the National level: the Brazilian Experience' Presentation by R. Paes de Sousa, Rio+ World Centre for Sustainable Development (Rio Centro Mundial Para o Desenvolvimento Sustentavel) UNDP, *http://ec.europa.eu/europeaid/sites/devco/files/presentation-pcd-challenges-national-level-brazil_20140612_en.pdf*

TCU (2016a), Framework for Evaluation of the Centre of Government TCU Publishing, Brasilia, *http://portal.tcu.gov.br/lumis/portal/file/fileDownload.jsp?fileId=8A8182A25454C5A801545DC1433145ED*

TCU (2015), ACÓRDÃO N° 1492/2015 - TCU – Plenário, *https://contas.tcu.gov.br/sisdoc/ObterDocumentoSisdoc?codVersao=editavel&codArqCatalogado=9022616*

TCU (2014a) Framework to Assess Governance in Public Policies, TCU Publishing, Brasilia, *https://www.google.fr/url?sa=t&rct=j&q=&esrc=s&source=web&cd=1&cad=rja&uact=8&ved=0ahUKEwiC_NK6_s7UAhWFVhoKHV6nAHUQFggmMAA&url=http%3A%2F%2Fportal.tcu.gov.br%2Flumis%2Fportal%2Ffile%2FfileDownload.jsp%3FfileId%3D8A8182A14DDA8CE1014DDFC404023E00&usg=AFQjCNH4lLkhnUily2eVQvpAsRwBQCMTVw*

TCU (2014b), Judgement 3580/2014, Survey Report, Plenary *https://contas.tcu.gov.br/juris/SvlHighLight?key=41434f5244414f2d434f4d504c45544f2d31333338303136&sort=RELEVANCIA&ordem=DESC&bases=ACORDAO-COMPLETO;&highlight=&posicaoDocumento=0&numDocumento=1&totalDocumentos=1*

TCU (2014c), Judgement 019.059/2014-0 *https://www.google.fr/url?sa=t&rct=j&q=&esrc=s&source=web&cd=1&cad=rja&uact=8&ved=0ahUKEwiQ45PujrfPAhWKBBoKHchmDV0QFggfMAA&url=http%3A%2F%2Fwww.tcu.gov.br%2FConsultas%2FJuris%2FDocs%2Fjudoc%2FAcord%2F20150528%2FAC_1205_18_15_P.doc&usg=AFQjCNGZk5nRgov_aiZQiMYvrNy9HkJIRg&bvm=bv.134495766,d.d2s*

TCU (2010), Judgement 1453/2010 *https://contas.tcu.gov.br/sagas/SvlVisualizarRelVotoAcRtf?codFiltro=SAGAS-SESSAO-ENCERRADA&seOcultaPagina=S&item0=39360* ;

TCU (2009), Judgement 2919/2009. Survey report. Plenary. *http://www.tcu.gov.br/Consultas/Juris/Docs/judoc/Acord/20091204/013-705-2009-6-MIN-JJ.rtf*

TCU (2008), Judgement 3038/2008 *http://www.tcu.gov.br/Consultas/Juris/Docs/judoc%5CAcord%5C20081215%5C018-215-2008-0-MIN-AN.rtf*;

TCU (2007), Judgement 1690/2007 *http://www.tcu.gov.br/Consultas/Juris/Docs/judoc%5CAcord%5C20070823%5CTC-010-107-2007-0.doc*

Brazil's Federal Court of Accounts
Insight and Foresight for Better Governance

Chapter 3

Auditing for more strategic and sustainable budgeting in Brazil

Guided by OECD's Recommendation of the Council on Budgetary Governance, this chapter promotes action that Brazil's supreme audit institution, the Tribunal de Contas da União (TCU), can take to encourage more sustainable and strategic budgeting over the long-term. In particular, this chapter looks at Brazil's budgetary structure with respect to four key trends that have emerged amongst OECD member countries in the last decade, including: (i) integration of medium-term perspectives in the budget, (ii) the integration of performance information into, evaluation and value-for-money into the budget, (iii) strengthening of fiscal discipline and (iv) long-term fiscal sustainability. Recommendations are made to TCU as to how to support improvements in each area through its audit and advisory work.

3.1. Introduction

The budget is the single most important policy document of governments. The budget clearly outlines which policy objectives have been prioritised. If those priorities are to be met, the budget should be both strategic and sustainable (OECD, 2002). Brazil's budgetary process has been evolving through incremental change. Since the introduction of the Fiscal Responsibility Law (LRF) in 2000, budgetary reforms in Brazil have tended towards budgetary equilibrium and fiscal responsibility (IDB, 2010). The trend continues, with current efforts to stimulate growth focused on placing limits on spending and establishing controls in high-risk areas.

Fiscal sustainability and responsibility require short-term action with a view towards developing more sustainable outcomes over the medium and long-term. Short-term decisions should not come unequivocally at the expense of medium-term perspectives and planning that is meant to adequately guide annual allocations in the Budgetary Guidelines Law (Lei de Diretrizes Orçamentárias or LDO) and the Annual Budget Law (Lei Orçamentária Annual or LOA), which are in turn meant to provide realistic fiscal frameworks through which entities can plan.

Cutting expenditures in the short-term may often shift perspectives away from medium-term efforts towards efficiency and effectiveness of such expenditure or towards "good budgetary governance."[1] In efforts to balance both, the OECD's Network of Senior Budget Officials used lessons learned from the financial crisis to develop international budgetary principles that could equip budgetary systems with the tools to meet the complex challenges of the future (OECD, 2015a). The current environment provides a window of opportunity for Brazil to align with good international principles in budgetary governance. While reforms since 2010 have largely been incremental, focusing on fine-tuning existing initiatives and institutions, the current proposals would suggest opportunity to bring about more meaningful change. In driving improvements for a more strategic and sustainable budget, TCU is a source of valuable and objective oversight and insight.

Brazil's supreme audit institution (SAI), the Tribunal de Contas da União (TCU), has been instrumental in improving fiscal responsibility in Brazil in accordance with its constitutional mandate to verify government accounts and audit the operations of the government. This role, and TCU's audit of the year-end consolidated accounts of Government, was the focus of the OECD's 2012 review "Brazil's Supreme Audit Institution: The audit of the consolidated year-end government report." TCU recently received much public interest for its opinion of the government's 2014 accounts, which played a central role in recent political turmoil. In addition to checks of compliance with financial and accounting rules, TCU is increasingly active in assessing the adequacy of Brazil's medium-term perspectives in the budget. For instance, TCU recently conducted an audit of the broader budgetary framework, using the principles of OECD's Recommendation of the Council on Budgetary Governance. Such audits can be useful inputs for budgetary decision making and policy making, provided that they are provided in timely and efficient manner.

This chapter focuses on the activities of TCU that provide oversight, insight and foresight for more strategic and sustainable budgeting. TCU could complement work it already does in this area, taking inspiration from other SAIs that are also looking to improve multi-annual programmes that affect citizen's well-being in the medium and long-term. The role of SAIs in this regard is not to second guess difficult policy decisions proposed by government and authorised by the Congress, but rather to aid in more effective, efficient and transparent spending.

3.2. Overview: budgeting at the federal level

The legal framework of the budgetary process in Brazil is primarily laid out in the 1988 Constitution, putting the main responsibilities of creating and executing the budget in the Executive. Article 165 of the Constitution establishes Brazil's budgetary framework is comprised of three budgetary instruments, as established in article 165 of the Constitution – the Multi-annual plan (*Plano Pluriannual or PPA*), the LDO and the LOA. The process begins with the PPA, which the President must present to congress during the first year in office. PPAs are presented every four years, thus covering three years of the current presidential term and the first year of the following.

The drafting of the plan is done between line ministries, the Ministry of Planning, Development and Management (*Ministério do Planejamento, Desenvolvimento e Gestão*, or MP) and the President's Office. The MP is responsible for ensuring consistency between programmes. The plan comprehensively covers all government expenditures in several hundred outcomes or output based programmes. Additionally, PPA highlights the political priorities of the government. Priority programmes are marked as mandatory, meaning they are protected from cuts in the presidential implementation decrees, and MP aids spending on these programmes rather than individual ministries (OECD, 2003).

The annual budget process then begins when the government presents the LDO to Congress by 15 April, which must then be approved by Congress by 30 June. According to the 2000 Law of Fiscal Responsibility (*Lei de Responsabilidade Fiscal*, LRF), LDO must include targets for the primary surplus for the next three years which Congress must approve (mandatory for the first year and indicative for the next 2 years – rolling process). In accordance with the constitution, LDO must also stipulate which expenditures and mandatory. The bill also contains information on lending policies of government financial institutions and a number of procedural issues (OECD, 2003).

The annual budget then begins with internal reviews of the Planning Secretariat and the Budget Secretariat of the MP. The Planning Secretariat reviews the results of the previous year's activities through inputs and outcomes and proposes amendments to the priority programmes. This review is then taken into account in the review by the Budget Secretariat, however for the most part this lengthy review focuses more on the amount of resources needed to carry out each organisation's activities, as well as analyses last year's spending. The Budget Secretariat's review will then determine the maximum amount of expenditure for each ministry, and this will also inform Congress's deliberation on the LDO. Ministries then have three weeks to input their detailed allocations which cannot exceed the amount set by the CMO. They can also appeal their maximum allocations, however ultimately it is set by the CMO. The Budget Secretariat is then responsible for finishing the LOA and presenting it to Congress before 31 August. Approval by Congress happens before 22 December (OECD, 2003).

As the understanding of the budgeting process widens, and as governments review budgetary processes and tools, SAIs are also evolving their work beyond fulfilment of the traditional mandate of monitoring compliance with budgetary laws. For instance, SAIs are assessing the link between the accuracy of the budget and the preparedness of government to deliver on long and short-term plans, programmes and policies (OECD, 2016a).

TCU, like its peer SAIs, has been active in assessing the budget, pursuant to Constitutional articles 70, 71 and 74 of Brazil's 1988 Constitution. Chief among TCU's responsibilities to this end include accounts proceedings, including the year-end audit of the President's accounts, and carrying out audits and supervisory proceedings of administrative units. Firstly, TCU is charged with examining the accounts rendered annually by the President of the Republic, and those of the administrators and other persons responsible for public monies, assets and values of the direct and indirect administration. TCU's audit of the year-end President Report, which focuses on financial compliance but also efficiency and effectiveness of individual sectors, is TCU's greatest means for assessing, in year Y, adherence to the LOA in year X-1. TCU has additional activities that contribute to strengthening the accuracy of the budget and medium-term planning individually (such as Executive planning or evaluation of fiscal forecasts), as well as the link between the two (evaluation of the PPA). The process and production of TCU's year-end audit was covered extensively in an OECD review in 2012.[2]

Secondly, TCU is charged with carrying out inspection and audits of an accounting, financial, budgetary, operational or property nature in the administrative units of the Legislative, Executive and Judicial Powers. TCU enjoys discretion in its audit planning and flexibility in determining the scope of inspection and analysis. Knowing the importance of all elements of the budget, both on the quantitative and qualitative dimensions of public spending, TCU is tackling a range of budgetary weaknesses. Its recent comprehensive audit using OECD principles indicates follow-up audits that drill down onto other critical elements of good budgetary governance, such as: clarity and adequacy of fiscal projections, and the quality of performance-related information.

TCU can continue to support greater alignment with international practices of budgeting – taking into account Brazil's challenges in good budgetary governance and particularly in linking strategy and budget, as well as the approaches already taken by TCU. Generally, TCU could systematise more concretely its targeting of other elements of the budget that support long-term sustainability, including assessing macroeconomic indicators, the effect of in-year adjustments to the budget, and the use of evidence in budgetary trade-offs and decisions, for instance and as discussed further below. The time is opportune, given the rapidly changing environment, demands for greater fiscal responsibility and the greater attention that TCU has drawn in its audits on the budgetary process. Specific recommendations are provided in Table 3.1.

The recommendations to TCU (Table 3.1) are not meant to suggest a role in long-term projections or conducting fiscal forecasting, but instead how it can support their quality and use them for pointing to the sustainability of the programmes being funded. The proposals advance objectives 6 and 8 of TCU's strategic plan. Objective 6 is to improve the availability and reliability of information of the public administration particularly of financial and performance related information (objective 6.2) and objective 8 is to encourage the monitoring an evaluation of performance of public administration, particularly to assess the effectiveness and sustainability of the financing of public policies (objective 8.4) (TCU, 2015a).

Table 3.1. **Recommendations: Auditing for more strategic and sustainable budgeting in Brazil**

TCU could encourage more meaningful medium-term perspectives in the budget by (a) auditing overall performance of multi-year sectoral plans, and (b) highlighting key findings on the alignment of annual budgetary allocations with multi-annual priorities, emphasising implications for entity-level planning.

- TCU could assess overall performance of medium and long-term sectoral plans, focusing on 1) adequacy and execution of annual allocations for achieving goals, 2) the impact of thematic programme goals set out in the multi-annual plan, and 3) the implications of performance for achieving the sustainable development goals.
- TCU could continue to assess and communicate key findings on the alignment of multi-annual priorities with annual budgetary allocations, emphasising the importance of entity-level planning with a longer time horizon.

TCU could help to improve the reliability of evidence and information for making performance-based budgetary decisions through assessments of key areas, such as expenditure programmes funded by earmarks and the effectiveness of operational cost measurement.

TCU could enhance its contributions to the dialogue on fiscal discipline by periodically assessing in-year progress reports to discern how adjustments to fiscal targets and plans affect the achievement of goals.

TCU could further assess whether adequate institutional procedures and safeguards are in place to ensure the quality, reliability and sustainability of budget forecasts and medium-term projections.

3.3. Encouraging more strategic and sustainable budgeting over the medium-term through audits of policy performance

TCU could encourage more meaningful medium-term perspectives in the budget by (a) auditing overall performance of multi-year sectoral plans, and (b) highlighting key findings on the alignment of annual budgetary allocations with multi-annual priorities, emphasising implications for entity-level planning.

Decades of OECD experience in working on good budgetary governance show a predominant trend in seeking a greater link between strategy and budget. Upstream allocation decisions of the budgeting process, including those decisions meant to be taken in the interests of citizens, determine which government priorities will or will not be funded. A mismatch between policy objectives and annual resource allocations can lead to unfulfilled strategic goals and objectives (OECD, 2014a; 2015b; 2016b).

Governments, particularly institutions within the Centre of Government (CoG) responsible for planning, often elaborate a vision or prioritisation that is relatively short-term. Medium- and long-term planning requires resources, capacity and skills that the CoG may not have. A long-term strategy has the benefit of setting priorities that span electoral cycles and thus that provide a general guideline against which governments should pursue, regardless of political platform. Brazil's political actors have been able to achieve broad consensus on long-term policy objectives that has been useful in poverty reduction, growth stimulation and depolarization of policy conflicts that came about during prosperous economic times (Bertelsmann Stiftung, 2016). Yet, Brazil does not have a long-term plan at the federal level. Medium and long-term plans exist within select sectors, ministries and regions. Brazil's commitment to the achievement of the Sustainable Development Goals for 2030 provides broad aims for the government over the long-term.

One of the major developments in budgetary governance since the turn of the century has been the increased focus on the multi-annual dimensions of budgeting. Medium-term perspectives in budgeting refers here specifically to the adoption of Medium-term Fiscal Frameworks (MTFFs) or Medium-term Expenditure Frameworks (MTEFs) that strengthen the ability of the government collectively, and the Ministry of Finance (*Ministério da Fazenda*, MF) in particular, to plan and enforce a sustainable fiscal path.[3] MTFFs are increasingly relevant in a context where the multi-annual character of policies require an extended time horizon, such as large capital projects, new programmes, and organisational reform and restructuring (OECD, 2014a; 2015b, 2016b).

If properly designed, an MTEF should force stakeholders to deal with the medium-term perspective of budgeting and budgetary policies, typically covering a period of three to four years. It should also facilitate stakeholders in identifying the policy choices and trade-offs that will be necessary in light of the estimates of what would happen in the following three to five years based on unchanged policies. From the point of view of managers, in-line ministries and agencies, medium-term frameworks put them in a better position to plan their policies and operations, to the extent that they have some level of visibility regarding the likely level of funding beyond the next budget (OECD, 2014b).

Brazil's PPA is not an MTEF[4], but shares characteristics with MTEFs of OECD member countries (OECD, 2014b). The aim of the PPA, like that of an MTEF, is to improve the quality and certainty of multi-annual fiscal planning (OECD, 2015a). The PPA includes a strategic dimension intended to guide the preparation of thematic programmes, which describe the government's agenda in different areas, such as social security and public investment. In setting entity-level objectives, public managers are encouraged to link their entities' goals to the main themes of the PPA. According to stakeholders within and outside of TCU, the PPA does not provide sufficient guidance or criteria for entities to plan.

The current PPA (2016-2019) seeks to enable the government to better demonstrate and facilitate an understanding of how the overall government strategy connects to objectives and goals at the entity level (MP, 2016a). The MP has played an important role, together with the Ministry of Finance, in trying to foster a link between planning and budget despite budget rigidity. However, in practice, there are misalignments that do not transfer the intended benefits of the PPA, as set out in the constitution, into reality. These limit the extent to which Brazil's budgetary framework can allow for a medium- or long-term strategy and sustainability. Amongst other effects, the misalignment also makes it difficult for managers to know their programme targets and to accurately project performance and results (TCU, 2016a).

The PPA's thematic programmes around important areas such as environment and regional development are meant to provide a framework for planning across sectors, such as in the National Education Plan (PNE). This reflects the strides made in recent years to adopt a more cross-cutting and forward looking view into its PPA – now structuring each 4-year PPA cycle around thematic outcomes. The Constitution spells out that the 3 budget laws – the PPA, the LDO and the LOA – should be aligned. In the absence of an explicit long-term plan at the federal level, long-term ambitions and indicators in Brazil are detailed through comprehensive sectoral plans, such as the National Education Plan (PNE). The PPA's thematic programmes provide policy goals over the medium and long term. However, in practice, there are misalignments that do not transfer the intended benefits of the PPA, as set out in the constitution, into reality. These limit the extent to which Brazil's budgetary framework can allow for a medium- or long-term strategy and sustainability. Amongst other effects, the misalignment also makes it difficult for managers to know their programme targets and to accurately project performance and results (TCU, 2016a).

Heavily funded programmes, which were incongruent with austerity measures, were evidence of a need to strengthen the link between planning and budget, even before the economic downturn (OECD, 2015c). The sustainability and strategic nature of Brazil's budgetary framework is influenced by the rigidity and large proportion earmarked to particular expenditures. A 2009 assessment using the Framework for Public Expenditure and Financial Accountability (PEFA) found that during the execution of the budget, Brazil's Executive restricts the release of funds for discretionary commitments and spending in a way that is often inconsistent with PPA. PEFA (2009) gave Brazil a grade C in 'frequency and transparency of adjustments to budget allocations'. In-year adjustments, according to TCU, mean that the LOA ends up leading to adjustments in the PPA itself, instead of the other way around. Finally, TCU has detected a lack of synergy between individual sector-based plans and the PPA.

Medium-term budgetary planning yields a number of benefits for governments, ensuring that policies and programmes deliver results for citizens. For instance, one benefit of effective medium-term budgetary planning is that it should work to mitigate particular activities that may be considered as classic budgeting "games", such as: *i)* capital projects being launched with changing operating costs; *ii)* programmes coming into effect late in the budget year, thus not exposing their full costs in the initial year; and *iii)* programmes' spending implications not being fully reflected under the circumstances prevailing during the budget year, but will become so in out-years.

Another benefit of effective medium-term budgetary planning is in the flexibility it grants in spending, allowing governments to fund programmes that require multi-year funding in order to realise policy goals. Brazil's budgetary framework allows for carryover of unused funds or appropriations from one year to another in order to facilitate multi-year budgeting for discretionary, operational and investment spending (OECD, 2014b). This flexibility in expenditure is important for multi-year programmes, when managed within reason, particularly in view of Brazil's otherwise rigid budget. Brazil is the only country in OECD's 2013 survey of select Latin American and Caribbean countries to allow line ministries to carry over unused funds without thresholds for both operational and investment expenditures (OECD, 2014). Of 32 OECD member countries, carry-over without threshold for operating expenditures is allowed in 34% of countries, and for investment expenditures in 43% of countries' (OECD, 2014b).

TCU has been active in auditing budgetary planning, including the PPA, Budgetary Guidelines and law (LDO and LOA). As these budgetary instruments are created as laws, and not programmes, TCU's corresponding work does not comment on the priorities chosen or merits within those laws, nor the recipients of the 35% 'priority' spending (OECD, 2003). Moreover, as an SAI, TCU does not audit the judgement behind the design of laws or policies. However, TCU can assess the reliability and achievement of objectives set within those laws. Many peer SAIs, like TCU, have been active in this space.

An OECD survey of 10 SAIs showed the extent to which they were active in assessing auditees against international budgetary standards. Nine of ten had assessed the adequacy of budgetary planning processes, including: to facilitate an alignment between budgeting and strategic objectives; to ensure reliability and quality of tools that underlie the budget; to manage public debt; to assess long-term sustainability; and to guide the multi-annual process of resource allocation. Ten out of ten SAIs surveyed had assessed the effectiveness of the procedures in place for managing, monitoring and overseeing financial allocations, including: the compliance and consistency of in-year budget reallocations; the adequacy of in-year budget execution reports (OECD, 2016a).

TCU recently released a comprehensive audit of Brazil's budgetary system using OECD principles espoused in the *Recommendation of the Council on Budgetary Governance* (OECD, 2015a). One main component of the audit focused on principle 2 of the Recommendation, on the need to "Closely align budgets with the medium-term strategic priorities of government". TCU found a weak alignment between the 3 budgetary documents (Box 3.1). The alignment, or misalignment, is found primarily in the lack of integration of the PPA's thematic programmes in the LOA. The low degree of implementation calls into question the ability of the programme goals to be met in by the year end, and thus by the end of the current PPA. Other key findings of this recent TCU audit in this area are summarised in Box 3.1.

Box 3.1. **TCU audit findings: misalignment between multi-annual priorities and annual budgets**

TCU's recent survey report provides a comparison of good practices in budgeting and established by the OECD and the International Monetary Fund (IMF). It outlines areas for improvement and good practices for Brazil's public administration, providing recommendations to Brazil's Ministry of Planning, Development and Management (*Ministério do Planejamento, Desenvolvimento e Gestão*, MP).

The key findings related to qualitative and quantitative elements of the budget were as follows:

- "Brazil does not have a medium-term plan aligned with government priorities; in view of the discrepancies in the forecasts of macroeconomic parameters, and changes in primary and nominal result targets, in order to adjust them to government spending, it is not possible to say that, in Brazil, budgets are being managed with clear boundaries, credible and predictable in fiscal policy." *This element of analysis pertains to OECD recommendation 1: Manage budgets within clear, credible and predictable limits for fiscal policy.*
- "A lack of consistency between planning and budgeting, and the administration's inability to achieve consistent and intact forecasts, results in the imposition of budgetary and financial constraints that are too high for sectoral bodies during the year. This failure has caused damage to the effective and efficient implementation of the actions of the LOA and the implementation of the PPA programs. TCU concluded that the Federal Public Administration is not adhering to the principles concerning the integrity of forecasts and budget execution". *This element of analysis pertains to OECD recommendation 10: Promote the integrity and quality of budgetary forecasts, fiscal plans and budgetary implementation through rigorous quality assurance including independent audit.*
- "In relation to the monitoring of budget implementation and evaluation of results, there is a lack of effectiveness indicators in the PPA; objectives of the plan have no indicators nor annual targets; there is no clear definition of those responsible for conducting the PPA objectives, especially those arising from cross agendas without national plans; the half-yearly monitoring proves to be inapposite to aid management; the current budget structure hinders the association between costs incurred and the results of policies; there is a lack of a co-ordination body responsible for oversight of budget execution and more effective accountability for results; and monitoring and evaluation processes are formal and not always feedback the planning system; We conclude from this that the Federal Public Administration is not adhering to the principles that address performance evaluation and cost-effective." *This element of analysis pertains to OECD recommendation 8: Ensure that performance, evaluation & value for money are integral to the budget process.*

Source: Adapted from TCU (2016a), TCU Judgement 033.142/2015-7 Survey Report, *http://bibspi.planejamento.gov.br/bitstream/handle/iditem/700/Acordao_TCU_948_2016.pdf?sequence=1)*

To help the government address these challenges, TCU can develop its audit portfolio to improve budget processes and planning, and provide meaningful insights for budgetary decision making in the Congress. Given the governments focus on short-term priorities, as discussed, TCU's audits and findings could continue to emphasise a perspective that looks beyond immediate objectives and challenges. This is particularly relevant in the coming years, as Brazil takes on the challenge of effectively designing and implementing policies to achieve the Sustainable Development Goals (SDGs). The SDGs, by their nature, have a medium to long-term horizon for the achievement of outcomes. In addition, the PPA is not as effective as intended in guiding annual allocations, making sectoral plans more critical for economic and social progress over the medium and long-term. Where sectoral plans exist, such as the National Education Plan (PNE) spanning from 2014 to 2024, they could feature more consistently as the focus of audits. As a result, TCU's work on medium-tern budgeting would not solely be tied to the PPA.

Building on TCU's existing work in this area, TCU could offer meaningful medium-term perspectives for improved budgetary planning in the following ways:

- TCU could assess overall performance of medium and long-term sectoral plans, focusing on 1) adequacy and execution of annual allocations for their goal achievement, 2) the impact of any relevant thematic programme goals set out in the PPA, and 3) the implications of performance for achievement of related SDGs; and
- TCU could continue to assess and communicate key findings on the alignment of multi-annual priorities with annual budgetary allocations, emphasising the importance of entity-level planning with a longer time horizon.

TCU could assess overall performance of medium and long-term sectoral plans, focusing on 1) adequacy and execution of annual allocations for achieving goals, 2) the impact of thematic programme goals set out in the multi-annual plan, and 3) the implications of performance for achieving the sustainable development goals.

Building on its current portfolio, as detailed below, TCU can induce help government to identify inconsistencies and gaps in formulation, implementation or evaluation of policies that may lead to falling short of sectoral or national goals. TCU's audits have linked poor execution of thematic programmes with the inability of the PPA to allow for realistic annual allocations. For instance, TCU's recent audit noted that the thematic programmes appearing in the PPA (2016-2019) such as Regional Development, Sustainable Land Management and Economics, Climate change and Urban Planning and Tourism, had executed less than 10% of the annual allocations in the first semester of 2016. Particular thematic programmes, such as Urban Planning, have executed less than 1% (TCU, 2016a). The low percentages of implementation are due to several factors, such as contingencies made by the Executive, lack of technical capacity of agencies to implement the policy, the occurrence of limiting factors unforeseen at the time was thought to politics, among others. TCU's audit found it impossible to say, with few exceptions, that the LOA reflects the medium-term planning of government in view of the difficulties faced by agencies when executing policies.

TCU audit teams attempted to assess the values set out for in the PPA of 2012 to 2015 (Law 12,593 / 2012), with the values throughout the execution of the plan. TCU found that, in reality, PPA programme values were updated yearly in accordance with the annual appropriations in the PPA. In other words, instead of the PPA guiding the preparation of the LOA, the actual appropriations in the LOA fuel a review process of the PPA, removing the planning utility of the PPA, since the overall thematic programme values, which should guide the allocation of resources in the LOA are not used as a parameter to draw up the budget law (TCU, 2016a).

This inverse process, whereby the LOA inspires review and updating of the PPA, would suggest that ministry or sectoral plans end up having more impact on the achievement of policy goals in particular policy areas than the PPA does. This renders these sectoral plans critical for social and economic progress in Brazil. Accordingly, TCU has assessed Brazil's national development policy from various angles, including its governance, indicators and alignment with the PPA (Box 3.2).

Box 3.2. **The SAI of Brazil – audit for national development policy**

Objective

A series of audits took place between 2009 and 2013 that focused on the national policy for regional development and aimed to understand and identify structural features that may be responsible for any successes and performance gaps. The dedication of effort and time in these audits was justified by the amount of public resources invested in the national policy for regional development (around BRL ten billion annually) and the importance of the issue to national development. This comprehensive work involved six audits and 214 business days at a cost of BRL 988 000 (approximately USD 325 000).

Scope and methodology

The scope included the whole governance structure for managing the national policy for regional development, including its formulation, rules, actors, monitoring and evaluations systems, transparency, plans and finance resources - as public funds dedicated to loans for entrepreneurships with favourable interest rates, tax expenditures and budget expenses.

To capture a systemic view of the policy, TCU included the following: Usage of many teams for auditing the various public agencies and finance tools, distributed by the Brazilian regions elected by the policy, co-ordinated by a common guidance and audit questions provided by the preliminary audit; assessment of compliance between the actions and the legal conception of the policy; usage of many performance audit tools (indicators analysis; problem tree method; mapping the logical model of the policy; stakeholder analysis; survey; consultation to experts); a study of international models, together with the executive bodies and agents responsible for the policy management ; and a strong interaction and open debate with the executive bodies and agents responsible for the policy management

The main findings (and related recommendations) include:

- The policy had not been assessed since it started.
- The predicted monitoring and evaluation system had not been built.
- There were no appropriate indicators of performance to guide the management and ensure transparency for the citizens.
- The formulation of the policy did not consider mechanisms to fight the major causes of the problems.
- There was no strong alignment between the diagnostic that guided the policy formulation and the regulation for using the majority of finance resources.
- There was a lack of co-ordination between the federal agencies concerning the policy.
- There was a lack of co-ordination between the federal, state and local level concerning the policy planning and implementation.

Box 3.2. **The SAI of Brazil – audit for national development policy** *(cont.)*

Many measures were adopted after the recommendations, these are listed below:

- The responsible government body promoted an assessment of the policy that covers the time between its formalisation and the year after the first audit recommendations.
- There was a stronger investment in developing the monitoring and evaluation system.
- A new set of indicators is being used and others are being developed by the government agencies.
- A new conception for the policy was formulated after intensive stakeholder participation across the country. This led to a new project of law and regulation for the policy that considers the need to improve the governance of the policy, especially regarding co-ordination issues.

Sources: TCU (2013a), Audit on the National Policy for Regional Development in the Multi-Annual Plan (PPA) and the Annual Budgets (TC 002 976 / 2013-7) *http://www.tcu.gov.br/consultas/juris/docs/conses/tcu_ata_0_n_2013_38.pdf*; TCU (2012a): Audit of the Accounts of the President of the Republic, (*Contas do Presidente da República*), 2012, *http://portal2.tcu.gov.br/portal/page/portal/TCU/comunidades/contas/contas_governo/Contas2012/index.html*; TCU (2012b), Monitoring of Recommendations of the Preliminary Audit (TC 015 133/2011-7) *http://www.tcu.gov.br/Consultas/Juris/Docs/judoc/Acord/20120124/AC_0042_01_12_P.doc*; TCU (2012c), Performance Audit on the Indicators of the National Policy for Regional Development (TC 037 079 / 2012-3) *https://contas.tcu.gov.br/etcu/AcompanharProcesso?p1=37079&p2=2012&p3=3*; TCU (2011a): Audit of the Accounts of the President of the Republic, (*Contas do Presidente da República*), 2011, *http://portal.tcu.gov.br/tcu/paginas/contas_governo/contas_2011/index.html*; TCU (2011b), Performance Audit on the Logic Model and Goals of the National Policy for Regional Development (TC 033.934.2011-8); *http://www.tcu.gov.br/Consultas/Juris/Docs/judoc/Acord/20141211/AC_3564_49_14_P.doc*; TCU (2009), Preliminary Audit on the National Policy for Regional Development (TC 013.705.2009-6); *http://www.tcu.gov.br/Consultas/Juris/Docs/judoc%5CAcord%5C20091204%5C013-705-2009-6-MIN-JJ.rtf*

In future audits, TCU could assess the interplay between sectoral goals, and overlap with related PPA thematic goals and the goals that Brazil has sought in signing for the SDGs. In support of such an approach, TCU could build on its experience in auditing sectoral plans in other areas, such as the National Education Plan (2014-2024), which spans beyond the PPA (2016-2019), but will end before the SDG goals are to be met (2030). In addition, SDGs is one element not considered in the series of audits of the national development policy.

In view of the aforementioned TCU findings, TCU could also assess adequacy of annual allocations for achieving government-wide goals. Where single sectoral plans exist, TCU can use this as a basis of analysis. TCU could ask whether the annual allocations reflect the government-wide priorities and thematic programmes set out in the PPA. TCU could also ask whether public managers have a sense of whether funding proposals and plans of particular sectors are linked to the PPA, or to one another, and are based on realistic funding projections. The 2009 PEFA report found a weak link between planning and budget, noting that sector strategies are not well costed and are not related to the aims set out in the PPA and LDO (PEFA, 2009).

Where no sectoral plan exists, TCU could assess a set of plans that cut across the sector or with other related sectors. For instance, this could include assessing objectives in health that touch upon education, or vice-versa. This would have the added benefit of allowing TCU to deepen its understanding on the policy interactions and policy effects within sectors and between sectors (see Chapter 2).

TCU could continue to assess and communicate key findings on the alignment of multi-annual priorities with annual budgetary allocations, emphasising the importance of entity-level planning with a longer time horizon.

Given the extensive activity that TCU has already undertaken to examine the alignment, or rather the misalignment, of the PPA, TCU could benefit from making clearer the importance of their findings for better budgetary governance. For instance, TCU could consider holding targeted seminars with the executive and legislative branches – particularly with Centre of Government entities with a responsibility for oversight of the government agenda.

In addition, TCU could amplify its focus during its audits with regards to the impacts the current PPA has on annual planning at the ministry level. A recent TCU audit demonstrated the extent to which sectoral bodies and the Federal Budget Secretariat (*Secretaria de Orçamento Federal*, SOF) discuss the policies of the PPA to be prioritized in the LOA of each year. Fifty-eight percent of sectoral bodies claimed that they always or almost always had this discussion, while 42% of agencies said that they sometimes, rarely or never had this discussion (TCU, 2016). These numbers suggest greater opportunities to improve such interactions. Further, as discussed below, the projections prepared for the LDO are often overestimated, and thus mean that entities plans are also overly ambitious and often need to be downsized. The questions in Box 3.3 below could help TCU to conduct audits that delve into the impact of the PPA, LDO and LOA on entity planning.

Box 3.3. **Potential questions in assessing PPA, LDO and LOA's impact on entity planning**

The following questions can inform an assessment of how government-wide budgetary provisions enable annual planning at the ministry level, so that strategies and activities are goal-oriented, realistic and measurable.

- Is the budget process used to align national priorities, reconcile sectoral objectives and foster policy integration?
- What efforts are being made to re-structure the budgetary process to reflect the increasing cross-cutting nature of policy-making?
- Why are the predetermined objectives and indicators important? How are indicators/ targets used to manage service delivery?
- In what ways are the policies and their associated resource allocations likely to reinforce each other for achieving sustainable development objectives?
- Have ex ante evaluations of capital and current expenditure programmes been undertaken?

Source: OECD (2016a), *Supreme Audit Institutions and Good Governance: Oversight, Insight and Foresight*, OECD Public Governance Reviews, OECD Publishing, Paris. *http://dx.doi.org/10.1787/9789264263871-en*; OECD (2015d), OECD (2016b), *Better Policies for Sustainable Development 2016: A New Framework for Policy Coherence*, OECD Publishing, Paris, *http://dx.doi.org/10.1787/9789264256996-en*.

The example of the Auditor General of South Africa (AGSA) and its activities to fulfil its mandate to undertake an annual *Budgetary and Strategic Review* can also be instructive for TCU. Although this activity is formally considered as a financial and compliance audit, it also incorporates a broader assessment of pre-determined objectives laid out in the budget. Specifically, AGSA reviews the relevance and measurability of pre-determined objectives and the measurability of targets to help ministries understand shortcomings in their planning. The Auditor General presents findings to relevant parliamentary committees (case study Box 3.4).

Box 3.4. **Audit of strategy and budget in South Africa**

In South Africa the portfolio committees of parliament and provincial legislatures undertake reviews, recommendations and reports on budgets before they are submitted to parliament and the legislatures for approval. In this process, the Auditor General of South Africa plays an important role in the budgetary and strategic plan review that uses the insight gained from the previous year's financial and compliance audits. The review considers each department's financial accountability records, assessments of internal controls and delivery on service objectives to assess the budgets audit preparations.

Specifically, procedures of the budget process are incorporated into the year-end compliance audits. AGSA reviews compliance with the *Public Financial Management Act of South Africa* in the areas of current annual budgets, virements, rollovers, adjustments and reporting. In addition, AGSA also performs procedures on predetermined objectives through interim auditing.

- In assessing the measurability of objectives, AGSA asks: Does the indicator/measure have a clear unambiguous definition? Is the indicator/measure defined so that data will be collected consistently? Based on discussions held with senior management and relevant information inspected, is the indicator/measure well-defined? Is it possible to verify the processes and systems that produce the indicator? Based on discussions held with senior management and information inspected, is it possible to conclude whether the indicator/measure is verifiable?
- In assessing the measurability of targets, AGSA asks: Is the planned target specific? Is the planned target measurable? Is the planned target time-bound?
- In determining the relevance of objectives, AGSA interviews relevant senior managers/officials to determine how indicator/measurement relates logically and directly to an aspect of the institutions mandate, and the realisation of strategic goals and objectives. The following questions are used as the basis of the discussion: Why are the predetermined objective and indicators important? How are the indicators/targets used to manage service delivery? AGSA then provides a conclusion.

These procedures on the budget process are then incorporated into a presentation to parliament's and provincial legislatures' portfolio committees.

Source: OECD (2016a), *Supreme Audit Institutions and Good Governance: Oversight, Insight and Foresight*, OECD Public Governance Reviews, OECD Publishing, Paris. *http://dx.doi.org/10.1787/9789264263871-en*

3.4. Strengthening performance-based budgeting with evidence and findings from audits

TCU could help to improve the reliability of evidence and information for making performance-based budgetary decisions through assessments of key areas, such as expenditure programmes funded by earmarks and the effectiveness of operational cost measurement.

Difficult budgetary decisions require objective and factual information on what works well and what does not. In 2015, the OECD recommended that Brazil's policy makers review the earmarking of public revenues and mandatory spending floors with a view towards making public spending more responsive and flexible to the policy priorities (OECD, 2015c). These proposals reflect international standards and good practices. For instance, OECD's recommendation on good budgetary governance stipulates that performance, evaluation and value for money be integral to the budget process (OECD, 2015a), including:

- evaluating and reviewing expenditure programmes – including associated staffing resources as well as tax expenditures – in a manner that is objective, routine and regular to inform resource allocation and re-prioritisation both within line ministries and across government as a whole (Principle 8d); and
- taking stock, periodically, of overall expenditure (including tax expenditure) and reassessing its alignment with fiscal objectives and national priorities, taking account of the results of evaluations; noting that for such a comprehensive review to be effective, it must be responsive to the practical needs of government as a whole (principle 8g).

In recent years, OECD and other countries have increasingly sought to develop a focus on the results achieved with the appropriations allocated through various approaches under the heading of "performance budgeting." Performance budgeting frameworks are widely found in OECD countries and are generally flexible in nature. In general, the different policy sectors aim to use performance information for setting allocations for programmes, line ministries and agencies, for strategic planning, for proposing new areas of spending, and for a reduction in spending.

In reality, there is currently no settled consensus on the optimal way of using performance information within the budgeting context. The issues arising range from the level of information being used, the problems inherent in measurement of public performance and concerns that performance budgeting would displace other mechanisms for accountability and monitoring of performance.

A 2013 OECD survey showed that, generally, when performance targets are not met, the consequences for managers of ministries can be limited. This suggested that performance information was not easily transformed into action, as was the case in Brazil (Table 3.2). More recently, case studies of 5 OECD member countries (Canada, Ireland, the Netherlands, the United Kingdom and the United States), demonstrated that the performance public managers are increasingly evaluated with use of performance information in mind (OECD, 2016b).

Brazil uses elements of performance-based budgeting (OECD, 2014b; IBP, 2016; Bertelsmann, 2016). However, the quality of the information used as inputs into the budget (underlying assumptions) and the results reported against the budget are questionable, according to TCU. There is oversight from constitutionally appointed bodies, such as TCU and the Ministry of Transparency, Supervision and Control (*Ministério da Transparência, Fiscalização e Controle*, CGU), as well as mechanisms that legally guarantee citizen engagement and feedback on programmes and services. In addition, there is a law (Complementary law 101/2000) which establishes a council to assess the performance of agencies and actors in the formulation of the budget, and the Senate is obliged to conduct annual evaluations.

In practice however, there are concerns with the quality of information and its meaningful use in making budgetary decisions (IMF, 2014; TCU, 2016a). Moreover, Brazil's LOA and LDO do not identify the budgetary impact of new policies, making it difficult to anticipate implications for the budget (IMF, 2014). When performance targets are not met, consequences for managers of ministries can be limited, as is the case in Brazil (OECD, 2014b). A recent OECD report on trends in performance-based budgeting found that general programme evaluations can be useful, but lack a budget focus. It suggests:

> *"Frequently, evaluation is designed and used to assist programme managers better understand the performance of their programme to comprehend how to do better given resource and*

policy constraints. These perspectives are legitimate frameworks for analysis, yet this process rarely generates the sort of evidence most useful to budget officials – data on the relevance of a programme, an understanding of the causal relationship between financial inputs and outputs/outcomes, and analysis of the efficiency and economy with which programmes deliver performance" (OECD, 2016b).

Table 3.2. **Performance budgeting practices at the central level of government (2013)**

Latin America and the Caribbean

	Existence of standardised performance budgeting framework for central government	Consequences for poor performance			
		No consequences	Organisational or programme's poor performance made public	More intense monitoring of organisation and/or programme	Budget decreases
Argentina	Yes	❍	O	❍	⊙
Barbados	Yes	❍	❍	O	⊙
Brazil	Yes	●	❍	❍	❍
Chile	Yes	⊙	●	⊙	⊘
Colombia	No, Line Ministries/Agencies have their own	⊘	❍	⊘	⊘
Costa Rica	Yes	O	●	O	⊘
Dominican Republic	No, Line Ministries/Agencies have their own	..	..	..	..
Ecuador	Yes	⊘	❍	O	⊙
El Salvador	No, Line Ministries/Agencies have their own	..	..	..	..
Guatemala	Yes	●	⊙	●	⊘
Honduras	No, Line Ministries/Agencies have their own	O	⊘	O	❍
Mexico	Yes	❍	●	●	❍
Panama	Yes	●	⊘	❍	⊘
Paraguay	Yes	⊘	⊙	⊙	❍
Peru	Yes	⊘	❍	O	❍
Total					
● Always		3	3	2	0
O Usually		2	1	5	0
⊙ Occasionally		1	2	2	3
❍ Rarely		3	5	3	5
⊘ Never		4	2	1	5
x Not applicable (information not produced or negotiations do not take place)		2	2	2	2
.. Not available		2	2	2	2

Source: OECD (2014b) 'Government at a Glance: Latin America and the Caribbean 2014,' Country Fact Sheet, OECD Publishing, Paris, *https://www.oecd.org/gov/brazil_en.pdf* Accessed 30 Sep 2016.

In decentralised systems, it is rare for a central budget authority to conduct evaluations themselves and instead rely on evaluation of ministries and programme managers. Thus, if evaluations are not producing results that are comparable, the evaluations become less useful from a budgetary perspective. To date, reviews that have a specific budget focus – such as spending reviews – tend to provide more focused evidence that can be input into the budgetary process (OECD, 2016b).

A further issue is that evaluations often lack commentary on efficiency or effectiveness, as well as the success or shortfalls in meeting programme expectations. Instead, evaluations are prone to equivocal explanations that, again, make it difficult for budget officials to take a horizontal, comparative view on performance implications for the budget (OECD, 2016b). Such expectations and pitfalls of performance-based budgeting frameworks will be useful for Brazil's government to keep in mind in this first year of the "Committee on Monitoring and Evaluation of Federal Public Policies" (CMAP), established by the federal government in

April 2016. Established as an inter-ministerial committee, CMAP seeks to improve actions, programs and public policies, as well as the application of resources and the quality of public spending (Internal ordinance Number 102) (MP, 2016b; 2016c; 2016d; 2016e). It aims to generate results from across the administration that can better inform performance, as well as to serve in the elaboration and execution of the budget. Learning from OECD member countries, the CMAP may benefit from integrating budgetary-focused reviews into its basket of evaluative tools.

SAIs have been attempting to link results of policies and programmes to the budgetary assumptions and decisions that underlie them in order to promote more informed and evidence-based decisions. In a survey of ten SAIs, eight had assessed whether there are adequate mechanisms to generate and capture quality performance information during the phase of budget execution (OECD, 2016a). TCU's own work on governance reflects this approach. One example is TCU's systemic report of the labour function (FISC-Trabalho) that looked at the allocation of resources to labour policies, the subsequent monitoring of indicators and progress, or lack of, with regards to previous audits. The audit pointed to sustainability issues with the Support Fund for Workers (Fundo de Amparo ao Trabalhador), and an imbalance between revenue and expenditure (TCU, 2015c).

TCU has also looked at elements of performance and value-for-money elements in budgeting through other activities. For instance, TCU undertook a monitoring report on the procedures for drawing up the PPA for (2008-2011), with emphasis on the analysis of performance indicators linked to the various programs that make up medium-term budget. The work aimed to map out a diagnosis of the main problems and challenges faced by the planning system involved in the PPA design task (TCU, 2009a).

Linking outcomes to budgetary decisions is a challenging pursuit, but doing so is critical for developing a clear picture of Brazil's federal performance year-on-year (TCU, 2016a). More reliable and relevant performance information, demonstrating what is working and what is not, would further help Brazil to determine trade-offs based on reliable evidence. This also helps to protect the budgeting processes from special interests, thereby creating trust in government spending decisions. TCU's audit reports can serve as critical inputs into the process. To effectively inform budget deliberations and resource allocations, TCU's report should be published in a timely, relevant and objective manner, in accordance with international standards (INTOSAI, 2013). In addition, TCU could further help to improve the reliability of evidence and information for making performance-based budgetary decisions. Areas TCU could consider as a focus of future audit work to this end include the following:

- **The usefulness of budget reviews and evaluations for decision-making**: TCU could look at existing reviews or evaluations for their link to the budget, as a separate endeavour to assessing evaluations for their reliability in general (discussed in chapter 5). A 2014 IMF review of Brazil's budgetary framework recommended the introduction spending reviews that would encompass mandatory expenditures (IMF, 2014). TCU could also assess the extent to which CMAP's provisions for gathering budgetary related results will yield informative and reliable findings.
- **Reliability of information of policies related to earmarking of public revenues:** The government has produced ad-hoc evaluations on tax expenditures, but the government does not provide systematic reviews or an overarching view of results obtained through these increased expenditures. In 2011, Brazil's tax revenue was highest amongst Latin American and Caribbean countries, amounting to 35% of GDP (OECD, 2014b), but much of

it earmarked and limits the flexibility of government to allocate spending between areas (OECD, 2015). These tax-related expenditures are approved by Law but by different legal instruments and at different times than the LOA. According to TCU officials, these are also not under same scrutiny by Congress. In 2015, the OECD recommended that Brazil's policy makers review the earmarking of public revenues and mandatory spending floors with a view towards making public spending more responsive and flexible to the policy priorities (OECD, 2015c). As mentioned, the IMF recommended that Brazil introduce spending reviews that encompassed mandatory expenditures (IMF, 2014).

- **Reliability of measurement of operational costs:** Another area for focus could be the periodic assessment of government's evaluations of its operational costs. This requirement was foreseen in the fiscal responsibility law of 2000. The Ministry of Finance (MF) began developing a system for measuring costs of activities as was predicted approximately 4 years ago. While the implementation has been gradual, there may be an opportunity for TCU to assess the quality of any existing reports as well as of the underlying review process itself. This could act to accelerate the process, anticipated in 2000. This process will be an important means of supporting budgetary trade-offs made to operational expenditure. TCU may be inspired by the Netherlands Court of Audit for instance (Box 3.5), which found that a merger, intended to produce savings for the government by cutting operational costs, would fail to materialise because of faulty projections on which the decision for the merger was based. This is a good example of SAIs using foresight to highlight the need for quality, objective evidence for more sustainable decisions.

More consistent evaluation by TCU in these areas would help to make off-budget expenditures or expenditures under different oversight processes, more transparent. Due consideration should be given in advance to the oversight procedures that have been established, and whether there is an opportunity for this to be strengthened before TCU engages.

Box 3.5. **The SAI of the Netherlands – linking evidence-based decisions with efficiency gains**

Audit Objectives

The Netherlands Food and Consumer Product Safety Authority (NVWA) was created on 1 January 2012 through the merger of three inspectorates: the General Inspectorate (AID), the Netherlands Plant Health Authority (PD) and the original Food and Product Safety Authority (VWA). The government had foreseen two opportunities to make savings with the new supervision methods of the NVWA:

1. The three merger partners' development and the introduction of new supervision methods was looked upon as a potential source of cost savings. By using risk-based working methods and giving more responsibility to the private sector, the NVWA would need fewer people.
2. As inspections, knowledge development, personnel and premises/operational management could be combined following the merger, economies of scale were anticipated.

The Court of Audit assessed whether the merger between the VWA, the AID and PD was evidence based, and whether it produced the desired efficiency gains by looking at 1) the cost savings ex post; and 2) the underlying premises of the merger. The audit took 650 working days.

Box 3.5. **The SAI of the Netherlands – linking evidence-based decisions with efficiency gains** *(cont.)*

Audit Outcomes

The audit determined that the government had failed to make a thorough analysis of the pros and cons of the merger before it decided to merge the inspectorates in 2007. The government had based its decision on general considerations and assumptions about potential efficiency gains. The conditions under which new supervision methods could cut expenditure, how much money would be saved and over what time period, had not been studied in advance. The inability to apply the new methods of supervision across the board meant that foreseen major savings were not realised in recent years. The new supervision methods are also unlikely to produce significant savings in the next four years because they will first require the investment of time and money. The expected economies of scale from the merger also proved too optimistic. Foreseeable risks, for example in the field of IT, were not taken fully into account. Furthermore, the overlap between the three organisations was never quantified, but was estimated to never be greater than 13%.

The considerable savings expected of the merger have so far failed to materialise, resulting in inevitable consequences for the feasibility of the planned savings. The intended structural saving of €50 million as from 2012 has not been achieved. The target of a further saving of €31.6 million as from 2018 was lowered by €11.8 million in 2013. The Court deemed it unlikely, however, that even this lower savings target will be achieved.

Following the audit, the State Secretary for Economic Affairs began implementing the NCA's recommendation to consider social risks and human resources before taking any decision on further changes to the NVWA's tasks and budget. The SAI received no response on its recommendation to monitor the achievement of savings, and has since encouraged the ministry to provide a clear overview of the initial budget, the savings targets and the price level in the annual budget and accounts.

Good pracices used

This was an innovative performance audit for the NCA as it not only evaluated the results of the decision (in this case, the savings) but also looked at the assumptions for the decision (the merger). Auditing if the assumptions of a decision were plausible helps to determine the causes of unsatisfactory results. Analysing the wording of relevant documents, figures, and interviews with those directly involved, broke down general concepts (such as "synergies") on which the decision was based into more operational concepts. The audit included a quantification of the overlaps – or lack of synergies – that existed between the merged entities.

At a very basic level, the Court found it useful to study the figures of the intended budget cuts. There appeared to be considerable uncertainty within the Ministry of Economic Affairs about the reference level from which the cuts had to be realised. Moreover, the effect of inflation is important in such long-term policy intentions and was not made explicit. Determining the causes helped to strengthen the Court's recommendations.

Lessons learned

In this study the Court tried to uncover whether the new organisation (NVWA) had enough resources for their tasks and, to this end, conducted many structured interviews with staff. At the end of the study, the Court considered much of the interview information as unreliable. The Court now views the reliability of information from interviews as a methodological problem to be solved by further integrating other scientific approaches with qualitative analysis.

Sources: Adapted from OECD (2016a), *Supreme Audit Institutions and Good Governance: Oversight, Insight and Foresight*, OECD Public Governance Reviews, OECD Publishing, Paris. *http://dx.doi.org/10.1787/9789264263871-en*; NCA (2013), Supervision of the Netherlands Food and Consumer Product Safety Authority Following the Merger, *www.courtofaudit.nl/english/Publications/Audits/Introductions/2013/11/Supervision_of_the_Netherlands_food_and_consumer_product_safety_authority_following_the_merger*.

TCU may be further inspired by the SAIs of Canada, Korea and the Netherlands in which the SAI assessed workforce sustainability of government plans to manage population ageing, which will also become an issue for Brazil (Box 3.6).

Box 3.6. **The SAIs of Canada, Korea and the Netherlands – using foresight to assess workforce sustainability and population ageing**

In 2012, the Netherlands Court of Audit undertook a review of Human Resource Management that focused on the strategy and planning for central government personnel. The audit analysed the preparedness of central government for increases in retirement and turnover in personnel predicted between 2012 and 2022. The Court of Audit concluded that the lack of a strategic personnel plan significantly undermined its ability to anticipate and oversee the consequences of personnel changes. Planned spending cuts to the civil service between 2012 and 2014 compounded the need for strategic planning to ensure that jobs necessary in the future were not cut. Lack of planning prevented central government from steering the development of staff and responding to evolving needs.

In 2012, the Korean Board of Audit and Inspection conducted an audit on the management practices of the Government Employee Pension Service (GEPS) and Teacher's Pension (TP), with the goal of determining the stability of the systems and restoring public trust. As a result it found the deficiencies in asset management and operations of the GEPS and TP, including inaccurate measuring of the value of assets, overpayment for management services compared to other pension systems and overstated revenues. The audit also found that ineligible recipients indeed received pension and severance payments. BAI provided recommendations for the GEPS and TP to better manage its assets, and notified the relevant ministries of ineligible recipients of pension payments so they could begin actions to recollect the money.

It found issues with the status of the assets managed by these systems, including inaccurate measuring of the value of assets held, overpayment for management services compared to other pension systems, and overstated revenues. The audit also found that some persons who were not eligible for the pension were allowed to receive pension and severance payments. The Board of Audit and Inspection provided recommendations for the GEPS and TP systems to better manage its assets, and notified the relevant ministries of ineligible recipients of pension payments so that they could begin to recollect the improper disbursements.

The Auditor General of Canada delivered its Fall Report in 2012, which included a chapter on the long-term fiscal sustainability of Canada. It looked particularly at the growing proportion of elderly Canadians and the resulting pressure on the health care and pension systems. The Auditor General focused on whether Finance Canada had analysed and publicised these long-term sustainability issues, as well as made decision makers aware of their findings. The Auditor General concluded that Finance Canada had made long-term sustainability analyses where appropriate, but made recommendations regarding the need to: 1) perform analyses of the overall long-term fiscal implications for the federal government of budget proposals, 2) inform the Minister of Finance before budget measures are decided and approved, and 3) publish overall long-term fiscal sustainability analyses for the federal government, as well as periodically publish an analysis for all governments combined (i.e. federal, provincial, territorial and municipal) to give a comprehensive perspective of Canada.

Sources: Adapted from OECD (2016a), *Supreme Audit Institutions and Good Governance: Oversight, Insight and Foresight*, OECD Public Governance Reviews, OECD Publishing, Paris. *http://dx.doi.org/10.1787/9789264263871-en*; NCA (2012), Central Government personnel: strategy and planning, Netherlands Court of Audit, the Hague, *www.courtofaudit.nl/english/Publications/Audits/Introductions/2012/05/Central_government_personnel_strategy_and_planning*; OAG (2012), 2012 Fall Report of the Auditor General of Canada, Office of the Auditor General of Canada, Ottawa, *www.oag-bvg.gc.ca/internet/English/parl_oag_201210_07_e_37351.html#hd5a*.

3.5. Assessing in-year progress reports to support the dialogue on fiscal discipline

TCU could enhance its contributions to the dialogue on fiscal discipline by periodically assessing in-year progress reports to discern how adjustments to fiscal targets and plans affect the achievement of goals.

With the introduction of the Fiscal Responsibility Law (*Lei de Responsabilidade Fiscal*, LRF) in 2000, Brazil moved towards a more established pattern of mid-term fiscal management that would provide more stability.[5] Further specifications on fiscal rules and responsibility were made in the supplementary Law 229, originating in 2009 and being updated in 2015, which outlines norms on planning, budget control and public accounting for public sector management (Brazil Senate, 2015). The requirements outlined in the LRF essentially act as fiscal rules, which are concrete indicators of fiscal management.[6]

Fiscal rules can play an important role in credibility of national budgeting by constraining politically-motivated spending to improve macroeconomic stability in the short-term, while contributing to long-term fiscal sustainability. Further, fiscal rules should make it easier to understand and to anticipate the government's fiscal policy course throughout the economic cycle (OECD, 2015d). Brazil's expenditure commitments, budget allocations, and revenue projections tend to be adjusted fluidly in year, weakening the institutional link between planning and budgeting in practice that is set out in the Constitution (IMF, 2014; PEFA, 2009; TCU, 2016a). The International Monetary Fund (IMF) found "the Constitutional powers of Congress to increase revenue estimates and the President's powers based on the LRF to issue decrees to reduce expenditures regularly lead to an inefficient and time-consuming budget process" (IMF, 2014).

Periodic in-year reporting on budget execution and revision of budget estimates has helped OECD member countries to detect and manage the impact of economic developments and other factors on the budget in a timely manner. Such reports identify any changes to the assumptions underlying the budget, as well as other relevant events that have transpired during the fiscal year. Thus, quality in-year reporting becomes important to ensure that entities can manage in accordance with fiscal adjustments, and continue to work towards the achievement of goals and objectives. In Brazil, executive entities provide reports on fiscal targets and compliance with fiscal rules bimonthly and every quarter, marking points of control, or "pontas de controle" (MP, 2016b). The LRF requires the Executive to report to the CMO every 4 months to explain the evolution of fiscal objectives. They are sent to CGU for review. The LRF also mandates that Brazil's TCU (and TCEs) audit the enforcement of the law's procedural rules.

There are fewer TCU examples targeted to this area of budgetary governance when compared to the other areas explored in this chapter. TCU touches on fiscal discipline as part of its accounts examinations process. It also featured tangentially in the review of budgetary governance, explored at length in recommendation 3.1.

Given the importance of in-year reporting and the potential of in-year adjustments to affect strategic goals, TCU could audit in-year progress reports to understand how adjustments to fiscal assumptions are affecting entity and programme outcomes at the end of the year. Specifically, such audits could help TCU and audited entities to understand how the quality and decision making related to in-year reporting and adjustments to fiscal targets affect the annual or multi-annual goal attainment of the specific entity or programme. This work would allow for real-time feedback on a key governance mechanism, so that additional adjustments could be made, as needed, to ensure the success of policies and programmes.

TCU would be well placed to contribute further to the discussion on fiscal discipline and responsibility. It can do so with both Congress and the Executive. Indeed, part of TCU's impact in strengthening more sustainable budgeting rests on improving communication particularly with the CMO. Further, TCU could consider more frequent communication of key findings with central entities involved in budget and planning (MP and MF).

3.6. Improving audits to support long-term fiscal sustainability

TCU could further assess whether adequate institutional procedures and safeguards are in place to ensure the quality, reliability and sustainability of budget forecasts and medium-term projections.

Public fiscal sustainability is the ability of public governments to maintain public finances at a credible and serviceable position over the long run, in light of the prevailing mix of spending and revenue policies. Prudent macroeconomic assumptions, sensitivity and risk analyses, as well as appropriate fiscal rules, are factors that can help to orient spending and revenue policies within sustainable levels in the short and medium term.

Long-term fiscal projections can play a useful role in identifying the expected future costs and associated debt of current policies in light of forecasted demographic and economic developments. In most OECD countries, the Central Budget Authority (CBA) is responsible for long-term fiscal projections. In some countries this responsibility is located in other departments of the Ministry of Finance other than the CBA or in other core ministries. Some OECD governments also present long-term fiscal challenges in a cross-generational perspective, in order to distribute benefits and cost in a reasonable way over generations.

In Brazil, projections are prepared jointly by the MP and the MF. Any ex-ante comparison of the government's macroeconomic and fiscal forecasts with those of other institutions goes unpublished (IMF, 2014). Past assessments of Brazil's preparation of multiyear fiscal forecasts and functional allocations have identified room for improvement (PEFA, 2009). Despite the strong institutional framework for creating projections, adjustments are made to the revenue projections and discretionary spending during the Congressional approval process (Hallerberg et al., 2009; PEFA, 2009; IMF, 2014; TCU, 2016a). The IMF has recently suggested that Congress should be required to use forecasts prepared by independent parties, which are perceived to be more objective in the event the Congress rejects the estimates of the MP and MF. This could also help to ensure that increases in revenue estimates by Congress, in exercise within its constitutional powers, are measured and evidence-based.

In Brazil, bodies of expertise that could provide insight on fiscal sustainability, apart from the MF, have come and gone. Establishment of an Independent Fiscal Institution (IFI) is one way in which OECD countries are trying to improve the credibility of budgetary forecasts and enhance independent oversight with regard to fiscal performance. A proposal to establish an IFI in the Brazilian Senate is currently incorporated into draft law number 65.[7] The creation of IFIs reflects a trend of invest in resources and institutions that facilitate Parliamentary engagement in the budget process. TCU, and other bodies in Brazil, can look to OECD's *Recommendation of the Council on Principles for Independent Fiscal Institutions* (OECD, 2014c), for both guidance in its establishment or criteria against which an eventual IFI could be evaluated.

An SAI is another institutional mechanism for supporting adequate institutional procedures and safeguards for quality economic and budgetary forecasts. OECD's "Supreme Audit Institutions and Good Governance: Oversight, Insight and Foresight" (2016a) demonstrates how SAIs are contributing to budget sustainability. They are active in using foresight to assess the reliability of fiscal projections in order to ensure that underlying assumptions of the budget are sound. Nine of 10 SAIs, including TCU, are looking to the reliability and quality of tools that underlie the budget. Eight of 10 had assessed the adequacy of other mechanisms for determining the quality and reliability of budgetary forecasts and fiscal plans, and managing accordingly (OECD, 2016a).

TCU is responsible for assessing compliance of entities with the Fiscal Responsibility Law, and its more traditional role has been to monitor fiscal targets. TCU's recent work in assessing the budgetary framework against OECD's *Recommendation of the Council on Budgetary Governance* looked at the ability of public administration to achieve consistent and intact budgetary forecasts. Select examples of TCU's work in this area include:

- **Evaluation of the revenue forecast of the year 2013**: Seeks to verify the adherence of the statements presented to the constitutional and legal requirements, particularly the Fiscal Responsibility Law (TCU, 2013b).
- **Audit of financial position of government**: Follow up report to check that the financial statements of Ministry of Finance reflect, in all material respects, the financial position at the end of year (TCU, 2015d).
- **Audit on the reliability of the budgetary forecasts and fiscal plans** like revenues, expenditures, fiscal targets, national economic forecasts and central government primary balance (TCU, 2015e).
- **Survey report to identify the criteria used to forecast macroeconomic indicators** that are used for preparing the Annual Budget Law, to compare the predicted values with the realized and to check for possible discrepancies and effects on the budget execution and government finances (TCU, 2014a).
- **Evaluation of the revenue forecast of the year 2014**: Seeks to verify the adherence of the statements presented to the constitutional and legal requirements, particularly the Fiscal Responsibility Law (TCU, 2014b).
- **Compliance and monitoring report, Follow-up:** Revenue forecast evaluation of the federal budget bill 2015, to assess the estimates of revenue contained in the Budget Bill of the Union for 2015. This report showed that projected revenue estimates did not match the market expectations (TCU, 2014c).

The recommendations are not meant to suggest a role for TCU in long-term projections or conducting fiscal forecasting, but instead how it can support their quality and use them for pointing to the sustainability of the programmes being funded. In fact, TCU's future audits could delve further into the subject, to assess whether Congress specifically is equipped with the institutional capacity, including independent professional advice and critique, to meet OECD principle 10 to "promote the integrity and quality of budgetary forecasts, fiscal plans and budgetary implementation through rigorous quality assurance including independent audit" (OECD, 2015a).

In addition, future TCU audits could use fiscal projections to ascertain progress or advancements in the quality of forecasts over time, and to more systematically assess sustainability of programmes, as has been done by the SAI of Mexico (Auditoría Superior de la Federación), which assessed the assumptions on which decisions related to the deficit were made. As a starting point, ahead of the establishment of the IFI, TCU could analyse and collect key findings from audits already conducted in order to identify the processes and conditions that produce quality fiscal targets. In addition, according to external stakeholders, TCU could integrate these conditions as criteria into its audits. Other approaches include those of the SAIs of Canada, the United Kingdom and the United States (Box 3.7).

Box 3.7. **SAI approaches to assessing fiscal sustainability**

Canada's Office of the Auditor General (OAG): Auditing long-term sustainability

Canada's OAG in past years has used audit as a tool to assess to what extent long-term sustainability is factored into budgeting and policy. For example, in 2012 the OAG examined how well the Department of Finance accounts for the impact of spending and taxing on long term fiscal sustainability before recommending policy. This audit also examined how long-term fiscal sustainability analyses are prepared and reported.

The audit found that the Department of Finance prepares long term fiscal analyses when they deem it relevant. As such, they will only make projections for the impact of fiscal measures past five years if they believe the impact of those taxes and spending measures is going to be significantly changed relative to the size of the economy. When the Department does deem it relevant to perform analyses, they assess the long-term impact of individual measures on revenues or expenditures but it does not always consider the effect on budgetary balance and public debt or overall fiscal sustainability.

Additionally the audit found that although the Department of Finance does provide results of fiscal sustainability analyses that project budgetary balance and debt in the long term, they do not provide it to Parliament with enough time before the budget is tabled to inform decisions. In fact, for a budget, the Minister is not informed of the overall long term fiscal impact until months after the budget measures have been adopted. Further, although fiscal sustainability assessments have been prepared since 2010, the Department does not make them public.

The United Kingdom National Audit Office (UK NAO): Audit of Forecasts

In 2014, the UK NAO conducted cross government reviews to assess how departments produce and use forecasts for effective public financial management. While the focus of the review was mostly forecasting that informs expenditure, the findings prove applicable to forecasting more generally, such as benefits from new investments.

The review found poor forecasting is an entrenched problem across the government. For example, forecasts often lacked ranges and sensitivity analysis, which detracts from the effectiveness of risk management. The audit found often decision makers need to introduce new measures quickly and do not fully manage the risks for the forecasts. Additionally, 'optimism bias' has a tendency to skew risk management by making forecasts which are more supportive for policy initiatives rather than realistic. The audit also found that the centre needs to do more in order to incentivise better forecasting as there are few examples of sanctions or rewards for quality forecasting. Additionally, because there is no consistent approach or framework for forecasting across government it is difficult to compare the quality of forecasts.

The United States Government Accountability Office (GAO): Long Term Fiscal Simulations

Since 1992, the GAO has published long term fiscal simulations showing the deficits and debts under different policy assumptions. Rather than precise forecasts or predictions of what will happen in the future, however, these are general illustrations of the outcomes of different sets of policy assumptions in order to provide a context for future policy options.

For the projections the GAO uses two types of simulations. The Baseline Extended follows the current year's baseline projections of the Congressional Budget Office, creating a simulation reflecting the current law taking into account caps and automatic enforcement procedures and inflation for the next ten years. Additionally, for the alternative simulation, federal debt as a share of GDP grows throughout the period and can be expanded for a number of decades.

Through these simulations, in 2004, the GAO demonstrated that without large scale entitlement reform and/or dramatic changes in tax and spending policies, the country will face persistent and escalating deficits.

Source: OECD (2016); *http://www.oag-bvg.gc.ca/internet/English/parl_oag_201210_07_e_37351.html*; *http://www.gao.gov/products/GAO-04-585T* and *https://www.nao.org.uk/wp-content/uploads/2015/01/Forecasting-in-government-to-achieve-value-for-money-summary.pdf*

Notes

1. "Budgetary governance" refers to the processes, laws, structures and institutions in place for ensuring that the budgeting system meets its objectives in an effective, sustainable and enduring manner (OECD, 2015a).
2. OECD's review "Brazil's Supreme Audit Institution: The audit of the consolidated year-end government report" focused extensively on this particular activity of TCU, this report does not seek to duplicate and focuses thus on the other operational audits of TCU (OECD, 2012).
3. The level of detail of such frameworks varies from country to country. The World Bank (2013) proposes some useful distinctions among MTEFs, in ascending order of sophistication and detail: medium-term fiscal frameworks (MTFFs, which focus upon fixed fiscal limits for budget-setting), medium-term budget frameworks (MTBFs, which aim to incorporate national and sectoral strategies within the MTFF) and medium-term performance frameworks (MTPFs, which include systematic use of performance information within funding envelopes).
4. As designated by Senior Budget Officials in Brazil, which reported to the OECD Budget Survey in 2013 to not have an MTEF at the federal level.
5. The LRF included: restraints for certain expenditures, such as personnel; clear debt ceilings; setting restrictions for public spending near election time in all levels of government; imposing clear responsibilities for budget managers; ceilings on personnel expenditure (including pensions); and binding the use of public resources to government programs defined in the budget.
6. A fiscal rule is seen as a fiscal policy expressed in terms of a summary indicator of fiscal performance has two fundamental characteristics. First, it presents a constraint that binds political decisions made by the Legislature and by the Executive. Second, it serves as a concrete indicator of the Executive's fiscal management (Kopits and Symansky, 1998).
7. As of September 2016, referring to draft law 65 that had been approved in Congress in March 2016.

References

Bertelsmann Stiftung (2016), Brazil: country report, Transformation Index 2016, *https://www.bti-project.org/fileadmin/files/BTI/Downloads/Reports/2016/pdf/BTI_2016_Brazil.pdf*

Brazil Senate (2015), Senate, Law on Fiscal Quality (Lei de qualidade fiscal) (229/2009), *http://www25.senado.leg.br/web/atividade/materias/-/materia/91341*

Hallerberg et al. (2009), Who decides the budget?, *https://publications.iadb.org/bitstream/handle/11319/6725/Who%20Decides%20the%20Budget%3F%20A%20Political%20Economy%20Analysis%20of%20the%20Budget%20Process%20in%20Latin%20America.pdf;jsessionid=B08C0802D35A2422CB26DEADDCA1605D?sequence=1*

IBP (International Budget Partnership) (2016), *http://www.internationalbudget.org/data-evidence/*, accessed online September 2016.

IDB (2010) 'The Political Economy of Fiscal Reform in Brazil: The Rationale for the Suboptimal Equilibrium' IDB Working Paper Series 117, *http://www.iadb.org/res/publications/pubfiles/pubIDB-WP-117.pdf*

IMF (2014), 'Budget institutions in G-20 countries – country evaluations' *https://www.imf.org/external/np/pp/eng/2014/040714d.pdf*

INTOSAI (2013), "International Standards of Supreme Audit Institutions 12 – The Value and Benefits of Supreme Audit Institutions – Making a Difference in the Lives of Citizens", INTOSAI Professional Standards Committee, Copenhagen, *www.intosai.org/issai-executive-summaries/view/article/issai-12-the-value-andbenefits-of-supreme-audit-institutions-making-a-difference-to-the-liv.html.*

Kopits, G. and S. Symansky (1998), "Fiscal Policy Rules", Occasional Paper, No. 162, International Monetary Fund, Washington, DC

MP (Ministry of Planning, Development and Management, Ministério do Planejamento, Desenvolvimento e Gestão (MP) (2016a), PPA 2016-2019, *http://www.planejamento.gov.br/secretarias/upload/Arquivos/ppa-2016/orientacoes_elaboracao_ppa_2016_2019_02.pdf*

MP (2016b), bimonthly reports and reports issued every quarter, for each year since 2004 are available here: *http://www.planejamento.gov.br/assuntos/orcamento/informacoes-orcamentarias/rel-de-avaliacao-fiscal-e-cumprimento-de-meta/relatorios-de-avaliacao-fiscal-e-cumprimento-de*

MP (2016c), "Government institutes Committee to monitor and evaluate public policies", Ministry of Planning, Development and Management, accessed February 2017, *http://www.planejamento.gov.br/noticias/governo-institui-comite-para-monitorar-e-avaliar-politicas-publicas*

MP (2016d), "Interministerial Committee discusses public policies and evaluates effectiveness of actions", Ministry of Planning, Development and Management, accessed February 2017, *http://www.planejamento.gov.br/noticias/comite-interministerial-discute-politicas-publicas-e-avalia-efetividade-de-acoes.*

MP (2016e), National Press (*Impresa Nacional*), Ministry of Planning, Development and Management, (now *http://pesquisa.in.gov.br/imprensa/jsp/visualiza/index.jsp?data=08/04/2016&jornal=1&pagina=79&totalArquivos=204;*

NCA (Netherland Court of Audit) (2013), Supervision of the Netherlands Food and Consumer Product Safety Authority Following the Merger, *www.courtofaudit.nl/english/Publications/Audits/Introductions/2013/11/Supervision_of_the_Netherlands_food_and_consumer_product_safety_authority_following_the_merger.*

NCA (2012), Central Government personnel: strategy and planning, Netherlands Court of Audit, the Hague, *www.courtofaudit.nl/english/Publications/Audits/Introductions/2012/05/Central_government_personnel_strategy_and_planning;*

OAG (2012), 2012 Fall Report of the Auditor General of Canada, Office of the Auditor General of Canada, Ottawa, *www.oag-bvg.gc.ca/internet/English/parl_oag_201210_07_e_37351.html#hd5a.*

OECD (2016a), *Supreme Audit Institutions and Good Governance: Oversight, Insight and Foresight*, OECD Public Governance Reviews, OECD Publishing, Paris. *http://dx.doi.org/10.1787/9789264263871-en*

OECD (2016b), «Performance budgeting practices and procedures», OECD *Journal on Budgeting*, Vol. 15/3. *http://dx.doi.org/10.1787/budget-15-5jlz6rhqdvhh*

OECD (2015a) 'Recommendation of the Council on Budgetary Governance', 18 Feb 2015, *https://www.oecd.org/gov/budgeting/Recommendation-of-the-Council-on-Budgetary-Governance.pdf*

OECD (2015b), Brazil Policy Brief: Public Governance: improving the effectiveness of public spending, Paris, *https://www.oecd.org/brazil/brazil-improving-effectiveness-of-public-spending.pdf*

OECD (2015c), *OECD Economic Surveys: Brazil 2015*, OECD Publishing, Paris. *http://dx.doi.org/10.1787/eco_surveys-bra-2015-en.*

OECD (2015d), The governance of inclusive growth *http://www.oecd.org/governance/ministerial/the-governance-of-inclusive-growth.pdf*

OECD (2014a), "Partners for Good Governance: Mapping the role of Supreme Audit Institutions", Analytical framework, OECD, *http://www.oecd.org/officialdocuments/publicdisplaydocumentpdf/?cote=GOV/PGC/ETH(2014)9&docLanguage=En*

OECD (2014b) '*Government at a Glance: Latin America and the Caribbean 2014*,' Country Fact Sheet, OECD Publishing, Paris. *https://www.oecd.org/gov/brazil_en.pdf* Accessed 30 Sep 2016

OECD (2014c), Recommendation of the Council on Principles for Independent Fiscal Institutions, OECD, Paris. *http://www.oecd.org/gov/budgeting/OECD-Recommendation-on-Principles-for-Independent-Fiscal-Institutions.pdf*

OECD (2013) Brazil's Supreme Audit Institution: The Audit of the Consolidated Year-end Government Report, OECD Public Governance Reviews, OECD Publishing. *http://dx.doi.org/10.1787/9789264188112-en*

OECD (2003) 'Budgeting in Brazil' OECD Journal on Budgeting, Vol. 3, No. 11, OECD Publishing, Paris. *https://www.oecd.org/brazil/40139608.pdf*

OECD (2002), «OECD Best Practices for Budget Transparency», *OECD Journal on Budgeting*, Vol. 1/3. *http://dx.doi.org/10.1787/budget-v1-art14-en*

PEFA (2009) 'Brazil: Federal Public Financial Management Performance Based on PEFA Methodology' December 2009, available at: *http://siteresources.worldbank.org/BRAZILEXTN/Resources/Brazil_PublicManagement_English.pdf* accessed 14 September 2016

Schick, A. (2003), «The Role of Fiscal Rules in Budgeting», *OECD Journal on Budgeting*, Vol. 3/3. *http://dx.doi.org/10.1787/budget-v3-art14-en*

TCU (2016a), TCU Judgement 033.142/2015-7 Survey Report, *http://bibspi.planejamento.gov.br/bitstream/handle/iditem/700/Acordao_TCU_948_2016.pdf?sequence=1*

TCU (2015a), Strategic Plan of Brazil's Federal Court of Accounts, 2015-2021 (Plano Estratégico do Tribunal de Contas da União para o período 2015-2021) PORTARIA-TCU N° 141, DE 1° DE ABRIL DE 2015, Brasilia, *http://portal.tcu.gov.br/tcu/paginas/planejamento/2021/index.html.*

TCU (2015b) TCU Judgement 732/2015, Plenary, Survey report. *https://contas.tcu.gov.br/pesquisaJurisprudencia/#/detalhamento/11/%252a/NUMACORDAO%253A732%2520ANOACORDAO%253A2015/DTRELEVANCIA%2520desc%252C%2520NUMACORDAOINT%2520desc/false/1*

TCU (2015c), FISC-Trabalho, *http://portal.tcu.gov.br/data/files/A2/77/25/4D/B4068510C57FF5851A2818A8/Fisc_Trabalho_web.pdf*

TCU (2015d), Audit of financial position of government, TCU Judgement 001.636/2015-4-Plenary, *https://contas.tcu.gov.br/pesquisaJurisprudencia/#/detalhamento/11/%252a/NUMACORDAO%253A001.636%2520ANOACORDAO%253A2015/DTRELEVANCIA%2520desc%252C%2520NUMACORDAOINT%2520desc/false/1*

TCU (2015e), Audit on the reliability of the budgetary forecasts and fiscal plans, TCU Judgement 927/2015- Plenary *https://contas.tcu.gov.br/pesquisaJurisprudencia/#/detalhamento/11/%252a/NUMACORDAO%253A927%2520ANOACORDAO%253A2015/DTRELEVANCIA%2520desc%252C%2520NUMACORDAOINT%2520desc/false/1*

TCU (2014a), Survey report to identify the criteria used to forecast macroeconomic indicators , TC 020.367/2014-7, *https://contas.tcu.gov.br/sagas/SvlVisualizarRelVotoAcRtf?codFiltro=SAGAS-SESSAO-ENCERRADA&seOcultaPagina=S&item0=529189*

TCU (2014b), TCU Judgement 1123/2014 – Plenary: Survey report, *http://www.tcu.gov.br/Consultas/Juris/Docs/judoc/RELAC/20140512/RL_0007_14_14_P_WDO.doc*

TCU (2014c), Plenary: Follow-up report. Revenue forecast evaluation of the federal budget bill 2015 (Judgement 3013/2014) (*http://www.tcu.gov.br/Consultas/Juris/Docs/judoc/Acord/20141107/AC_3013_44_14_P.doc*)

TCU (2013a), Audit on the National Policy for Regional Development in the Multi-Annual Plan (PPA) and the Annual Budgets (TC 002 976 / 2013-7) *http://www.tcu.gov.br/consultas/juris/docs/conses/tcu_ata_0_n_2013_38.pdf*;

TCU (2013b) Evaluation of the revenue forecast of the year 2013, TCU Judgement 223/2013 – Plenary: Survey report.. (*http://www.tcu.gov.br/Consultas/Juris/Docs/judoc/Acord/20130225/AC_0223_05_13_P.doc*)

TCU (2012a): Audit of the Accounts of the President of the Republic, (Contas do Presidente da República), 2012, *http://portal.tcu.gov.br/tcu/paginas/contas_governo/contas_2012/index.html*

TCU (2012b), Monitoring of Recommendations of the Preliminary Audit (TC 015 133/2011-7) *http://www.tcu.gov.br/Consultas/Juris/Docs/judoc/Acord/20120124/AC_0042_01_12_P.doc*

TCU (2012c), Performance Audit on the Indicators of the National Policy for Regional Development (TC 037 079 / 2012-3) *https://contas.tcu.gov.br/etcu/AcompanharProcesso?p1=37079&p2=2012&p3=3*

TCU (2011a): Audit of the Accounts of the President of the Republic, (Contas do Presidente da República), 2011, *http://portal.tcu.gov.br/tcu/paginas/contas_governo/contas_2011/index.html*

TCU (2011b), Performance Audit on the Logic Model and Goals of the National Policy for Regional Development (TC 033.934.2011-8); *http://www.tcu.gov.br/Consultas/Juris/Docs/judoc/Acord/20141211/AC_3564_49_14_P.doc*

TCU (2009a), Performance Audit on the system of planning and budget management (TC 014.899 / 2009-2), *http://www.tcu.gov.br/Consultas/Juris/Docs/judoc/Acord/20110204/AC_0117_02_11_P.doc*

Brazil's Federal Court of Accounts
Insight and Foresight for Better Governance

Chapter 4

Auditing for more robust internal control and risk management systems

This chapter explores select challenges the Brazilian government faces related to internal control and risk management, considering the role of numerous actors, and emphasising the contributions of Brazil's supreme audit institution, the Tribunal de Contas da União (TCU). This chapter offers recommendations for TCU to nuance its work in this more traditional area in a way that promotes risk management, control and integrity that is more targeted to the changing policy landscape. Recommendations are framed around international principles in (i) government-wide systems of internal control and risk management (ii) entity-level ownership and capacity for implementation of internal control and risk management and (iii) capacity for use of tools for implementation. The time is now for actors in Brazil to prioritise a more robust internal control and risk management system that supports the government in achieving objectives, while reducing risks of fraud, corruption, waste and abuse.

4.1. Introduction

A key function of good governance is an internal control system and risk management function that supports government in the achievement of its policy priorities and ministries in pursuit of related objectives. This includes policies and procedures, established by the Centre of Government (CoG) or relevant audit body, as well as mechanisms and tools for implementing internal control systems at the entity level. In addition, an internal control and risk management framework helps to reduce risks of fraud, corruption, waste and abuse, providing a reasonable level of assurance of an entity's efficiency, performance and compliance with laws, regulations and standards.

In Brazil, the internal control system and risk management function is continually evolving, yet the recent environment places greater urgency for continued and lasting change towards a greater culture of integrity in the Brazilian administration. One step on this path is the recent creation of new internal control and risk management standards, based on international good practices, including COSO's 2013 Internal Control-Integrated Framework. These standards, and policy formulation for the internal control system in general, is the remit of the Ministry of Planning, Development and Management (*Ministério do Planejamento, Desenvolvimento e Gestão*, MP) and Brazil's internal control body, the Ministry of Transparency, Supervision and Control (the Ministério da Transparência, Fiscalização e Controle, CGU), formerly the Comptroller General of the Union (CGU). Another evolutionary step is in the introduction of Monitoring and Evaluation Committee Of Federal Public Policies (*Comitê de Monitoramento e Avaliação de Políticas Públicas Federais*, or CMAP), which is donned the responsibility of improving policies and actions of the Federal Executive and improving the allocation of expenditure. As part of its evaluation of cross-cutting programmes of the federal government, the initiative is meant to include an analysis of risks to achievement of their objectives (MP, 2016a; 2016b; 2016c; 2016d). The initiative being new, there is little evidence yet on the effectiveness of this promising initiative.

The MP and CGU spearhead the policy making and guidance related to internal control and risk management activities in Brazil, among other activities. Brazil's supreme audit institution, the Tribunal de Contas da União (TCU), is another key contributor to this function in government. Through its audits, guidance and reviews of contracts, TCU contributes to the oversight for internal control system as well as the integrity of the system as a whole. From this perspective, TCU is a critical actor in the broader governance of Brazil. This aligns with OECD's Recommendation of the Council on Public Integrity, among others, which highlight the important role of SAIs in preserving and strengthening integrity systems. In addition, TCU plays a role in providing insight and foresight, anticipating the vulnerabilities, challenges and opportunities for the Brazilian government to address integrity risks and systemic vulnerabilities. In its compliance and judicial role, TCU has other activities that contribute to integrity and accountability, including the ability to issue sanctions and non-binding resolutions. This chapter focuses more on proactive, rather than reactive mechanisms for strengthening integrity through internal control and risk management.

As described in this chapter, TCU makes numerous contributions to more effective and efficient internal control systems and risk management in the Brazilian government. TCU's traditional role is in assessing compliance with financial law, as evident through the comprehensive audit of the year-end government report. However, strategic objective 7 of TCU's 2015-2021 Strategic Plan notes a core aim of TCU "to induce the improvement of risk-management and internal controls of public administration." TCU's external control strategy for 2015 to 2017 estimates a resource allocation of 12% to this objective, which gives it the third largest resource allocation of all external control objectives (TCU, 2015a). TCU has made the strategic and financial commitment to play a key role in strengthening integrity in the Brazilian government.

This chapter explores select challenges that the Brazilian government faces related to internal control and risk management, considering the role of numerous actors – particularly those in the Centre of Government (CoG). This chapter looks at what TCU is doing with a view towards opportunities for greater, more effective contributions to this governance function. In particular, this chapter proposes the following actions for TCU to consider in strengthening its role as an inducer of better internal control and risk management in government.

4.2. Overview: internal control and risk management at the federal level

The internal control system, its risk management functions and resulting internal controls activities are not ends themselves, but means to achieving objectives and better governance largely by detecting and hindering mismanagement and misuse. Thus, they are also means of achieving integrity in the public sector. Control activities should be balanced and risk-based to avoid being overly burdensome. Frameworks for internal control systems vary, with different institutional, policy and managerial arrangements. An array of standards and international good practices exist, such as those produced by the Committee of the Sponsoring Organisation of the Treadway Commission (COSO), the Institute of Internal Auditors (IIA) and others, to help guide entities in developing a robust internal control system and risk management function. In addition, countries have developed their own frameworks, based in part on these international good practices, such as the Standard Model of Internal Control (Modelo Estandar de Contro Interno, or MECI) of Colombia and Mexico.

An internal control and risk management system unfolds at two levels. The first is at the central level – whereby a central agency or agencies provides top down guidance and oversight of implementation of IC and RM mechanisms at the entity level. The second then, is the entity level. Effective risk management is critical because it drives the selection and adaptation of internal control activities, which could involve both the augmenting and reduction of controls, depending on the results of risk assessments. Risk assessments can inform managers about the perceived likelihood and impact of risks, allowing for prioritisation and effective resources allocation the highest risks. Among other activities, risk management involves the systematic implementation of policies, procedures and practices to identify, analyse, respond, and monitor risks.

Effective systems involve a number of external actors. For the 'supervision of accounting, finances, and budget,' Brazil's Constitution establishes a system of internal control to be maintained, in an integrated way, in the Legislature, Executive and Judiciary (Article 70; 74).[1] As such, the effectiveness of the internal control system relies on the contributions of an array of institutions, including the National Congress, the supreme audit institution (TCU), the Attorney General's Office, the Judiciary and the Office of the Prosecutor General within the Federal Public Ministry (Ministério Público Federal, or MPF). The Office of the Prosecutor

General is an autonomous agency responsible for holding parties accountable for acts of corruption and wrongdoing under the civil, administrative and criminal law code.

Ensuring accountability and integrity in government relies not only on effective top-down design, but also on implementation of internal control and risk management. While an internal control system is primarily the responsibility of managers within the entity, co-ordination and joint actions between the MPF, CGU and TCU, among other actors, are necessary for promoting greater integrity, accountability and transparency in the Brazilian government. This includes audits and evaluations to achieve the goals set out in Brazil's multi-year plans (Plano Plurianual de Acao, or PPAs). In addition, the CGU and TCU co-ordinate in their respective processes in order to render the opinion on the consolidated year-end government report, the Accounts of the President of the Republic (Contas do Presidente da República, or CPR), which is a core element of the federal government's financial reporting framework established by the 1988 Constitution of the Republic of Brazil and the 2000 Law on Fiscal Transparency (Complementary Law 101/2000). As OECD noted in 2013, the CPR does not include an assessment of the functioning of the Internal Control System of the Federal Public Administration. OECD recommended that the CPR include such an assessment to demonstrate progress in enhancing internal control systems and delivering on policies (OECD, 2013).

Developing robust internal control mechanisms can be seen as an iterative process aimed at strengthening integrity of the entity, as well as improving performance and governance. With the introduction of the 1988 Constitution and in line with reforms and public management trends in the 1990s, the system of internal control in Brazil evolved from a focus on compliance to assessments of management and operations.[2] In addition, in 2003, Brazil centralised the internal audit function, which was once dispersed in ministries, to a single body with ministerial status, the Comptroller General of the Union (CGU) (Olivieri et. al, 2015).[3] Figure 4.1 illustrates the arrangement of other countries with regards to the internal audit function.

Figure 4.1. **Centralised and decentralised internal audit functions in different countries**

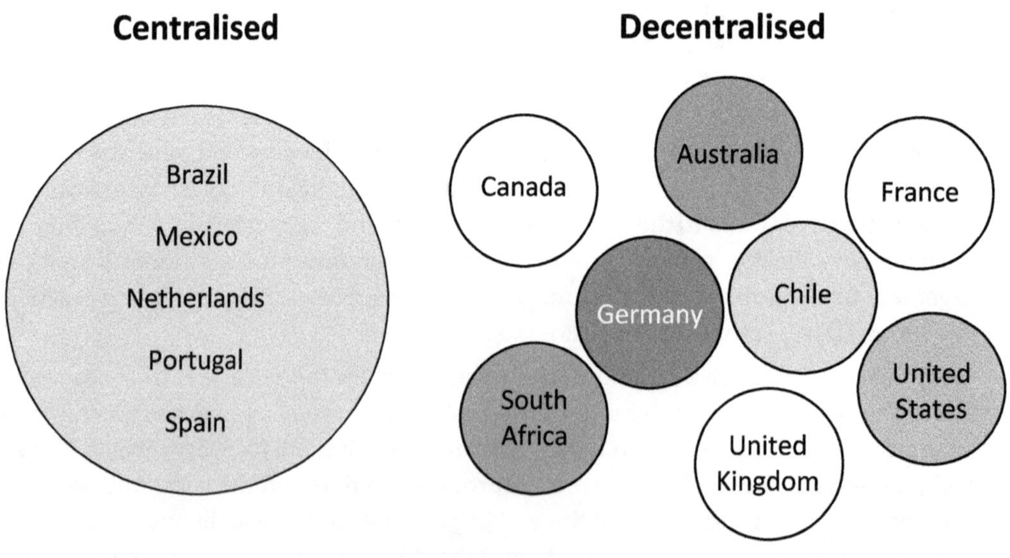

Source: OECD Secretariat

In May 2016, the CGU was renamed as the Ministry of Transparency, Supervision and Control, but it still maintains its core mandate, which is to support the President and the Executive Branch in matters related to internal control activities, anti-corruption and public audit, among others (Government of Brazil, 2016).[4] Within the CGU, there are entities for ensuring integrity and accountability in government, including the Commission of Co-ordination of Internal Control and the Secretariat of Transparency and the Prevention of Corruption. In addition, in 2000, the Internal Control Co-ordination Commission (CCCI) was established as a collegiate body with an advisory function in the Executive Branch for the internal control system. CCCI aims to conduct analyses and make proposals and suggestions for procedures for evaluation and improvement of internal control across the federal government. The internal control system has the following purposes:

- Evaluating the attainment of the goals established in the Multi-annual plan (*Plano Pluriannual*, PPA), the implementation of government programmes and of the budgets of the Union;
- Verifying the lawfulness and evaluating the results, as to effectiveness and efficiency, of the budgetary, financial and property management in the agencies and entities of the federal administration, as well as the use of public funds by private legal entities;
- Exercising control over credit transactions, collateral signatures and guarantees, as well as over the rights and assets of the Union;
- Supporting external control in the exercise of its institutional mission (Constitution 1988).

In May 2016, the MP and the CGU published new standards for internal control, risk management and governance (MP/CGU, 2016). The standards offer top-down guidance to help institutionalise and strengthen the internal control system in government. For instance, the standards emphasise that managers of each government entity should be responsible for the design, implementation, monitoring and improvement of the internal control system and risk management function (MP/CGU, 2016). This reflects a fundamental notion of management control, which places ownership of the internal control system inside an entity (i.e. the 1st line of assurance). In other words, in the public sector context, the primary "owners" of an internal control system and its related components are executive branch managers, as opposed to other actors, such as the internal audit bodies. Brazil's Constitution of 1967 recognised this, assigning responsibilities of the internal control system to the executive branch (Article 71). The CGU within the executive branch constitutes the 3rd line of assurance, responsible for assessing the effectiveness of other actors that have the primary responsibility of designing and implementing internal control and risk management activities.

Brazil's internal control standards also provide for the creation of Governance, Risk and Internal Committees within all ministries. Each committee should be composed of top managers and heads of units within ministries, with the support of CGU's Special Advisor for Internal Control. Per the standards, these committees are meant to play a lead role in various activities, such as: institutionalising the internal control system, ensuring compliance with laws and regulations, setting policies, supervising risk assessment activities and making recommendations to improve internal control and risk management. In Brazil, the development of such institutional mechanisms illustrates a positive step forward in the country's efforts to develop a capacity and structure to further institutionalise internal control and risk management in the public sector.

SAIs have a unique role for establishing and maintaining effective internal control mechanisms. As noted above, the three lines of defence in the public sector context include entities within the executive branch. A fourth line of defence is the external auditor, i.e., TCU in the Brazilian context. Traditionally, SAIs' compliance and financial audits have aimed primarily at assessing financial expenditure and financial conduct in accordance with controls. SAIs' audit scopes cover how controls are set in an attempt to ensure that controls facilitate the achievement of the policy goals they are aiming to protect (OECD, 2016a). In looking at the efficiency and effectiveness of internal controls and risk management, SAIs have been able to gather insight into what does and does not work. SAIs are also actively assessing processes for the development of guidance around internal control and risk management; some SAIs are even responsible for developing guidance themselves. In OECD's (2016a) "SAIs and good governance: Oversight, Insight and Foresight", six out of ten peer SAIs provide written guidance on establishing rules and controls, and five out of ten undertake research in this area.

TCU supports internal control and risk management in 3 main ways. First, TCU conducts performance audits and evaluations aimed at improving internal control systems and risk management in government. Second, on the basis of its compliance and financial audits, TCU can issue sanctions and binding resolutions in response to non-compliance with law. Third, TCU provides advisory services to external stakeholders, such as representatives of the executive branch and the Congress. TCU officials pointed out that recently TCU has provided inputs to Congress on 3 bills related to the topic. In addition, in 2017, TCU established an internal Department of Institutional Relations on Fight Against Fraud and Corruption, charged with collaborating with other entities (e.g. the Federal Police and prosecutors) to improve information sharing, strengthen audits and conducting relevant trainings. As discussed in the next section, TCU has also developed guidance for the executive branch to help improve fraud risk management, among other issues. Through these activities, TCU contributes to the effectiveness of the internal control system and strengthens the integrity of government.

TCU's external control activities in this area have focused both on issues within an entity or sector, as well as broader, systemic internal control and risk management issues. For example, in 2012, TCU evaluated the maturity level of risk management across sixty six entities of the indirect administration, including the MP. The audit focused on municipalities, foundations, public enterprises and joint stock companies, assessing risk management environments, processes, partnerships and results (TCU, 2012). Subsequent sections further explore TCU's contributions to this governance function.

TCU faces heightened expectations to contribute to the reduction of corruption in the country, as evidenced by a recent survey commissioned by Brazil's National Industry Confederation that showed 90 % of respondents thought TCU is an important actor for fighting corruption. This role is aligned with TCU's mandate. TCU can meet these expectations not only by maintaining the effectiveness of its compliance audits and judicial function, but also by undertaking new approaches that take into account systemic issues at the central level, implementation at the entity level, and tools for tackling on the ground.

TCU can build on this work to strengthen its contributions to this function of government, as discussed in the sections below. Amidst low government trust and corruption-related scandals, TCU is in a position to rise above the short-term politics of the moment in support of a long-term vision for improving this governance function. However, the expectation is not that TCU exercise functions that are already being serviced by, or should be serviced by, another expert body or institution. SAIs should not compensate for a lack of maturity in internal control. An SAI's role should be to support, not displace, other public entities.

The OECD makes recommendations to below (Table 4.1) to support TCU in this endeavour of driving improvements in public administration through improved monitoring and evaluation. The following recommendations aim to support TCU in the fulfilment of its mandate and, particularly the achievement of strategic objective 7 of TCU's 2015-2021 Strategic Plan: "to induce the improvement of risk-management and internal controls of public administration" (TCU, 2015a). The external control strategy (2015-2017) estimates a resource allocation of 12% to this objective, which gives it the third largest resource allocation of all external control objectives (TCU, 2015b).

Table 4.1. **Recommendations: Auditing for more robust risk management and internal control at the federal level**

TCU could strengthen the effectiveness and consistency of internal control and risk management approaches across government by identifying and communicating systemic and high-risk areas for central entities to address, including the Ministry of Planning, Development and Management and Comptroller General of the Union.
TCU could induce managers to overcome implementation challenges and further institutionalise key risk management and control activities.
• TCU could take steps, such as applying change management paradigms, to further institutionalise management ownership over internal control systems and risk management.
• TCU could enhance guidance and audits about how to improve the culture of integrity across government, in co-ordination with the key actors.
TCU could help strengthen the capacity of government to prevent fraud and corruption through audits and additional guidance that ensure the effectiveness policies and use of tools, such as data analytics.

4.3. Identifying systemic, high-risk areas for better internal control systems and risk management at the whole-of-government level

TCU could strengthen the effectiveness and consistency of internal control and risk management approaches across government by identifying and communicating systemic and high-risk areas for central entities to address, including the Ministry of Planning, Development and Management and Comptroller General of the Union.

A key element of good governance is an internal control and risk management system that supports the entire government in the achievement of its policy priorities and ministries in pursuit of related objectives. Moreover, the rise in cross-cutting initiatives in OECD member governments necessitates a broader, more holistic view, of the risks that are presented and how they can be controlled. This context highlights the critical role that the Centre of Government (CoG) can play in guiding the effective design and implementation of the internal control system. In a study of OECD member countries, 52% of CoGs share the responsibility for risk management and strategic foresight with another body, while 18% have the primary responsibility (OECD, 2014a). The contributions of central institutions to a more robust internal control system and risk management function include the following:

- The CoG can a responsibility to manage risks to the overall government strategy at the highest level. This means having processes to identify and manage the most pressing risks to the achievement of policy objectives and government priorities.
- The CoG provides policies and procedures in support of more consistent and effective design, implementation, monitoring and improvement by managers at the entity level.
- The CoG can play a role in oversight of management ownership and execution.

In order to ensure that central entities can adequately fulfil their role, they must have the policies, procedures and capacity to take a horizontal view across government. It is here that SAIs can play a key role. The comparative advantage of an SAI, in relation to other actors in an accountability system, is its ability to take a government-wide view of key governance functions in order to identify systemic issues affecting multiple agencies. SAIs are incorporating into their strategic plans and audit programming such systemic reviews, which provide a perspective on the overall quality of internal control and risk management in government. This can include a focus not only implementation of these functions in government, but also the formulation of policies, procedures and guidance. This cross-cutting work can complement audit and oversight activities that are more reactive and focus on short-term risks. Box 4.1 below provides an example of government-wide reviews conducted by various SAIs.

Box 4.1. **Supreme audit institution and government-wide studies for improved integrity, internal control and risk management**

Institutional mechanisms, policy interactions, contextual factors and effects are all examples of elements that contribute to policy coherence (OECD, 2016b). SAIs are in a unique position to look across government agencies to assess an issue and the extent to which governments are achieving policy and operational coherence. For instance, they offer perspectives of oversight, insight and foresight to reviews of policies and programme planning, such as the integration of government-wide objectives into current strategies and planning and the preparedness of government to tackle future goals.

Mexico's ASF:

Every year since 2012, ASF has conducted at least one government-wide integrity review that touches on elements of coherence, looking specifically at the strategies and mechanisms of federal public institutions to strengthen integrity and prevent corruption. These studies focus on what government is doing in these areas, particularly activities related to internal control systems and risk-management functions. Examples of these studies include the following:

- *Study about the Strategies for Combating Corruption in the Public Sector* – ASF conducted this study to understand the actions federal public sector institutions had been making to tackle corruption, based on the applicable standards and international best practices, in order to identify areas of opportunity and promote the implementation of an integrity programme (ASF, 2014).
- *Technical Study for the Promotion of a Culture of Integrity in the Public Sector* - ASF analysed and described the best international practices in integrity, as well as implementation of anti-corruption controls, to help government institutions formulate an integrity programme for strengthening the culture of transparency, probity and accountability (ASF, 2015).

Canadian Office of the Auditor General (OAG): assessment of entities risk management frameworks

In Canada the Auditor General has been assessing entities controls for integrated risk management. In responses to audits 2003 and 2006 the OAG found government entities did not have adequate integrated risk management frameworks. In 2009 then, the OAG performed an audit on the Treasury Board of Canada Secretariat, Office of the Comptroller General and seven large federal departments to assess the progress of the recommendations and commitments from the previous audits. Importantly, this audit did not assess appropriateness or completeness of internal controls or the risks identified in their Corporate Risk Profiles, but rather focused on whether the departments were assessing their internal controls and practices and their approach to risk management.

In regard to developing policies, frameworks and relevant guidance on internal controls, and implementing risk management measures, departments made satisfactory progress. Each of the selected departments has developed a corporate risk profile that summarises the assessment of the department's key risks with processes to update the profiles regularly. The departments have also incorporated that risk profile into business planning, priority setting, and decision making and reporting. They still have not, however, assessed their internal control systems in order to address weaknesses. Further, the Comptroller General has yet to establish processes for monitoring the completion of these assessments or assessing actions taken by departments to address internal control issues.

Box 4.1. **Supreme audit institution and government-wide studies for improved integrity, internal control and risk management** *(cont.)*

The Netherlands Court of Audit: assessing financial risk exposure of government

The Netherlands Court of Audit assessed the risk of financial ties between the government and eight international financial institutions following the financial crisis in 2008. In order to do this, the Court prepared eight factsheets that show the ties between the government and these eight institutions, highlighting their financial profiles and the measures the Dutch government has taken to mitigate risks. This allowed for exposure of public finances to be easily mapped out, and provided the Parliament with better insights into which risks are shared, how institutions mitigate risks, the institutions' precautionary balances and the risk to the Netherlands.

Portuguese Tribunal de Contas: Audit of internal audit in state owned enterprises.

The Portuguese Tribunal de Contas in order to strengthen overall governance of selected entities, assessed the internal audit function of state owned enterprises. Through a performance audit of 20 state owned enterprises, the Court evaluated internal audit function in each of the public enterprises and compared it to international best practices. The audit also assessed the influence of governance models on the effectiveness of the internal audit function. On the 20 entities that responded to the survey, 16 had an internal audit unit, however only 5 of those 16 were familiar with the full breadth of internal audit concepts. Additionally, half of the respondents of the survey had internal audit units that reported to the board, however, many of the boards did not have non executives on them which largely compromise the independence of the audits.

Hungarian State Audit Office: Cross-government integrity surveys

Since 2011, the State Audit Office of Hungary has been carrying out a series of integrity surveys of public sector institutions, ranging from national to regional and local levels, and covering a wide range of public sector branches. These integrity surveys are based on integrity questionnaires, which were inspired by the Dutch methodology of integrity assessment used in many countries. The integrity surveys consider three main components of integrity:

- Inherent risks which emanate from the legal standing and permanent tasks of the organisation, such as providing public services
- Risk-increasing factors which result from everyday organisational functioning and structure, such as recruitment practices
- Level of controls which encompass the system of control mechanisms, such as based on a code of conduct. The survey focuses on organisational experience, events and actions taken, not on perceptions or attitudes.

The annual survey has already been implemented six times. Analyses on the results of the surveys available on the website of SAO, have been essential in informing the work on integrity in the Hungarian public sectors. The approach and terminology regarding integrity has been widely acknowledged by all levels of public management and by the broader public. SAO complements this survey with annual international seminars that are dedicated to strengthening public sector integrity.

Source: OECD (2016a), *Supreme Audit Institutions and Good Governance: Oversight, Insight and Foresight*, OECD Public Governance Reviews, OECD Publishing, Paris. *http://dx.doi.org/10.1787/9789264263871-en*; OECD (2017a), *Mexico's National Auditing System: Strengthening Accountable Governance*, OECD Public Governance Reviews, OECD Publishing, Paris. *http://dx.doi.org/10.1787/9789264264748-en*; ASF (Office of the Auditor General of México, or Auditoría Superior de la Federación) (2015), "Technical Study for the Promotion of a Culture of Integrity in the Public Sector", *https://www.asf.gob.mx/uploads/180_Estudios/1173_Estudio_Tec_para_la_Promocion_de_la_Cultura_de_Integridad_en_el_Sec_Pub.pdf*; ASF (2014), "Study about the Strategies for Combating Corruption in the Public Sector", *https://www.asf.gob.mx/Trans/Informes/IR2014i/Documentos/Auditorias/2014_1642_a.pdf*; OAG (Office of the Auditor General of Canada), Chapter 1, Financial Management and Control and Risk Management, *http://www.oag-bvg.gc.ca/internet/English/parl_oag_201106_01_e_35369.html*; NCA (Netherlands Court of Audit) (2011), financial risks to the Netherlands, *www.courtofaudit.nl/english/Publications/Audits/Introductions/2013/09/Financial_risks_to_the Netherlands_of_international_guarantees*; NCA (2011), Risks to Public Finances, *http://www.courtofaudit.nl/english/Publications/Audits/Introductions/2012/06/Risks_to_public_finances*; *http://www.courtofaudit.nl/english/Publications/Audits/Introductions/2011/05/Spending_Cuts_Monitor_2011*. TdC (Tribunal de Contas de Portugal) (2011), The internal audit function in the State Owned Enterprises, *www.tcontas.pt/en/reports/audit_report_08-2011-2s_abstract.pdf*.

In the last few years, TCU has conducted research and evaluations that provide a systemic view of issues related to internal control and risk management, including the following examples:

- **Framework to Assess Governance in Public Policies**: After reviewing and building upon various national and international models of governance in public policies, TCU developed a model for governance evaluation in public policies comprised of eight components. One of them is comprised by a gathering of good practices concerning risk management and internal controls. (TCU, 2014b).
- **Sector-level review of risk management maturity in government:** In 2013, TCU conducted a survey of risk management activities at the sector level. In this evaluation, TCU assessed the maturity of risk management in various sectors of the federal government with the help of its indicator based on COSO's Enterprise Risk Management Framework, ISO 31000 on Risk Management and governmental models of risk management in Canada and the United Kingdom. The participating institutions were then classified into five categories of maturity. At the time, 67% of organisations were in the bottom two classifications. The risk management maturity levels were higher in oil (61%) and financial sectors (65%) than transportation (28%) and regulatory sectors (31%) (TCU, 2013a).
- **Survey on the governance system focused on implementation of public policies**: Evaluation of the co-ordination efforts and the Brazilian internal control system compared with main international standards (TCU, 2013b).
- **General Criteria for Internal Control in Public Administration:** A study of the models and the disciplinary regulations in different countries. The study explores the role models for internal risk management and controls and how the surveyed countries have addressed the issue in their legal systems. The goal is to support the discussion, in the Federal Senate, of a bill to define general criteria of internal controls, risk management and governance in the Brazilian government (TCU, 2009b).

Building on this body of work, TCU could help to strengthen the effectiveness and consistency of internal control and risk management approaches across government by emphasising, in its audits and evaluations, areas for the central entities to act. Specifically, TCU could help to ensure an effective internal control system and risk management function across government by identifying and communicating systemic issues and high-risk areas.

The design and implementation of an effective internal control system and risk management function is first and foremost the responsibility of the Executive Branch, as reflected in international standards and indicated in Brazil's Joint Normative Instructions (MP/CGU, 2016). Nonetheless, TCU can play a critical role in ensuring that systemic and high-risk areas in government are addressed by identifying and communicating issues for the central entities (e.g. the MP and CGU) to address. As discussed in chapter 2, systemic issues often highlight the need for better coherence and co-ordination between government entities that have shared activities or a collective impact on national policy goals. Systemic issues include vulnerabilities and areas for improvement that are cross-cutting and can affect multiple public entities or programs.

The perspective of "systemic errors" by the European Court of Auditors (ECA), in its review of the management and control systems of member states of the European Union, is instructive. According to the ECA, an error is considered as systemic when there is a high probability that the same problem may affect other projects in a similar manner." The ECA further notes that it is necessary to identify the extent of this systemic error (ECA 2012).

For instance, multiple public entities may uniformly be interpreting and applying procurement rules incorrectly, leading to reduced effectiveness and efficiency, as well as increased risks of fraud, waste and abuse.

As indicated in the ECA's definition, analysing systemic issues is not just about identifying problems, but also understanding the extent of them. TCU's own work offers an example of evaluations that focus on systemic issues, whether that was explicitly the purpose. For example, in addition to those noted above, in 2014, TCU conducted a survey of 7,700 public entities to evaluate their governance practices, including those related to risk management. TCU assessed the maturity of risk management based on a set of criteria. Among the 380 federal public entities surveyed, 80% of organisations were in the early stage of risk management, 13% the intermediate stage and only 7% have the ability to structure improved risk management. Based on the survey, TCU concluded that there are inefficiencies in risk management in public sector entities (TCU, 2014a). Such surveys not only illustrate potentially systemic issues across different government entities, but also suggest high-risk areas and institutions that could help the CoG to direct resources efficiently and effectively.

Few entities in government have the remit, resources and expertise to conduct such evaluations. TCU could further leverage this comparative advantage by systematising its evaluations of systemic issues and high-risk areas, and linking its findings to areas where the CoG can act to improve policies upstream. As the CoG works to institutionalise its Normative Instructions, and TCU advances its framework for managing fraud risks, such evaluations could be beneficial for refining policies and enhancing the co-ordination and consistency of how the standards and leading practices are applied across government. The comparative evidence from evaluations and surveys can be a beneficial input for the CoG, as well as TCU itself, to promote a common interpretation of standards and frameworks for internal control and risk management. The evidence can also inform TCU's recommendations directed at the CoG itself for amending policies, rules or guidelines to improve government-wide performance.

In addition to government-wide evaluations and surveys, TCU can incorporate systemic perspectives into the design of its audits. This can involve scoping the audit to include multiple entities within a specific part of the audit universe, sector or type of institution, incorporating research objectives that focus explicitly on the systemic aspects of a particular issue. For instance, in 2014, the Ministry of Veteran Affairs of Canada conducted an audit of four programs to provide assurance that processing of overpayments was done in compliance with laws, policies and regulations. The audit design included specific research objectives to identify systemic issues among the programs that caused overpayments. The audit revealed, among other things, that oversight, monitoring, and reporting of overpayments could be strengthened to determine and address systemic issues (Veteran Affairs Canada, 2014). In the last few years, TCU has conducted several audits that were systemic in design and scope, including the following:

- **Evaluation of internal controls of Roraima's municipalities**: Members of the Public Management Control Framework, including TCU, CGU and the State Court of Accounts of Roraima, reviewed the entities and activities of municipalities of the State of Roraima to identify systemic issues and assess the maturity of the internal control systems in the State's municipalities (TCU, 2014c).
- **Audit of internal controls of university hospitals procurement**: Evaluation of internal control of bidding and contract area of university hospitals. The audit addressed key aspects of the internal environment, with emphasis on the internal audit and control activities applied on a sample of processes (TCU, 2013c).

- **Performance audit of internal control units of Executive, Legislature and Judicial Branches:** The audit found need for improvements in the institutional structures for performance and development of staff. (TCU, 2009a).

To the extent TCU emphasises systemic issues within its audits, whether at an institutional or sector level, it could further develop approaches to aggregate the findings from those audits to paint a bigger picture of cross-government issues. Doing so could help TCU to identify the extent of systemic challenges, but also the viability and scalability of potential solutions. In this role, TCU can act as an interlocutor between government entities for innovation and change, facilitating dialogue on how multiple institutions can better address shared issues. For instance, identification of systemic issues with the bidding and contracts related to hospitals could be analysed against similar issues in other sectors and among different institutions, since procurement policies, rules and practices are often shared. TCU is in a unique position to identify the linkages between different parts of Brazil's governance structure, and communicate solutions formally through its recommendations and informally through dialogue, forums and trainings.

To complement a view towards systemic issues, TCU could consider a more systematic approach to identifying, analysing and communicating the highest risks in government, particularly with regards to strengthening integrity through risk management and internal controls. Findings and recommendations that focus on the highest risks could highlight for the CoG possible improvements to policies, guidance and inter-entity co-ordination. In addition, identifying sectors, programs or institutions that are high risk can help to focus resources on key challenges, and motivate managers responsible for those programs to act. In the context of internal control and risk management, high risk areas can include those that are most vulnerable to fraud, corruption, waste and abuse. TCU's existing evaluations, surveys and audits, such as those described above, can help to identify the highest risks.

SAIs can take different approaches for determining high risks. For instance, beginning in 1990, the U.S. Government Accountability Office (GAO) has analysed and reported on the progress of government entities in addressing high-risk areas, focusing on areas that are vulnerable to fraud, waste, abuse and mismanagement, or those that are in need of transformation (GAO 2017). The criteria GAO uses for assessing whether a program is a high risk include leadership commitment, capacity, action plan, monitoring and demonstrated progress (GAO 2017). GAO based its methodology for its High Risk List on its publication, *Determining Performance and Accountability Challenges and High Risks*, which guides auditors in making assessments about the challenges government faces. In it, the guide highlights the following criteria for determining government-wide high risks, noting that any material weakness must:

- "Be evident at multiple agencies
- Affect a significant portion of the government's total budget or other resources
- Stem from a deficiency that should be monitored and addressed through individual agency actions as well as through Office of Management and Budget [i.e. Centre of Government] initiatives, legislative action, and/or congressional oversight (GAO 2000)."

GAO developed a body of work for analysing and reporting on high-risks; however, many SAIs conduct similar processes as part of their risk-based audit programming, as described in chapter 1. GAO's process draws from existing audits, applying its high-risk criteria to recent findings. The example demonstrates an opportunity for SAIs to use their own work, information and data to provide a broader view of the functioning of government. Aligning with objective 7 of its strategic plan, TCU could also enhance analysis of its own work to identify potential vulnerabilities in the internal control system, and areas where the CoG can act. For instance, TCU conducts audits and investigations that highlight individual instances of potential fraud, corruption, waste or abuse. These cases can serve as a rich dataset for analysing risks in government and potential systemic weaknesses in the control environment. TCU could also collect data and information from the CGU, and use these cases as inputs to inform its own audit programming and planning to ensure its audits focus on the highest risks. They could also act as inputs for performance audits that are taking a broader look at internal control and risk management in government. Such approaches could help TCU to connect its reactive work to its more proactive portfolio, which is more preventive in the context of internal control and risk management.

4.4. Advancing risk management and internal control at the entity level by overcoming implementation challenges

TCU could induce managers to overcome implementation challenges and further institutionalise key risk management and control activities.

In 2014, TCU conducted a survey in co-ordination with the Rui Barbosa Institute, the Association of Members of the Brazilian Courts of Accounts (Atricon), and 28 subnational audit entities, that highlighted the systemic need for improved risk management and control in government. Specifically, TCU surveyed public entities to evaluate their governance practises, including those related to risk management. TCU assessed the maturity of risk management based on a set of criteria, and identified immaturity and inefficiencies in risk management in public sector entities. The figure 4.2 below depicts the results of the survey of federal organisations. It indicates that among the 380 federal public entities surveyed, 80% of organisations (column C11) were in what TCU defined as the early stage of risk management (i.e. inexistent, insufficient or initial), and 13% were in the intermediate stage (TCU, 2014a). The remaining 7% of organisations showed more advanced (or "improved") risk management.

The reasons for the low levels of capacity of risk management vary, but such surveys point to challenges related to implementation rather than design. In Brazil, the framework for the internal control system is generally aligned with COSO's Internal Control-Integrated Framework, as described in greater detail below. This framework embodies the internal control system within the governance architecture, which also includes the risk management function and internal control activities (see Figure 4.3).

Policy making and guidance related to internal control and risk management activities in Brazil is spearheaded by the Ministry of Planning, Development and Management (Ministério do Planejamento, Desenvolvimento e Gestão, MP), considered part of the CoG, and Brazil's internal control body, the Ministry of Transparency, Supervision and Control (Ministério da Transparência, Fiscalização e Controle, CGU). In May 2016, the MP and the CGU published a new framework and standards for internal control, risk management and governance (MP/CGU, 2016).

Brazil's new standards for internal control, risk management and governance (MP/CGU, 2016) assign responsibilities for these areas to managers' in the executive branch, underscoring the importance of management ownership. The framework is structured, and includes internal control components according to relevant international standards, such as the 2013 COSO Internal Control-Integrated Framework, the Enterprise Risk Management-Integrity Framework and standards of the International Organisation of Supreme Audit Institutions. The framework recognises a key relationship between organisational objectives, internal control components and the Three Lines of Defence Model, as depicted in figure 4.4 In addition, the standards call for executive branch managers to actively manage and assess various risks.

Figure 4.2. **TCU government-wide survey on risk management in public sector entities**

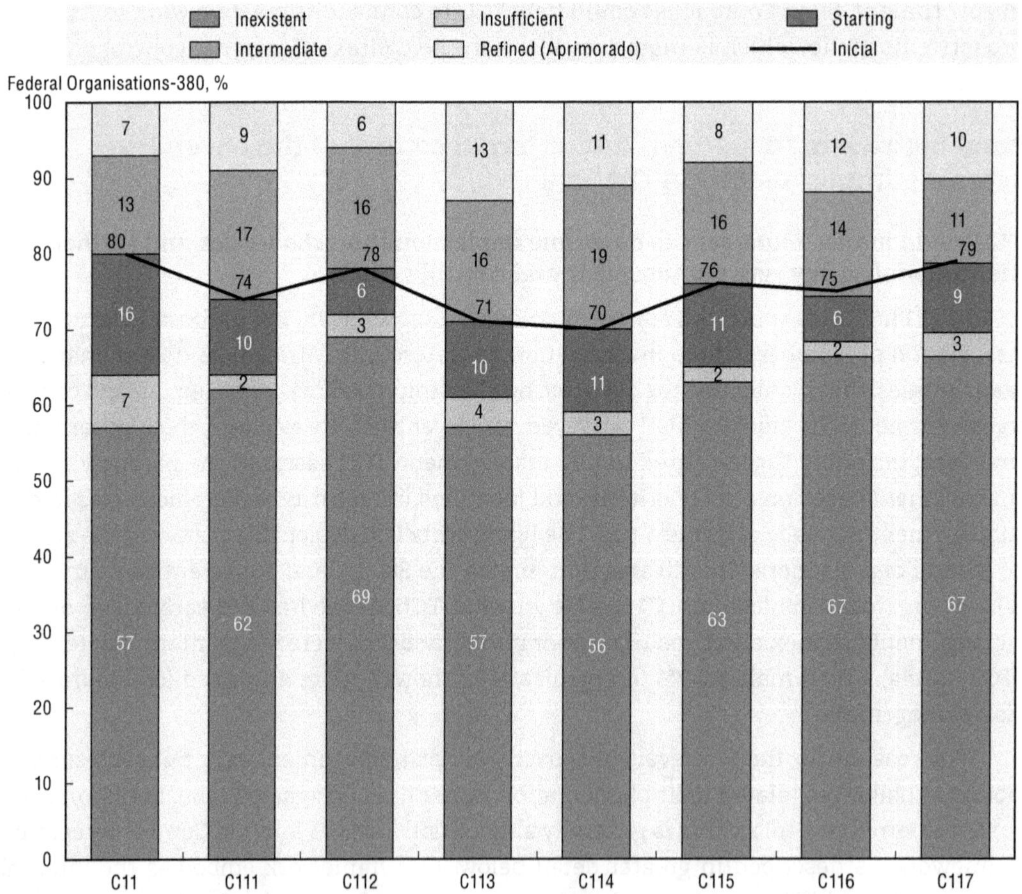

Legend:

C111: Risk guidelines for management and establishment of internal controls are set, and include the development of tolerance to risk, roles and responsibilities, classification criteria risks

C112: The management process of risk is implemented and includes the following components: control environment; fixation objectives; evaluation of risks; control activities; information and communication; monitoring activities

C113: Risk criteria of the organisation is identified

C114: Internal controls to mitigate the identified critical risks are deployed

C115: Continuity plan related to critical elements of the area of expertise is deployed

C116: The responsibility for co-ordinating the management structure of the risk attributed to the organisation

C117: The internal governance uses the information resulting from the management of risk to support their decision-making processes

Source: TCU (2014a), Survey of Risk Management in Public Governance, Gestão De Riscos Levantamento De Governança Pública, *http://portal.tcu.gov.br/lumis/portal/file/fileDownload.jsp?fileId=8A8182A24E08D405014E0D42E95B3708*

Figure 4.3. **Entity-level internal control systems and relationship to other components**

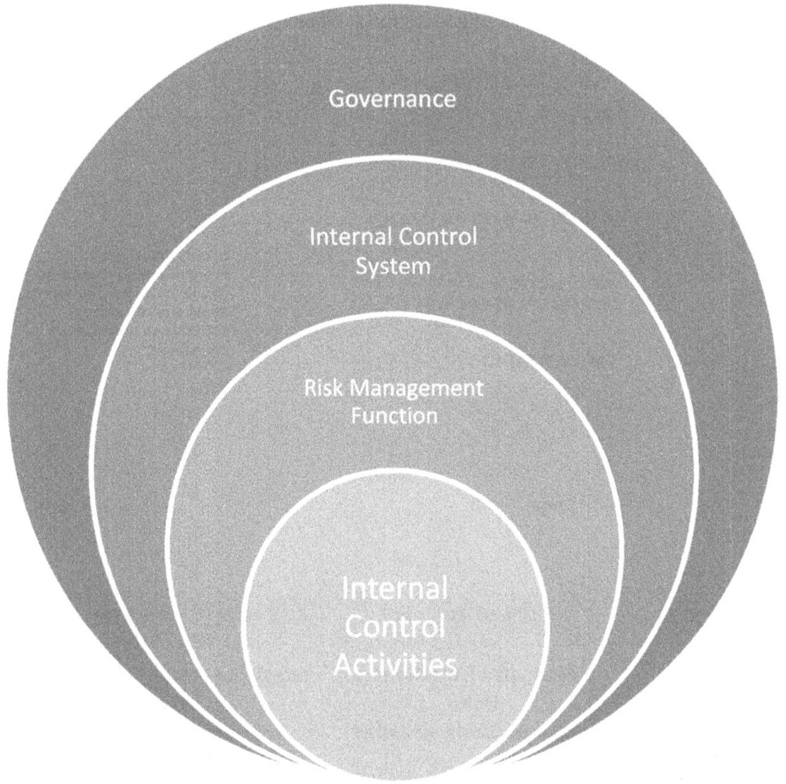

Source: Adapted from COSO Internal Control-Integrated Framework (2013).

As discussed further in the recommendations below, the perspective of managers with regards to internal control and risk management, characterised by an externalisation of the function to other entities, indicates that a culture of integrity is lacking in many entities of the Brazilian government. As a result, such a culture can limit the extent to which controls can be an integrated and aligned with the entities' strategy (OECD, 2013). To aid managers in overcoming the implementation challenge related to new internal controls standards, TCU and can build on existing audit work and other activities to focus on skill development, awareness raising and cultivating a culture of integrity. TCU already has developed a number of products to aid the government in strengthening risk management at the entity level (Box 4.2). This work is in line with objective 7 of TCU's strategic plan, and includes a Maturity Assessment in Risk Management in Public Administration, the General Criteria for Internal Control in Public Administration and the Basic Governance Reference Guide. TCU also is developing a Fraud Risk Management Framework to aid managers in implementing new standards for assessing fraud risks. TCU could complement this guide and other efforts by further developing its support for implementing good risk management practices. In particular, TCU could further strengthen its efforts to guide managers in overcoming implementation challenges for further institutionalising key risk management and control activities to address high-risks by:

- TCU could take steps, such as applying change management paradigms, to further institutionalise management ownership over internal control systems and risk management; and
- Aligning and disseminating guidance with high-risk areas, in co-ordination with the key actors and building on existing efforts to improve fraud risk management in government.

Figure 4.4. **Relationship between an organisation's objectives, the internal control components and the three Lines of Assurance Model**

Core Organisational Objectives

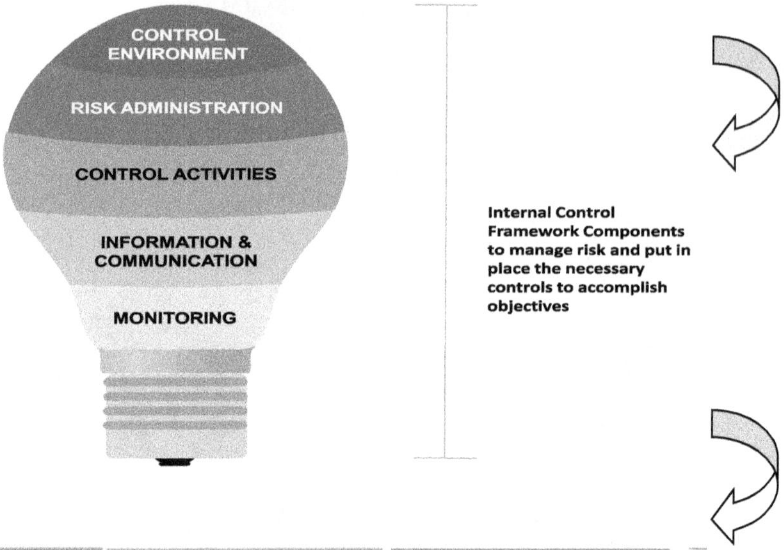

1st Line of Assurance	2nd Line of Assurance	3rd Line of Assurance
Operational level- Own and manage the risks • Good policy and performance data • Monitoring statistics • Risk registers	**Independent from delivery Units** • Compliance assessments or reviews • Program and project management • Direct reporting line to senior management and the Minister	**Independent internal audit function** • Assess and provide assurance over the effectiveness of the 1st and the 2nd lines arrangements • Risk based approach on addressing gaps or inefficiencies in the assurance system

The Three Lines of Assurance model

Source: Adapted by the OECD Secretariat with inputs from the Committee of Sponsoring Organisations of the Treadway Commission (COSO); COSO (2013), An Update of COSO's Internal Control – Integrated Framework, Committee of Sponsoring Organisations of the Treadway Commission, *www.coso.org/documents/cosoicifoutreachdeck_05%2018%20 12.pdf*; IIA (2013), IIA Position Paper – Three Lines of Defense in Effective Risk Management and Control, The Institute of Internal Auditors, Altamonte Springs, *www.theiia.org/goto/3Lines*; IIA (2015): Three Lines of Defence Model, Assurance Maps presentation-PIC EU-28 Conference 2015, *http://slideplayer.com/slide/10129777/*.

Box 4.2. **TCU activities in support implementation of risk management and internal control at the entity level**

Evaluation of units of internal control and internal audit: Assessed the internal audit units, internal control unit and internal control consultants of entities in the federal public administration. Recommended strengthening management and rationalization of control actions (TCU, 2014d).

Performance audit on risk maturity of Central Bank: Assessed risk management, activity in implementation, reaching units, activities and processes of Brazil's central bank. Also evaluated adherence to the guidelines of best practice guides (TCU, 2015e).

Evaluation of risk management maturity of Electrosul: Entity maturity considered intermediate in risk management, both in relation to the environment and the processes (TCU, 2015f).

Box 4.2. **TCU activities in support implementation of risk management and internal control at the entity level** *(cont.)*

Audit of risk management of Secretariat of Ports: TCU verified the risk management of Ports Secretariat on National Dredging Program. There was an institutionalised absence of procedures for identifying and assessing risks. (TCU, 2014e).

Source: Adapted from OECD (2016a), *Supreme Audit Institutions and Good Governance: Oversight, Insight and Foresight*, OECD Public Governance Reviews, OECD Publishing, Paris. *http://dx.doi.org/10.1787/9789264263871-en*; TCU (2014d), Evaluation of units of internal control and internal audit, (Acordao TCU 821/2014) *http://www.lexml.gov.br/urn/urn:lex:br:tribunal.contas.uniao;plenario:acordao:2014-04-02;821*; TCU (2015e), TCU Judgement 0548/2015, Acordo TC-020.137/2014-1 – Plenary, Performance Audit *http://www.tcu.gov.br/Consultas/Juris/Docs/judoc/Acord/20150320/AC_0548_09_15_P.doc* ; TCU (2015f), Evaluation of risk management maturity of Electrosul , TCU 605/2015, Acordo TC-019.140/2014-2, *http://www.tcu.gov.br/Consultas/Juris/Docs/judoc/Acord/20150330/AC_0605_10_15_P.doc*; TCU (2014e), Audit of risk management of Secretariat of Ports, Judgement 735/2014 – Plenary, Acordo TC 009.504/2013-3, Performance audit, *http://www.tcu.gov.br/Consultas/Juris/Docs/judoc/Acord/20140402/AC_0735_09_14_P.doc*

TCU could take steps, such as applying change management paradigms, to further institutionalise management ownership over internal control systems and risk management.

In Brazil, internal control is often seen as the remit of internal audit, not managers within the executive branch. TCU officials noted that managers do not see internal control and risk management as one of their core responsibilities, and TCU's surveys, discussed above, provide further evidence of this mentality, reflecting a low level of awareness or misunderstanding about this governance function. In addition, documents of Brazil's internal audit body itself, the CGU, illustrate the need for improving the culture of integrity through a greater emphasis on communicating the importance of management ownership over the internal control system. For instance, CGU's "Operational Plan of Decentralised Actions: Transparency and Prevention of Corruption," describes the role of the Secretariat of Transparency and Corruption Prevention (STCP) as the body responsible for the prevention of corruption in the Federal Public Administration (CGU, 2015). While the STCP plays an important role, such statements draw an incomplete picture. Managers within the executive branch are also responsible for preventing fraud and corruption, per international standards and Brazil's Normative Instructions. Failure to address this issue poses a threat to the implementation of these new standards.

An OECD review of the contributions of SAIs to strengthening internal control systems showed that the majority of SAIs that are effectively contributing to this area focus on the entity level. In a survey of ten SAIs, nine had assessed processes for the development of internal control guidelines, including the incorporation of risk management, the openness and consultation of the process and the alignment with international principles. Only half (five of ten) had reviewed leadership in establishing a culture conducive to risk-management and control. There is an opportunity for TCU to focus further on the latter, given its importance for change within an institution and system more broadly (OECD, 2016a).

TCU has already taken a number of actions to contribute to stronger internal control and risk management in the executive branch by improving skills and raising awareness. One recent effort is TCU's creation of a guide to help managers to evaluate fraud and corruption risks. TCU can build on this initiative by engaging CGU, the MP and other executive branch entities in implementing the practices and tools it promotes in both the guidance and its audits. Doing so would help to institutionalise Brazil's Normative Instructions, and advance international standards. For instance, ISO 31000 notes that the introduction of risk management and ensuring its continued effectiveness relies on strong and sustained commitment by managers, as well as rigorous and strategic planning to build commitment at all levels of an entity (ISO 2009).

Having standards and guides, Brazil now faces the challenge of further institutionalising internal control and risk management through greater management ownership. Applying change management principles and practices can help TCU to shift paradigms to help address this challenge. Various factors can undermine effective implementation of internal control and risk management, including institutional legacies, failure to understand complexity and a lack of leadership support. Institutionalisation also has a strong behavioural component involving the beliefs, habits and motivations of individuals. Common behavioural elements when faced with change include (Stoop, 2016):

- Feeling threatened by change, as a result of consequences on power structures, prestige, individual opportunities, or careers;
- A lack of understanding of the need for change or the implications of the change;
- Not having confidence in the promoters of change.

There are myriad of change management models that could be applied to the improving management ownership in Brazil, and ultimately the internal control and risk management functions. For instance, in the 1950s, renowned psychologist Kurt Lewin suggested that effective change requires successful completion of a three-step process of "unfreezing" the existing behaviour, moving to a new level and "refreezing" at the new level (Hayes 2014). Over the years, the process has evolved in different contexts to include concrete activities for each step. In the context of strengthening integrity in Brazil, this approach can be instructive for TCU, particularly as it enhances its own capacity and reorients its strategy to reduce fraud and corruption in government. Lewin's theory argues that "pull" strategies, whereby restraining forces are removed to strengthen a culture of integrity, are more effective than "push" strategies (i.e. outside pressure for change), because they are more likely to increase commitment and result in permanent change (Hayes 2014). Through its audits, evaluations, guidelines and convening power, TCU can act a strong pull agent to complement other entities in government.

Another preeminent change management model, developed by Harvard University professor John Kotter, employs an 8-step process (Kotter 2014):

1. Create a sense of urgency
2. Build a guiding coalition
3. Form a strategic vision and initiatives
4. Enlist a volunteer army
5. Enable action by removing barriers
6. Generate short-term wins
7. Sustain acceleration
8. Institute change

TCU could develop concrete activities mapped against these steps with the goal of refining its recommendations and findings related to management ownership, and addressing the behavioural aspects of institutionalising reforms. For instance, recent turmoil and scandals in Brazil could help TCU to justify in its audits the urgency for more robust risk management and internal control systems across government to regain citizens' trust in government. The importance of successfully implementing the new Normative Instructions issued by MP and CGU can also add a sense of urgency at the entity level. Moreover, to Kotter's second point on building a coalition, TCU could enlist the Internal Control Co-ordination Commission (Comissão de Co-ordenação de Controle Interno (CCCI)), of which TCU is a part. Founded in 2001, the commission includes high level officials and is chaired by the Chief Minister of the Comptroller General (CGU, 2016b). The group has only met 4 times in 15 years, and initiatives to improve management ownership and improve co-ordination between responsible entities to implement the Normative Instructions could reenergise the network. A strategic vision, related to Kotter's third point, could focus on policy outcomes and highlight the public value that is derived from strengthening internal control and risk management, such as reductions in loss of public funds to corruption and fraud and improved execution of the budget (OECD, 2017b).

Numerous change theory models exist that can help entities to address these issues, and understand "where they are" and "where they want to go" with regards to management ownership and building a culture of integrity. TCU could also adapt existing models, such as those described above, to its unique context. Indeed, one of the benefits of applying change management paradigms is that they can be flexible enough to be tailored to the individual contexts of institutions. They also are based on the notion that change is not an end state that can be reached through programmed steps, but rather an ongoing process (Paton 2008). In the Brazilian context, change management can help to bridge theory, as defined in new standards and guidelines to promote integrity, with practice in individual entities. It also provides insights on how to manage resistance to change, which could include the following techniques (adapted from Stoop, 2016):

- Demonstrate that the status quo cannot be maintained and why;
- Collect information concerns and rationale for the current situation, and provide factual and considerate responses;
- Understand and use resistance to change for making improvements;
- Engage those that are promoting change;
- Create new perspectives that are sustainable, rooted in the medium and long-term, not only the short term.

There are other ways that TCU could incorporate change management paradigms into its audits, evaluations and other initiatives. For instance, TCU could integrate the concepts into the audit process by having auditors take into account the drivers and inhibitors of change in the behaviour of auditees. TCU could also disseminate the concepts of change management paradigms through trainings and awareness-raising with audit teams, promoting more constructive approaches with auditees that focus on the process of change and holding auditees accountable for behaviour-based improvements. In addition, TCU could audit the change management or behaviour change as a specific subject unto itself. For instance, the U.K. National Audit Office (NAO) conducted a review, "Auditing behaviour change," that looked at the government's ability "to encourage individuals to change their behaviour in a way that will help Government achieve its policy goals." The NAO undertook this audit in view of "...a growing belief that policy goals may be achieved more effectively if the design and use of interventions incorporate a better understanding of behaviour." This concept can similarly be applied to behavioural change of auditees with regards to management ownership, with the belief that TCU recommendations may be achieved more effectively if audits incorporate a better understanding of the drivers and barriers to change in the context of improving internal control systems (NAO, 2011).

Finally, marginalising or ignoring the input of those who may resist change can slow or impede the process of change as a whole. In discussing findings with the auditee, and in line with the change management principles above on understanding resistance to change (Stoop 2016), TCU could emphasise in internal trainings and communication the importance of understanding the action (or inaction) of the auditee to facilitate a more constructive outcome. TCU may find the audit of the Netherlands Court of Audit instructive in this regard. In an audit of entities' fulfilment of requirements to assess policies with social aims, the NCA found that some ministries did not fulfil its obligations. The NCA reported on the non-fulfilment, without inquiring as to why evaluations were not carried out. Following some ministries' questioning of this approach, the NCA conducted a follow-up audit that looked specifically into the reasons why ministries did not evaluate the effectiveness of these policies.

Ministries provided, in several cases, reasonable explanations to have not evaluated particular programmes. The follow-up audit led to a recommendation that struck a balance, "if a minister thinks an effectiveness audit is neither feasible nor desirable for a particular policy measure, the reasons should be explained to the House of Representatives and the minister should reconsider the benefit and need for the policy, with the possible outcome being that the policy is terminated". The NCA treated this as a lesson learned (OECD, 2016a). A change management mindset of the auditor may provide contextual sophistication to an audit, eventually leading to more practical and constructive recommendations that do not risk raising resistance to the audit or auditors.

TCU could enhance guidance and audits about how to improve the culture of integrity across government, in co-ordination with the key actors.

Given the publication of new Normative Instructions, which requires managers to conduct risk assessments, future initiatives of TCU, as well as the CoG, could focus on the "how to" aspects of managing risks. These would complement existing guidance that provides a picture of risk management in government, but not necessarily practical applications and tools. In developing such guidance and engaging audited entities and the CoG, TCU should be mindful of maintaining its independence, to avoid designing risk management functions that it will ultimately audit.

TCU is well-positioned to improve risk management systems by building on past work and engaging more strategically with existing networks. For example, in addition to those discussed above, TCU has developed a number of products to aid the government in strengthening risk management. This work is in line with its strategic plan, which notes an objective to induce improvement of risk management and internal control of public administration through assessments (objective 7). Examples of TCU's work in this area include the following:

- Brazil's TCU report, *Maturity Assessment in Risk Management in Public Administration*, classifies government agencies by the level of development of their risk management mechanisms, from low formalisation ("initial" and "basic") to fully optimised ("enhanced" and "advanced"). The assessment enabled TCU to rank the maturity of risk assessment in public entities based on 4 axes: i) risk management environment; ii) risks management processes; iii) risks management in collaborations; and iv) achieved results with risks management (see Figure 4.5).

Figure 4.5. **TCU's axes for ranking maturity of risk management in federal entities**

Source: TCU (2013a), Measuring the degree of maturity of public entities in the management of risks, TC 011.745/2012-6, Relatório,Voto e Acórdão 2467/2013 - TCU/Plenário, *http://portal.tcu.gov.br/lumis/portal/file/fileDownload.jsp?inline=1&fileId=8A8182A14D92792C014D928003212A5A*

- *General Criteria for Internal Control in Public Administration*: This TCU study explores role models for internal risk management and controls, and shows how surveyed countries have addressed this issue in their legal systems. The study's goal was to support federal senate discussions concerning a bill to define the general criteria of internal controls, risk management and governance in the Brazilian government. The study revealed that the Brazilian internal control system did not comply with international standards (TCU, 2009b).
- *Basic Governance Reference Guide*: TCU's best governance practice guide provides important definitions for risk management and other relevant concepts. Good practices in the guide include, 'establish risk management and internal control systems' and 'monitor and evaluate the risk management and internal control system," in order to ensure that it is effective and that it contributes to the improvement of organisational performance' (TCU, 2014f).

As noted, TCU also is developing a guide with a framework for managing fraud risks in the public sector to aid managers in implementing new standards for assessing fraud risks. TCU could complement this guide and other efforts by further developing its support for implementing good risk management practices. Given the publication of new standards for internal control and risk management, which requires managers to conduct risk assessments, future initiatives of TCU could focus on the *"how to"* aspects of managing risks, such as data analytics as described in the next section. These would complement some of the other efforts of TCU that provide a picture of risk management in government, but are less useful for managers themselves as practical guidance.

These products are useful tools for managers and help to promote a culture of integrity, but dissemination and institutionalisation of the leading practices they communicate is critical. In addition, TCU could focus its performance audits to promote a culture of integrity through effective trainings and awareness-raising. Indeed, Designing and implementing internal control and risk management processes, beyond a mere compliance exercise, requires trainings and awareness raising that are tailored to the needs of leadership, line managers and staff. Trainings and awareness raising efforts can emphasise the following policies and practices, which TCU could incorporate into its analytical frameworks when conducting performance audits (adapted from IIA 2013a and GAO 2015):

- **Are employees required to attend trainings, including managers?** Attendance of managers at trainings not only helps to develop their knowledge and skills, but also demonstrates a tone-at-the-top and ownership of the internal control and risk management responsibilities. Requirements to attend trainings the focus on integrity, internal controls and risk management, particularly for new hires, can demonstrate the entity's commitment to the function.

- **Are the right people being trained, and the right people involved as trainers?** Effective internal control systems rely on the contributions of many actors. Some of these actors reside within the organisation, at different levels. Trainings can bring managers together with staff. Other actors are external to the entity. For instance, external actors like the internal audit function, contractors and investigators may be responsible for or contribute to key internal control processes. Trainings can help to bring these actors together and avoid siloes for information sharing and generating insights about the system.
- **Are the trainings tailored to the context, highlighting relevant and specific risks?** While internal control systems should follow standards, in particular those recently issued by the CGU, no one system is alike. Within entities, systems and the challenges they face can vary based on resources, expertise, types of risks, entity-level political economy, leadership and other factors. Trainings not only help to educate participants about the risks the entity faces, but they can also be a tool for managers to identify risks raised through exercises and discussions between different levels and teams within the entity. Other content that trainings and awareness raising campaigns can convey include the following:
  - Increase understanding of political leadership and senior public officials about the linkages between an effective internal control system and the achievement of the entity's objectives.
  - Provide concrete examples of how the early identification of risks can help avoid future problems, and thus save valuable time and resources.
  - Demonstrate concrete ways to integrate specific integrity policies at the entity-level planning and operations.
  - Explain the assurance as well as the consulting role of the internal audit function and the value of evidence based policy choices consolidating on existing audit reports.
- **Does the entity use different mediums to educate and raise awareness about internal control and risk management?** Trainings, on their own, may not be sufficient, particularly if they are periodically administered. Consistent messages using various mechanisms, such as newsletters, brochures, dedicated events and time period (e.g. anti-corruption week), can help to raise the profile of internal control and risk management policies and procedures. Importantly, the messages can communicate the benefits of an effective internal control system, including the demonstration of prevented fraud or corruption cases. Publicising the entity's integrity efforts externally is also valuable, not only for demonstrating impact, but as a deterrent for would-be corrupt actors.

In developing awareness and a culture of integrity, it is important that TCU focus not just on what the government may be doing wrong, but also on what it is doing right. Success stories and detailed case studies are important tools for communicating and illustrating an effective approach to managers. TCU could encourage entities to do this through its own reviews and recommendations in order to facilitate constructive dialogue and positive exchange of ideas. For instance, in Peru, an initiative of the supreme audit institution (the Contraloría General de la Republica, or CGR), calls on public entities to publish all the activities, good practices and achievements related to the implementation of the National Control System (through web and other tools such as internal newsletters). The new directive also requires public entities to elaborate awareness campaigns and capacity development plans within the 90 days following the publication of the directive. In addition to the new directive, some specific guidelines for the dissemination of internal control inside the public entity (*Lineamientos sugeridos para la difusion del Control Interno al interior de la entidad*) have been developed by the CGR. The guidelines suggest, for example, publishing news on the status of the implementation of the pilot projects (CGR, 2016).

Finally, other mechanisms exist for dissemination of key concepts, such as engaging in existing networks and developing seminars on select topics, as other SAIs have done. For instance, TCU is a member of the Internal Control Co-ordination Commission, a co-ordination-centre that aims to improve the effectiveness of the control function over public management. TCU could more proactively use the Network to draw attention to systemic issues, propose joint solutions and build awareness around the importance of managerial responsibility over the internal control system.

4.5. Improving use of tools, methodologies and guidance for effective risk management and control

TCU could strengthen the capacity of government to prevent fraud and corruption through audits and additional guidance that ensure the effectiveness of policies and use of tools, such as data analytics.

Aforementioned studies of TCU demonstrate the need for stronger capacities for managing risks in government. Moreover, new internal control standards place a greater emphasis on managers addressing implementation challenges. Effective implementation relies on managers to be proactive and to take responsibility over the internal control system, thereby promoting a culture of integrity. Policies, procedures, structures and tools are all part and parcel of a culture of integrity and critical for effective management of integrity risks. TCU recognised the need for managers to have a framework that touches on each of these elements to help guide their fraud risk management activities. TCU can build on this initiative by focusing its audits, additional guidance and engagement with the executive branch with an eye towards improved implementation of its framework and internal control standards.

A key area where TCU could focus its efforts, particularly audits and awareness-raising, is on the preconditions for successful fraud risk management within an entity, including policies and structures. Knowing the laws, government-wide policies and standards that set requirements is the first step for managers to know what policies should be in place to guide institutional efforts. The Australian Attorney-General's Department developed a Fraud Control Framework that outlines requirements for fraud control, including that government entities establish a comprehensive fraud control program covering prevention, detection, investigation and reporting strategies (Australian Attorney-General's Department, 2014). Australia's approach, among others, can help TCU to ensure its audits and awareness-raising effectively target the preconditions for effective fraud and corruption risk management. Key questions to consider include (adapted from Australian Attorney-General's Department 2014 and IIA 2013a):

- Does the entity have an effective and articulated fraud risk management framework (policies, assigned roles, procedures and controls) in place that represent activities to prevent, detect, respond and monitor?
- Is the framework, as well as key information (e.g. values, code of conduct, conflict of interests policies) easily accessible to employees and communicated early in the hiring and often?

- Are there policies and requirements for training related to fraud and corruption risk management for all levels of the entity?
- Is there a central point of contact for fraud risk management within the entity?
- To what extent does an external body (e.g. CGU or the Internal Control Co-ordination Commission) have a role in overseeing the development and implementation of the fraud risk assessment and fraud control plan?

TCU's guide for managing fraud risks highlights other areas then those covered above that could be adapted into concrete tools for auditors to hone the focus of their audits on fraud and corruption risk management. In doing so, TCU can induce change in alignment with the leading practices it sets out in its guide. In addition, TCU could create complementary guidance to aid auditor in incorporating the standards and practices into their plans, interviews, and findings. Box 4.3 below provides an example from the supreme audit institution of Costa Rica in the context of auditing to strengthen ethics in the public sector.

Fraud and corruption risk management is a multi-faceted function with many applications involving varied types of risks, depending on the context. The value of audit recommendations, guidance and consultations improves with more tailored, specific insights on the types of risks facing a particular entity or sector. For instance, the types of fraud risks inherent in the procurement cycle can different from those in the delivery of services for health and education. In addition, risk management relies on key tools and methodologies, such as risk assessments and data analytics. Such topics, whether sector-specific or about risk management techniques, require specific types of guidance and targeting in audits, given the unique nature of risks, skills and challenges they each have. TCU could build on existing frameworks for managing fraud risks with follow-on guidance that focuses on specific areas. Such guidance can be directed to managers in the executive branch and auditors alike.

One area TCU could explore, building on its leadership and initiatives in this area, is the harnessing of "big data" and the use of data analytics for integrity. Individuals who engage in fraud and corruption are effectively making cost-benefit analyses to better themselves at the expense of others, and data analytics can increase the risk and cost of being discovered (Persons 2016). TCU has evolved into a leader in this area, not only within the Brazilian government, but among supreme audit institutions as well. For instance, in 2015, TCU conducted numerous audits in an effort to go beyond a conventional "pay and chase" model of oversight, to more preventive actions to avoid fraud, corruption, waste and abuse through use of data analytics.

TCU has employed statistical methods, the analysis of images and geo-referencing techniques, among other approaches, to reduce the time allotted for analyses and encourage more cost-effective auditing (TCU 2015g). In one review, TCU applied Benford's Law as a data mining tool to conduct pricing analysis of a public works project. Benford's Law is one specific form of anomaly detection that can be used to identify potential fraud, and it states that numbers from sufficiently large data sources are typically distributed in a specific, non-uniform way (ACL 2013). Specifically, the number 1 typically appears as the first digit in the largest percentage of numbers in a data source (about 30%), with each successive number typically appearing as the first digit in a decreasing percentage of numbers in the data source, with the number 9 appearing as the first digit in just under 5 percent of numbers in any given data source. Deviations from this pattern are statistically unlikely in randomly occurring data sets and could indicate potential fraud (IIA 2009).

Box 4.3. **Auditing for Ethics in Costa Rica**

In 2008, the Office of the Comptroller General of the Republic of Costa Rica (CGR) developed a technical guide (*Guía Técnica para el Desarrollo de Auditorías de la Ética*, or Guide) to support internal auditors in performing ethics audit, which the CGR defines as the systematic, objective and professional process for evaluating the functioning and effectiveness of the institution's ethical framework, in order to promote its strengthening. Such guidance was provided after realizing that there was little knowledge about the audit of ethics both among Costa Rica's auditors as well as within the world's audit community.

The legal basis and standards supporting ethics audit in Costa Rica lays in several domestic and international instruments such as the Internal Control General Law (*Ley General de Control Interno*), the Manual to conduct internal audit in the Public Sector (*Manual de normas para el ejercicio de la auditoría interna en el Sector Público*), the International Standards for the Professional Exercise of Internal Audit (*Normas Internacionales para el Ejercicio Profesional de la Auditoría Interna* 2100, 2130, 2130 A1) and the Institute of Internal Auditor Practice Advisory 2130-1 (*Consejo para la práctica* 2130-1).

Ethics audit are carried out by those responsible of internal audit function within their competences and duties. Object of the audit is the institutional ethical frameworks, which includes the following three components:

- The ethical program: formal factors regarding ethical matters set out in the organization, such as the statement of institutional values, the code of ethics, the vision and mission, the definition of indicators of ethical management, and a formal strategy for strengthening ethics.
- The ethical environment: shared values, beliefs and behaviours of the organization's members. It includes observable informal factors such as the organizational climate, the management style, the models of decision making, the verbal expressions, and the behaviours of individuals.
- The integration of ethics within the institution's management systems: incorporation of ethical controls in the systems and procedures used in processes that are particularly sensible and exposed to ethical failure and corruption, such as human resources, financial management, administrative contracting and activities with potential political interference.

Considering the sensitiveness and complexity of the issues surrounding ethics, the Guide stresses the importance of the ethics auditors' professional competence and expertise. At the same time, the audited entity is also called to ensure a set of basic conditions for the ethics audits to be possible such as high management commitment with ethics, as well as support and an open-mind attitude prior to, during and after the audit process.

Next to the Guide, which sets out the methodology of ethics audit, the CGR has put at disposal of auditors a set of additional tools to support them in the systematic development of evaluations on ethical frameworks and which include:

- General work plan;
- Guide for evaluating the institutional ethical framework;
- Guide for the analysis of strengths, opportunities, weaknesses and threats;
- Ethics maturity model;
- Guides for interviewing high and middle management and others;
- Survey on the institution's ethical environment;
- Summary sheet of findings.

Although the users of the guide are internal auditors, it is also directed to the management when deciding to perform a self-evaluation of ethical issues as well as to external auditors.

Source: CGR (2008), *Guía Técnica para el Desarrollo de Auditorías de la Ética*, *https://cgrfiles.cgr.go.cr/publico/jaguar/Documentos/control_interno/secretaria/2009/Auditoria%20de%20la%20etica/mo_aud_etica_final.doc*; CGR's website: *https://www.cgr.go.cr/04-documentos/normativa/auditoria-etica.html*

As a result of TCU's review using Benford's Law, it found 17 services that were overpriced in the budget, amounting to 72% of the total overpricing found and nearly 150 million reals (nearly 47 million euros, adjusted for 2014) (TCU 2014g). This particular data analytics approach, like others, can reduce the amount of time auditors spend analysing large datasets, and help them to identify the highest risks for potential follow up audits. TCU has a number of other initiatives to improve the use of data analytics in government as well as its adoption by auditors, including trainings and projects as part of its innovation lab, the "Co-Participation Laboratory" (coLAB-i) (TCU, 2015g). Box 4.4 below describes another example of using data mining in the context of public procurement, with the additional benefit of developing an index that could produce comparative data on risks.

Box 4.4. **Data mining to identify corruption in public procurement in the European Union**

In recent years, a team of sociologists developed a new system to identify potential corruption in public procurement in Europe. The research team developed a "Corruption Risk Index" (CRI) that could mine available information related to public procurements to identify potential corruption issues. To develop the CRI, the lead researcher spoke with experts on public procurement to identify 13 "red flags" that could indicate corruption in an individual contract or tender. Among others, these red flags included very short tender periods (e.g., a tender issued on a Friday and awarded the following Monday), very specific or suspiciously complex tenders compared with others in the field, tender modifications leading to bigger contracts, inaccessible tender documents, and very few bidders in highly competitive markets. The flags were then weighted to determine a risk ranking for each contractor or firm. In a proof-of-concept conducted using data from Hungary, Slovakia, and the Czech Republic, the research team found that firms with a higher CRI score made more money than firms with lowers CRIs, and were also more likely to have politicians involved as either managers or owners and to be registered in tax havens.

Source: Research Center Budapest (2014), *http://mihalyfazekas.eu/wp-content/uploads/2015/08/Fazekas-Toth_State_capture_PP_2014Nov.pdf;*

In addition to data mining, a number of other techniques can be used to apply data analytics in the area of integrity. Data-analytic techniques allow entities to analyse large volumes of transactions or other data more effectively and efficiently than with manual techniques. For example, as shown above data-mining tools can facilitate comparisons, matching datasets can speed up and improve the accuracy of investigative results and predictive modelling as well as data visualisation can help to identify complex patterns in large datasets to identify fraudulent transactions (UN-INTOSAI 2013). In addition, data analytics can be used to test the effectiveness of internal controls. For example, the Office of the Auditor General of Western Australia recommends that agencies consider the use of data analytics to identify fraud or errors after a new system or process has been implemented, or after key controls have been modified as the identification of such issues can highlight gaps in the new or revised controls (Western Australia OAG 2016).

Detailing the leading practices for implementing the varied techniques is beyond the scope of this report; however, TCU could further support the executive branch in its use of data analytics through additional guidance and audits, focusing on both the process of using data analytics for integrity (as well as in other contexts) and leading practices related to specific techniques. With regards to the former, the steps described below (as well as

Figure 4.6) for implementing data analytics for integrity purposes could help guide TCU's work. The steps are applicable both to auditors using data analytics for their reviews, as well as managers within government who are responsible for preventing and detecting potentially fraudulent or irregular behaviour.

Figure 4.6. **Steps for Implementing Data Analytics for Integrity Purposes**

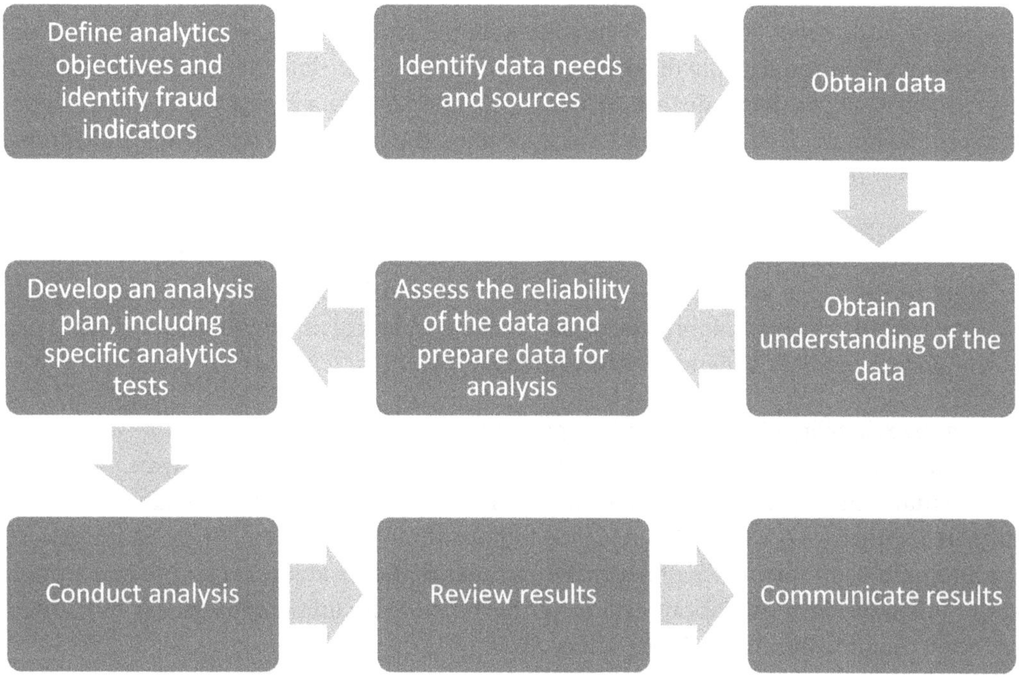

Source: OECD Secretariat

Define analytics objectives and identify fraud indicators. The first step in implementing data analytics for integrity purposes is to determine the objective. As a good practice, conducting a risk assessment can help the analytics team understand the areas in which fraud, corruption, or other integrity risks are most likely to occur, which can help focus the analysis. After defining the objective, the analytics team could identify the fraud or corruption indicators or "red flags" they plan to identify with the data-analytics test. When identifying fraud indicators, the analytics team could consider experience, typical business rule limits, and common fraud schemes (EY 2014). Understanding rules, processes and 'normal' behaviour, before implementing analytics tests, can help reduce false positives.

Identify data needs and sources. The next step is to identify the data that will be needed to identify the fraud or corruption indicators defined in the first step, as well as to identify the sources of that data. This may include data that exist within the entity, data from other government agencies, or data from external, non-government entities. The specific data needed to conduct the analysis will depend on the analytics objectives and the specific indicators the analytics tests will be used to identify.

Obtain data. The next step is to obtain the data necessary to conduct the analysis. As previously noted, the amount of time spent on this step may vary considerably depending on whether the data are available in-house or need to be obtained from external entities.

Obtain an understanding of the data. The next step is to obtain an understanding of the data. As previously noted, some understanding of the data is necessary in order to develop a formal data request; thus, this step may occur in conjunction with the prior step.

One good practice to assist the analytics team in obtaining and understanding of the data is to obtain the data dictionary, if one is available. Data dictionaries explain each field within the data and, as such, are a main source of information for data analysts (Auditor General of South Africa 2016). Data dictionaries are particularly useful when the data analysis involves combining data from different sources. In particular, data dictionaries help ensure everyone is using the same definition (GAO 2013) and help data analysts understand when different terms are used for the same thing or when the same term has different meanings across government entities or programs (Henderson and Hammersburg 2013).

Another good practice is to work with both system owners and information-technology experts to obtain an understanding of the data. System owners can provide information on how transactions are processed in the system and information-technology experts, particularly the database administrator, can provide technical information such as the rules of the system (Auditor General of South Africa 2016).

Assess the reliability of the data and prepare data for analytics. The next step is to assess the reliability and integrity of the data and to take steps as necessary to clean the data to ensure that it can be used in the analysis. This may include converting the data to a format suitable for analysis (EY 2014). In its "Guide to Data Mining as a Tool in Fraud Investigation," the Supreme Audit Institution of South Africa notes that data analysts can use one or more of the following data-validation tests to verify the integrity and completeness of the data provided (Auditor General of South Africa 2016):

- Verify the data types against the record layout and data dictionary (for example, text fields contain text)
- Confirm the record count with the control totals received
- Confirm the hash totals of numeric fields with the control totals received
- Identify missing data (for example, blank fields or gaps in sequences)
- Check for duplicate data and confirm whether any duplicates identified are false positives
- Reconcile the data to accounting records
- Perform reasonability tests (for example, calculate the number of transactions per month and determine if the number is near the number that would reasonably expected in a month)
- Perform period testing to determine if the data cover the requested period

Any discrepancies identified should be addressed before performing the analysis, which may include re-requesting the data (Auditor General of South Africa 2016). Care should be taken at this step to understand and assess any discrepancies or outliers identified as a result of data validation tests or data cleaning procedures as outliers or anomalies may be indicative of fraud or corruption.

Develop an analysis plan, including specific analytics tests. The next step is to develop an analysis plan that describes the data to be analysed, the specific analytics tests that will be performed, and the frequency with which the analytics will be performed. When using data analytics for integrity purposes, particularly for fraud detection and testing the effectiveness of internal controls, public-sector entities should:

- Analyse all relevant data: Public-sector entities should apply analytics tests to the full data population. Random sampling is useful for identifying problems that occur relatively consistently throughout data populations. However, as fraudulent transactions do not occur randomly, sampling may not be sufficient to identify fraud (ACL 2013). The INTOSAI Working Group on IT Audit notes that, by using data-analytics tools, auditors can look at all data, which makes it possible to spot connections and details that may be difficult to notice as the amount of information increases. By analysing all data, the auditor can identify anomalies or high-risk areas for further review (INTOSAI 2015).
- Design data-analytics tests based on the identified fraud indicators: The analytics team should translate the specific indicators of fraud or corruption identified at the beginning of the analysis into specific analytical procedures.
- Determine whether the analysis will be conducted on an ad hoc, repetitive, or continuous basis: Data-analytics tests can be applied ad hoc or can be applied on a repetitive or continuous basis, and the frequency with which to run data-analytics tests depends on the purpose for which analytics are being used. For example, data-analytics tests can be applied on an ad-hoc basis to identify potential issues that may indicate opportunities exist for fraud to occur (ACL 2013). This approach may be sufficient for an auditor using data analytics to test the effectiveness of an agency's internal controls. However, program managers using data analytics to maintain program integrity should automate data-analytic tests to monitor for fraud indictors on a continuous, real-time basis, if possible (GAO 2015). If data-analytics tests cannot be automated to occur on a continuous basis, such as when data can only be obtained on a periodic basis, performing data-analytics tests on a regular, periodic basis, can still be informative. For example, implementing data-analytics tests during monthly transaction cycles can help ensure that risks are being mitigated throughout the year, rather than on an annual basis (Mazur 2015).

Perform the analysis. At this stage, the analytics team implements the analysis plan to perform the analysis.

Review the results. After performing the analysis, the analytics team reviews the results. Data-analytics tests cannot confirm fraud; rather, such tests identify the existence of indicators that then need to be reviewed. Analysts can review the results and determine whether there is a logical explanation for why specific indicators were identified or if there are signs of fraudulent activity (GAO 2013). As reviewing results can be time consuming, taking time at the beginning of the analytics process to obtain a strong understanding of the process can help the analytics team develop more refined analytics tests that may produce fewer false positives.

Communicate the results. Once analytics tests have been implemented and the results have been reviewed, the analytics team communicates the results to relevant parties. When data analytics are used for identifying fraud or corruption, this may include providing information on potential fraudsters to law-enforcement entities for investigation. This may also include communicating information necessary to address control weaknesses or risks that managers may need to take steps to address. Good practices for communicating the results of analytics tests include understanding the needs of the audience and using data-visualization tools. Tailoring the output of data analytics to the intended audience can help ensure the results are usable, which helps ensure the overall success of the data-analytics initiative (GAO 2015). Data visualization tools, such as dashboards and maps, or even simple charts and figures, can illustrate areas of greater risks more clearly than spreadsheets, statistics, and lists of transactions. In addition, communicating the results to potential fraudsters can also be beneficial for reducing fraud and corruption, as described in the example in the box below (Box 4.5).

Box 4.5. **USDA's use of data analytics to reduce fraudulent crop insurance claims**

The U.S. Department of Agriculture (USDA) experienced a dra-matic drop in fraudulent claims for crop insurance after they implemented data analytics ap-proaches. The Federal Crop Insurance Corporation (FCIC), managed by the USDA's Risk Management Agency, offers insurance to farmers and other agricultural entities to for crop failures in the event of bad weather, as well as revenue losses when the price of commodities drop. USDA's Crop Insurance Program Compliance and Integrity Data Warehouse used multi-ple datasets to prevent and detect potentially fraudulent claim payments, resulting in billions of dollars in savings. Specifically, USDA data analysts used 170 data sour-ces, including terabytes of policy information, weather and satellite data, and millions of crop insurance policies across 3,200 countries, to cross-check potentially fraudulent claims with data from other sources, such as satelli-te images and weather records.

USDA's response to atypical patterns involved both conventional activi-ties (i.e. investigative approaches) as well as "soft" ap-proaches, like sending letters of inquiry to suspected fraudsters. The latter approach exemplifies the deterrent effect of communicating the results of the data analytics. Following the letters, there was a dramatic drop in claims, indicating that program participants were now aware of USDA's new ability to detect fraud or suspected fraudulent activities.

Source: Persons, Timothy, Chief Scientist of the U.S. Government Accountability Office (2016), Interview with TCU, Revista do TCU, Issue 135, *http://portal.tcu.gov.br/lumis/portal/file/fileDownload.jsp?fileId=8A8182A25AC9F28A015ACE19A18D4354*

The amount of time spent on each step may vary considerably depending on circumstances. For example, an institution with a centralized data warehouse that plans to analyse existing data owned and maintained within the institution may spend very little time obtaining data needed for the analysis. On the other hand, an institution that needs access to data held by an external entity—such as another government agency—may need to spend considerable time and resources in establishing processes and procedures to obtain the data. In Brazil, for instance, much of the procurement data involves government-wide databases and sources, such as the Integrated Federal Financial Administration System (Sistema Integrado de Administração Financeira do Governo Federal, SIAFI), Integrate System of Administration of General Services (SIASG), and Comprasnet, Brazil's central procurement website and e-procurement portal. TCU's Logistics Procurement Secretariat (SELOG) incorporates data analytics into its audits, referring to these systems. In this context, TCU's audits and reviews of data analytics can have application to numerous entities that provide input to and rely on these systems for their own work.

Notes

1. Article 74 of Brazil's Federal Constitution of 1988 outlines requirements for the system of internal control. The legislative, Executive and Judicial Powers shall maintain an integrated system of internal control for the purpose of: i) evaluating the attainment of the goals established in the Multi-annual Plan (plano pluriannual, PPA), the implementation of government programmes and of the budgets of the Union; ii) verifying the lawfulness and evaluating the results, as to effectiveness and efficiency, of the budgetary, financial and property management in the agencies and entities of the federal administration, as well as the use of public funds by private legal entities; iii) exercising control over credit transactions, collateral signatures and guarantees, as well as over the rights and assets of the Union; iv) supporting external control in the exercise of its institutional mission. Paragraph 1. The persons responsible for internal control shall, upon learning of any irregularity or illegality, inform the Federal Audit Court about it, subject to joint liability. Paragraph 2. Any citizen, political party, association or labour union has standing under the law to denounce irregularities or illegalities to the Federal Court of Accounts.
2. Other benefits that accrue through internal control include oversight and evaluation of operations, which are discussed in further detail in chapter 4.
3. See Decree 8.109/2013.
4. On 12 May, 2016, the former Office of the Comptroller General of the Union (CGU) became the Ministry of Transparency, Supervision and Control, as per provision N° 726, of 12 May, 2016 (Government of Brazil, 2016). The CGU was established to support the President concerning the protection of government property and increasing the transparency of management by means of internal controls and public audit, preventing and fighting corruption and was ombudsman (CGU, 2016a).

References

ACL (2013), Detecting and Preventing Fraud with Data Analytics, *https://www.acl.com/pdfs/ACL_fraud_ebook.pdf*

ASF (Office of the Auditor General of México, or *Auditoría Superior de la Federación*) (2015), "Technical Study for the Promotion of a Culture of Integrity in the Public Sector", *http://asf.gob.mx/uploads/180_Estudios/1173_Estudio_Tec_para_la_Promocion_de_la_Cultura_de_Integridad_en_el_Sec_Pub.pdf*

ASF (2014), "Study about the Strategies for Combating Corruption in the Public Sector", *http://informe.asf.gob.mx/Documentos/Auditorias/2014_1642_a.pdf*

Australian Attorney-General's Department (2014), Commonwealth Fraud Control Framework, *https://www.ag.gov.au/CrimeAndCorruption/FraudControl/Documents/CommonwealthFraudControlFramework2014.pdf*

Auditor General of South Africa (2016), "Guide to Data Mining as a Tool in Fraud Investigation," November 3, 2016, *http://content.intosaicommunity.org/library/audit-of-information-technology/guidelines/75-data-mining/file*

CGR (Comptroller General of the Republic of Peru, Contraloría General de la Republica) (2016), Directiva N°013-2016-CG/GPROD, Implementación del Sistema de Control Interno en las Entidades del Estado, *http://doc.contraloria.gob.pe/Control-Interno/web/documentos/normativa/RC_N149-2016-CG.zip*

CGU (Ministry of Transparency, Supervision and Control) (2016), website, *http://www.cgu.gov.br/* (accessed September 2016).

CGU (2016b), CCCI, *http://www.cgu.gov.br/assuntos/auditoria-e-fiscalizacao/comissao-de-coordenacao-de-controle-interno-ccci/composicao*

CGU (2015), Operational plan of decentralized actions for transparency and prevention of corruption, Second semester of 2015, *http://www.cgu.gov.br/sobre/institucional/planejamento-estrategico/arquivos/plano-operacional-stpc-2015.pdf*

COSO (2013), An Update of COSO's Internal Control – Integrated Framework, Committee of Sponsoring Organisations of the Treadway Commission, *www.coso.org/documents/cosoicifoutreachdeck_05%2018%2012.pdf.*

Eklund, Aapo Länsiluoto Annukka Jokipii Tomas, (2016),»Internal control effectiveness – a clustering approach», Managerial Auditing Journal, Vol. 31 Iss 1 pp. 5 – 34 *http://dx.doi.org/10.1108/MAJ-08-2013-0910*

Ernst and Young (2014), Y, "The Role of Data Analytics in Fraud Prevention," *http://www.ey.com/Publication/vwLUAssets/EY_-_Forensic_Data_Analytics/$FILE/EY-Data-Analytics-The-role-of-data-analytics-in-fraud-prevention.pdf*

European Commission (2014), Compendium of the Public Internal Control Systems in the EU Member States, *http://ec.europa.eu/budget/pic/lib/book/compendium/HTML/index.html*, accessed 23 November 2015

European Court of Auditors (2012), Structural Funds: Did the Commission Successfully Deal with Deficiencies Identified in the Member State's Management and Control Systems? Special Report No. 3 *http://www.eca.europa.eu/Lists/ECADocuments/SR12_03/SR12_03_EN.PDF*

Government Accountability Office (GAO) (2017), High-Risk Series: Progress on many high-risk areas, while substantial efforts needed on others (GAO-17-317), accessed February 2017, *http://www.gao.gov/assets/690/682765.pdf*

Government Accountability Office (GAO) (2015), A Framework for Managing Fraud Risk in Federal Programs (GAO-15-593SP), accessed March 2017, *http://www.gao.gov/assets/680/671664.pdf*

Government Accountability Office (GAO)(2013), "Data Analytics for Oversight and Law Enforcement." Washington, D.C., July 15, 2013. *www.gao.gov/products/GAO-13-680SP*

Government Accountability Office (GAO) (2000), Determining Performance and Accountability Challenges and High Risks (GAO-01-159SP), accessed February 2017, *http://www.gao.gov/assets/210/200448.pdf*

Government of Brazil, Provision N° 726, of 12 May, 2016, *http://www.planalto.gov.br/ccivil_03/_Ato2015-2018/2016/Mpv/mpv726.htm*

Henderson, Greg, and Carl Hammersburg (2013), "An Enterprise Approach to Fraud Prevention and Detection in Government Programs." SAS. Accessed December 16, 2016. *http://www.sas.com/en_us/whitepapers/enterprise-approach-fraud-detection-prevention-government-106136.html.*

Hayes, John,(2014), The Theory and Practice of Change Management, Palgrave Mammillan, United Kingdom

IIA (Institute of Internal Auditors) (2015), Three Lines of Defence Model, Assurance Maps presentation-PIC EU-28 Conference 2015, *http://slideplayer.com/slide/10129777/*

Institute of Internal Auditors (IIA) (2013), IIA Position Paper – Three Lines of Defense in Effective Risk Management and Control, The Institute of Internal Auditors, Altamonte Springs, *www.theiia.org/goto/3Lines*

Institute of Internal Auditors (IIA), American Institute of Certified Public Accountants, and Association of Certified Fraud Examiners (2013a), Managing the Business Risk of Fraud: A Practical Guide *https://www.acfe.com/uploadedFiles/ACFE_Website/Content/documents/managing-business-risk.pdf*

Institute of Internal Auditors (IIA) (2009), Global Technology Audit Guide (GTAG) 13: Fraud Prevention and Detection in an Automated World, *https://chapters.theiia.org/montreal/ChapterDocuments/GTAG%2013%20-%20Fraud%20Prevention%20and%20Detection%20in%20a%20Automated%20World.pdf*

International Organisation for Standardisation (ISO) (2009), ISO 3100 – Risk Management, *http://www.iso.org/iso/home/standards/iso31000.htm*

INTOSAI Working Group on IT Audit (2015), "Big Data Management and Data Analytics," June 2015. *http://www.intosaiitaudit.org/working_group_paper_lists/20.*

Kotter, J. (2014), Accelerate, *https://www.kotterinternational.com/8-steps-process-for-leading-change/*

KPMG (2015), "How Big Data Affects Auditing,"

Mazur, Edward J (2015), "Data Analytics-a Tool for Building Trust in Government." *The Journal of Government Financial Management*, July 2015.

MP (Ministry of Planning, Development and Management) (2016a), Bimonthly reports and reports issued every quarter, accessed online, September 2016, *http://www.planejamento.gov.br/assuntos/orcamento/informacoes-orcamentarias/rel-de-avaliacao-fiscal-e-cumprimento-de-meta/relatorios-de-avaliacao-fiscal-e-cumprimento-de*

MP (2016b), government Establishes Committee to Monitor and Evaluate Public Policies: *http://www.planejamento.gov.br/noticias/governo-institui-comite-para-monitorar-e-avaliar-politicas-publicas*

MP (2016c), Interministerial Committee Discusses Evaluation of Public Policies, *http://www.planejamento.gov.br/noticias/comite-interministerial-discute-politicas-publicas-e-avalia-efetividade-de-acoes*

MP (2016e), National Press (Impresa Nacional), Ministry of Planning, Development and Management, "Ministério do Planejamento, Orçamento e Gestão" (now Ministério do Planejamento, Desenvolvimento e Gestão), *http://pesquisa.in.gov.br/imprensa/jsp/visualiza/index.jsp?data=08/04/2016&jornal=1&pagina=79&totalArquivos=204;*

MP/CGU (2016), Joint Normative Instructions MP/CGU No 01, *http://www.cgu.gov.br/sobre/legislacao/arquivos/instrucoes-normativas/in_cgu_mpog_01_2016.pdf* (accessed September 2016)

NAO (National Audit Office) (2011), Auditing Behaviour Change, accessed February 2017, *https://www.nao.org.uk/wp-content/uploads/2011/09/NAO_Auditing_Behaviour_Change.pdf*

NCA (Netherlands Court of Audit) (2011), Financial risks to the Netherlands, *www.courtofaudit.nl/english/Publications/Audits/Introductions/2013/09/Financial_risks_to_the_Netherlands_of_international_guarantees*

NCA (2011), Risks to Public Finances, *www.courtofaudit.nl/english/Publications/Audits/Introductions/2012/06/Risks_to_public_finances*

NCA (2011), Spending Cuts Monitoring, *www.courtofaudit.nl/english/Publications/Audits/Introductions/2011/05/Spending_Cuts_Monitor_2011*

OAG (Office of the Auditor General of Canada), Chapter 1, Financial Management and Control and Risk Management, *http://www.oag-bvg.gc.ca/internet/English/parl_oag_201106_01_e_35369.html*

OECD (2017a), *Mexico's National Auditing System: Strengthening Accountable Governance*, OECD Public Governance Reviews, OECD Publishing, Paris. *http://dx.doi.org/10.1787/9789264264748-en*

OECD (2017b), "Observatory of Public Sector Innovation: Working with Change: Systems Approaches to Governance" Conference agenda, 28 February, 2017, Paris.

OECD (2016a), *Supreme Audit Institutions and Good Governance: Oversight, Insight and Foresight*, OECD Public Governance Reviews, OECD Publishing, Paris. *http://dx.doi.org/10.1787/9789264263871-en*

OECD (2016b), *Better Policies for Sustainable Development 2016: A New Framework for Policy Coherence*, OECD Publishing, Paris. *http://dx.doi.org/10.1787/9789264256996-en*

OECD (2016), Recommendation of the Council on Public Integrity (forthcoming)

OECD (2014a) 'Centre Stage: Driving Better Policies from the Centre of Government' OECD Publishing, Paris, *https://www.oecd.org/gov/Centre-Stage-Report.pdf*

OECD (2013), *Brazil's Supreme Audit Institution: The Audit of the Consolidated Year-end Government Report*, OECD Public Governance Reviews, OECD Publishing, Paris. *http://dx.doi.org/10.1787/9789264188112-en*

Olivieri, C. et al, (2015), Public Management Performance in Brazil: Challenges for Co-ordination. *http://dx.doi.org/10.5539/ibr.v8n8p181*

Paton, Robert A and James McCalman, (2008), Change Management: A Guide to Effective Implementation, Third Edition, SAGE Publications, London

Persons, Timothy, Chief Scientist of the U.S. Government Accountability Office (2016), Interview with TCU, Revista do TCU, Issue 135, *http://portal.tcu.gov.br/lumis/portal/file/fileDownload.jsp?fileId=8A8182A25AC9F28A015ACE19A18D4354*

Stoop, P. (2016), Concepts for facilitating and managing change: challenges in institutional and organisational development, with respect to the processes of regionalisation of a Supreme Audit Institution, presentation, Rabat, 2016, not available.

TCU (Tribunal de Contas da União) (2017), PORTARIA-SEGECEX N° 5 DE 7 DE MARÇO DE 2017 [Department of Institutional Relations for Control on Fight Against Fraud and Corruption], Brasilia.

TCU (2015a), Strategic Plan of Brazil's Federal Court of Accounts, 2015-2021 (Plano Estratégico do Tribunal de Contas da União para o período 2015-2021) PORTARIA-TCU N° 141, DE 1° DE ABRIL DE 2015, Brasilia, *http://portal.tcu.gov.br/tcu/paginas/planejamento/2021/index.html.*

TCU (2015b), External Control Plan of Brazil's Federal Court of Accounts (Plano de Contrôle Externo do Tribunal de Contas da União) April, 2015, Brasilia, *http://portal.tcu.gov.br/lumis/portal/file/fileDownload.jsp?fileId=8A8182A153234E0A01535D1006D60567.*

TCU (2015d), Survey of Public governance, Summary, *http://portal.tcu.gov.br/lumis/portal/file/fileDownload.jsp?fileId=8A8182A14F613FB5014F6B5206735279.*

TCU (2015e), TCU Judgement 0548/2015, Acordo TC-020.137/2014-1 – Plenary, Performance Audit *http://www.tcu.gov.br/Consultas/Juris/Docs/judoc/Acord/20150320/AC_0548_09_15_P.doc*

TCU (2015f), Evaluation of risk management maturity of Electrosul , TCU 605/2015, Acordo TC-019.140/2014-2, *http://www.tcu.gov.br/Consultas/Juris/Docs/judoc/Acord/20150330/AC_0605_10_15_P.doc*

TCU (2015g), Innovation at the Service of Control, Annual Report 2015, *https://portal.tcu.gov.br/lumis/portal/file/fileDownload.jsp?fileId=8A8182A25A4C7F07015A4D5527C25DAC*

TCU (2014a), Survey of Risk Management in Public Governance, Gestão De Riscos Levantamento De Governança Pública, *http://portal.tcu.gov.br/lumis/portal/file/fileDownload.jsp?fileId=8A8182A24E08D405014E0D42E95B3708*

TCU (2014b), Framework to Assess Governance in Public Policies, TCU Publishing, Brasilia, *http://portal2.tcu.gov.br/portal/pls/portal/docs/2686056.PDF*

TCU (2014c), Evaluation of internal controls of Roraima's municipalities, TCU Judgement 568/2014 – Plenary, Survey report. *http://www.tcu.gov.br/Consultas/Juris/Docs/judoc/Acord/20140314/AC_0568_07_14_P.doc*

TCU (2014d), Evaluation of units of internal control and internal audit, (Acordao TCU 821/2014) *http://www.psc-intosai.org/media/16694/tcu_performance_audit_manual.pdf;plenario:acordao:2014-04-02;821*

TCU (2014e), Audit of risk management of Secretariat of Ports, Judgement 735/2014 – Plenary, Acordo TC 009.504/2013-3, Performance audit, *http://www.tcu.gov.br/Consultas/Juris/Docs/judoc/Acord/20140402/AC_0735_09_14_P.doc*

TCU (2014f), TCU's Basic Governance Reference Guide for Public Sector Organizations, 2nd version, accessed February 2017, *http://portal.tcu.gov.br/lumis/portal/file/fileDownload.jsp?fileId=8A8182A253234F6C015333B3DE131B3F*

TCU (2014g), Benford's Law and Public Works Audit: an analysis of overpricing in the maracanã remodelling, Revisita do TCU, Issue 131, *http://revista.tcu.gov.br/ojs/index.php/RTCU/article/viewFile/63/327*

TCU ((2013a), Measuring the degree of maturity of public entities in the management of risks, TC 011.745/2012-6, Relatório,Voto e Acórdão 2467/2013 - TCU/Plenário, *http://portal.tcu.gov.br/lumis/portal/file/fileDownload.jsp?inline=1&fileId=8A8182A14D92792C014D928003212A5A*

TCU (2013b), Survey on the governance system focused on implementation of public policies, *https://contas.tcu.gov.br/etcu/AcompanharProcesso?p1=17064&p2=2013&p3=9*

TCU (2013c), Audit of internal controls of university hospitals procurement, *http://www.lexml.gov.br/urn/urn:lex:br:tribunal.contas.uniao;plenario:acordao:2013-06-26;1610*

TCU (2009a), Survey report. Search for information about the performance of the internal control bodies of the three branches: executive, legislative and judicial, *http://www.tcu.gov.br/Consultas/Juris/Docs/judoc/Acord/20090521/025-818-2008-4-AUD-WDO.rtf*

TCU (2009b), Survey report, General Criteria for Internal Control in Public Administration A study of disciplinary models and norms in various countries, *http://portal.tcu.gov.br/lumis/portal/file/fileDownload.jsp?fileId=8A8182A15A4C80AD015A4D5CA9965C37*

TdC (Tribunal de Contas de Portugal) (2011), The internal audit function in the State Owned Enterprises, *www.tcontas.pt/en/reports/audit_report_08-2011-2s_abstract.pdf*

United Nations and the International Organisation of Supreme Audit Institutions (UN-INTOSAI) (2013), A UN-INTOSAI Joint Project: Collection of Important Literature on Strengthening Capacities of Supreme Audit Institutions on the Fight against Corruption, *http://www.intosai.org/fileadmin/downloads/downloads/4_documaents/publications/eng_publications/E_UN_INTOSAI_Joint_Project.pdf*

Veteran Affairs Canada (2014), Audit of Overpayments, *http://www.veterans.gc.ca/pdf/deptReports/2014-audit-of-overpayments.pdf*

Western Australia Office of the Auditor General (2016), "Audit of Payroll and Other Expenditure Using Data Analytic Procedures," May 6, 2016, *https://audit.wa.gov.au/wpcontent/uploads/2016/05/report2016_06-DataAnalytics.pdf.*

Brazil's Federal Court of Accounts
Insight and Foresight for Better Governance

Chapter 5

Auditing for more effective government-wide monitoring and evaluation

Supreme Audit Institutions play a unique role in supporting monitoring and evaluation across government as third-party evaluators of government institutions, processes, policies, programmes as well as by evaluating evaluators within the Executive branch. Brazil's supreme audit institution, the Tribunal de Çontas da União (TCU), has similarly played both roles. This chapter explores the current approaches to evaluation in Brazil's federal administration vis-à-vis international principles and practices at three levels, looking at (i) the system of monitoring and evaluation across government, (ii) monitoring and evaluation at the entity or programme level, and (iii) the communication and co-ordination in improving the culture of monitoring and evaluation. Recommendations are consequently made to TCU as to how it can reorient external control approaches towards supporting more consistent and reliable generation of evidence on policies and programmes in Brazil's federal administration.

5.1. Introduction

Monitoring and evaluation (M&E) involves the systematic collection of evidence on the outcomes of policies and programmes in order to judge their relevance, performance and potential alternatives.[1] It is fundamentally about creating and using evidence to inform decisions and better policy making. M&E is not a process, but a management tool for making informed choices about current and future policies and programmes. The information produced from M&E should feed back into the cycle in order to make it possible to derive whether the implementation mechanisms of public policies are working effectively, efficiently and economically.

A recent and promising effort towards more coherent and comparable government-wide M&E stemmed from the 2016 establishment of the Committee on Monitoring and Evaluation of Federal Public Policies (*Comitê de Monitoramento e Avaliação de Políticas Públicas Federais*, or CMAP) (MP, 2016a; 2016b; 2016c). Given its recent inception, the impact of this Committee on improved M&E is yet to be seen. The effectiveness and objectivity of this Committee could support restoration of citizens' trust in face of increased demands for greater accountability and transparency in recent years. It can also serve to address the various references by domestic and international actors[2] to a need for higher quality information and indicators on government performance in Brazil. In OECD member countries, monitoring of the government programme is a top responsibility of the Centre of Government (CoG). The fulfilment of this role, whether through CMAP or otherwise, will be key to the production and quality of comparable results across the public administration.

Brazil's supreme audit institution, the Tribunal de Contas da União (TCU), is both an evaluator itself of policies and programmes as well as an "evaluator of the evaluators" in government. That is, TCU audits and evaluates the effectiveness of the M&E system and those responsible for it. TCU has historically played a central M&E role from a broader governance perspective in Brazil. Specifically, TCU has conducted audits, produced indices and developed guidance to provide greater accountability for government expenditures and budgetary goals, as well as aid auditors and executive branch managers alike in conducting better M&E. This chapter highlights some of TCU's work related to the M&E governance function in Brazil, and explores opportunities to further enhance its contributions to a more effective M&E system both at the whole-of-government and entity level. The opportunities are grounded in an analysis of some of the key challenges facing the Brazilian government with regards to M&E, bearing in mind international standards and good practices.

5.2. Overview: monitoring and evaluation at the federal level

M&E serves different purposes, including informing budget decision-making, providing information on the actual or likely performance of government programmes and supporting government planning, such as the development of national plans. In addition, M&E can improve the governance by guiding managers' decision making based on evidence of programmes' effectiveness and efficiency (World Bank, 2006). Definitions for M&E vary. Monitoring can be seen as systematic, ongoing collection of data on specified indicators that provide management, and other stakeholders, with an idea on progress towards objectives. Similarly, performance monitoring is a continuous process of collecting and analysing data to compare how well a project, program, or policy is being implemented against expected results (OECD, 2002). Effective monitoring allows governments to change course when problems arise instead of waiting until the end of a programme when public resources have been fully expended.

An evaluation is a systematic and objective assessment of an on-going or completed project, programme or policy, including its design, implementation and results. Evaluations help managers and other stakeholders to determine the relevance and fulfilment of objectives, as well as the efficiency, effectiveness, impact and sustainability of a particular initiative. As discussed in greater detail below, an evaluation should provide information that is credible and useful, enabling the incorporation of lessons learned into the decision-making processes (OECD, 2002).

The underpinning concepts of M&E in Brazil's public administration have evolved from bureaucratic (1980's), to managerial (1990's) to strategic (2000), as shown in Table 5.1 below. This evolution coincided with developments in the type of evaluation or tools used, as well as with the implementation of various initiatives to strengthen M&E in government. For instance, M&E within the Brazilian government, until the 1980s, was primarily limited to the audit function, including financial and compliance audits, until TCU introduced operational (i.e. performance) audits in 1982 (Vaitsman et. al, 2013). Such audits can be seen as a form of evaluation, as they go beyond compliance with laws and regulations and offer insight on the effectiveness, efficiency and economy of a particular policy or programme.

Table 5.1. **Implementation of the evaluation function in Brazil**

Predominant concept of public administration	Type of evaluation	Important events for M&E
1980s Bureaucratic	Operational audits	1970: Evaluation of Graduate Programmes; Accounting audits 1980: Yellow book translated and operational audits begin 1988: Federal Constitution 1991-95: First PPA
1990s Managerial	Managerial monitoring	1995-99: PPA Brazil in Action 1995: State Reform Plan 1998: Decree 2829, 28 Oct 1998 (links programmes and PPA) 2001: SIGPLAN created
2000s Strategic	Strategic evaluation	2000-03: PPA 'Go Brazil' 2004-7: PPA 'Brazil for All' 2004: SAGI created by MDS 2005: GESPÙBLICA 2008-11: PPA 'Development with Social Inclusion' 2009: 'Citizens' Charter' 2012: Access to Information Act 2012-15: PPA 'Brazil without Extreme Poverty'

Source: Adapted from Vaitsman, et. al (2013), *http://dx.doi.org/10.1080/13876988.2015.1110962*

Much of the driving force behind Brazil's M&E initiatives is linked to the PPA and efforts to strengthen performance-based budgeting. From the late 1980s, Brazil organised its budget process and activities around multi-year plans (Plano Plurianual de Acao, or PPAs), the Budgetary Guidelines Law (Lei de Diretrizes Orçamentárias, or LDO) and the Annual Budget Law (Lei Orçamentária Annual, LOA). These mechanisms and the budgetary process helped to institutionalise the evaluation function into the public administration in Brazil. For instance, the LDO refers to M&E, noting that executive branch entities should evaluate compliance with quarterly fiscal targets. The current PPA (2016-2019), in particular, intends to translate the government agenda into practical steps for implementation, including responsible actors and indicators for evaluations.

Responsibility for Brazil's evaluation function is shared between various entities that are both internal and external to the policy or programme being evaluated. The M&E system is meant to unfold on three levels, whereby the first evaluation is undertaken by programme management, the second by the sectoral ministry in verifying the entire programme, and the third by the Ministry of Planning, Development and Management *(Ministério do Planejamento, Desenvolvimento e Gestão,* MP) in taking an evaluation of the whole plan (World Bank, 2006). The MP is designated in Decree No 6,601 (2008) as the central body responsible for co-ordinating the M&E processes related to the PPA, as well as provide methodological guidance and technical support for line ministries and their M&E units (Government of Brazil, 2008a). In addition, the Institute for Applied Economic Research (IPEA), a public foundation affiliated with the MP, provides technical and institutional support for the Brazilian government, including a publication on planning and evaluating public policies in Brazil. This publication represents an excellent resource for TCU to bolster its audits with research, logic models and other tools to analyse the effectiveness of M&E of government programs (IPEA 2015).

Trends towards a results-based M&E system and performance-based budgeting have been coupled with increasing expectations on central entities or the CoG to understand what is happening across government. One of the top four responsibilities of CoG institutions in OECD member countries is in monitoring the implementation of the government programme – with cross-cutting programmes on the rise (OECD, 2014a). As part of their responsibility in communicating results and providing accountability, good practice in the CoG includes ensuring that cross-governmental standards exist for reporting and explaining information about policies and results (IADB, 2014).

In Brazil, the MP provides some level of centralisation, but self-evaluation remains a core principle of M&E in the Brazilian government. Units within line ministries have the responsibility for designing and conducting evaluations themselves (Government of Brazil, 2001). These efforts are often linked to specific programs or initiatives. For instance, the Ministry of Social Development and the Fight Against Poverty (Ministério de Desenvolvimento Social e Combate à Fome) evaluates social policies and programs. The Secretariat of Evaluation and Information Management (Secretaria de Avaliação e Gestão da Informação, SAGI) also conducts M&E activities related to key social development policies and programmes. Brazil conducts evaluations on a predominantly annual basis, but sectoral or multi-annual goals of PPA may be evaluated over a longer time horizon, such as those specifying M&E in sectoral plans like the National Education Plan (PNE).

In addition, the federal government established in April 2016 the CMAP to "improve public policies, programmes and actions, as well as the application of resources and quality of public spending" (Article 1) (Brazil, 2016). This inter-ministerial initiative groups together key CoG institutions: Ministry of Planning, Development and Management *(Ministério do Planejamento, Desenvolvimento e Gestão, MP)*, Ministry of Finance *(Ministério da Fazenda, MF)*, Ministry of Transparency *(Ministério da Transparência, Fiscalização e Controladoria-Geral da União,* CGU) and the Office of the President of Brazil *(Casa Civil)* (MP, 2016a; 2016b; 2016c). In looking to cross-cutting policies and programmes, the first initiative of CMAP was to evaluate social programmes – for instance, looking at the presence of fraud in Bolsa Familia (Veja, 2016).

For the achievement of its objectives, the CMAP can: select and propose the guidelines for the M&E of selected policies, programmes or initiatives for evaluation (Article 3); establish thematic commissions for M&E (Article 3); request information and opening of databases used for M&E, save for instances of financial secrecy (article 5); propose Guidelines to entities responsible for M&E to facilitate its work (Article 6). Article 7 stipulates that the activities of the CMAP do not replace the M&E activities that are developed at the entity and programme level (MP, 2016a; 2016b; 2016c). The clarification of interaction between the central and entity level will be important, given that Brazil's M&E system has traditionally been based on entities' self-evaluation (World Bank, 2006). The CMAP initiative is the latest in the evolution of Brazil's M&E system, and appears to be a diversion from the historical tie of M&E to the budget.

TCU is a key M&E actor in Brazil through the fulfilment of its mandate to examine government accounts and to perform supervision and audit of an accounting, financial, budgetary, operational and patrimonial nature (Constitution, article 71). Its accountability function is part of a wider network of other constitutionally appointed bodies, such as the Office of the Comptroller General (Controladoria-Geral da União, or CGU), and in conjunction with constitutional mechanisms that allow for citizen engagement and feedback on programmes and services. Civil society and coordination mechanisms also play a part in strengthening M&E in Brazil. Brazil's M&E Network (Rede Bra-sileira de Monitoramento e Avaliação), a chapter of the broader Latin American and Caribbean (LAC) Monitoring and Evaluation Network established by the World Bank and the Inter-American Development Bank (IDB), promotes dialogue between various M&E actors, including the Parliament and civil society organisations. The Network functions as a community of practice for M&E practitioners and knowledge-sharing, particularly through the use of a collaborative online platform (Rede Brasileira, 2016). Like audits, which can have a coercive effect on government entities, such efforts can help to promote coherence and effective M&E through the institutionalisation of standards and good practices. Moreover, ombudsmen provide an important avenue for civil society to provide feedback and submit complaints related to government programmes and services.

Through their audit and advisory work, supreme audit institutions (SAIs) like TCU are helping executive branch entities to improve the design and implementation of M&E policies and practices at the whole-of-government level and the entity level. Their audits, reviews and advisory work can provide government entities and policy makers with evidence about which policies and programmes are working, and why. For instance, in an OECD survey of 10 SAIs, 7 of 10 had assessed; the existence of a reasoned evaluation programme in each ministry, including: the mechanisms for ensuring reliable, quality, auditable financial and non-financial performance information; mechanisms for integrating performance information in objectives; coherence between objectives, outcomes and government vision (OECD, 2016a).

In addition, SAIs conduct evaluations themselves, and their work can contribute to solutions for different challenges that governments face in evaluating results. OECD's 2016 report, *Supreme Audit Institutions and Good Governance: Oversight, Insight and Foresight*, highlights good practices and government trends in M&E, and provides good examples of the various ways in which SAIs are helping to improve this function within government (OECD, 2016a). This work underpins the recommendations below. TCU's current strategic plan assigns objective 8 to encourage the monitoring and evaluation of performance by the Public Administration. The strategic plan highlights the need for TCU to contribute to the capacity of entities, and encourage the production and dissemination of objectives, targets and performance indicators that support decision-making processes (TCU, 2015a).

The following recommendations provide nuanced ways in which TCU can achieve its own strategic objectives and can support the federal government in reaching international good governance principles in M&E, such as (OECD, 2016a):

- Evidence-based decision-making through improved M&E systems at the whole-of-government level;
- Results-based management through reasoned evaluation at the programme and entity level;
- Greater information sharing for transparency;

OECD's recommendations, and expected outcomes, are provided in Table 5.2.

Table 5.2. **Recommendations: Auditing for more effective government-wide monitoring and evaluation (M&E)**

TCU could strengthen the effectiveness of M&E across government by further emphasising the role of the Centre of Government (CoG) and the need to further standardise results-based management.
• TCU could conduct periodic evaluations of government-wide M&E policies and mechanisms, putting greater emphasis on the CoG's ability to foster more consistent, results-based management and M&E of cross-cutting initiatives.
• TCU could strengthen efforts to assess the extent and effectiveness of entities in using M&E results for decision making.
TCU could help entities to improve institutional and programme evaluations by auditing their readiness, capacity and indicators to manage for results.
• 2.A. TCU could periodically conduct readiness assessments of selected entities to evaluate their effectiveness and maturity of M&E and their culture of results-based management.
• 2.B. TCU could strengthen reviews of entity and programme results, particularly indicators, for assessing their value for decision making and achieving medium to long-term goals.
TCU could assess the communication and coordination mechanisms, including interoperability of information and data systems, to improve M&E of cross-cutting government policies and programmes.

5.3. Emphasising the role of the Centre of Government in strengthening M&E systems from a government-wide perspective

TCU could strengthen the effectiveness of M&E across government by further emphasising the role of the Centre of Government and the need to further standardise results-based management.

Brazil's evaluation function is shared between various entities that are both internal and external to the policy or programme being evaluated. The current M&E system in Brazil is decentralised. The MP provides some level of co-ordination and centralisation, yet units within line ministries retain the responsibility for designing and conducting evaluations (Government of Brazil, 2001). Moreover, government-wide M&E policies are evolving, but efforts made be ad-hoc or vary by sectors as well as across states (Rosenstein, 2015). The 2016 establishment of CMAP involving central government entities (MP, CGU and Casa Civil) may help to systematize M&E across government.

The variance in approaches in M&E has implications for standardisation and institutionalisation of M&E practices, as well as comparability of results. On the one hand, the flexibility afforded to units and line ministries is important to ensure that results generated from M&E are tailored enough to speak to the successes and failures of particular initiatives. On the other hand, standardisation and institutionalisation of M&E across government has a myriad of benefits, including comparability of government performance and safeguarding initiatives against undue influence. Indeed, political sensitivities and special interests can undermine robust M&E systems, since underperforming or failed initiatives can tarnish reputations of politicians or high-level officials. In such circumstances, incentives for deemphasising potential problems or minimising publicity of failures could result in indicators that are unreliable, as well as inaccurate assessments that convey overly positive results.

As mentioned above, the evaluation of M&E in Brazil has largely been linked to the PPA and efforts to strengthen performance-based budgeting. In 2010, the Brazilian government published a decree (N° 7.133) that established guidelines, general criteria and procedures for reviewing individual and institutional performance (Chamber of Deputies, 2010). The decree notes that institutional performance evaluations aim to assess organisational goals and targets in line with the PPA, the LDO and LOA (Chamber of Deputies, 2010). It refers to both "global" and "intermediate" targets. The decree provides some general guidelines for conducting evaluations and using their results, such as the need for using objective criteria and publishing results, yet key M&E practices and concepts are not readily apparent or explicit as a framework. Moreover, much of the discussion about M&E in the decree is discussed in the context of individual performance (as opposed to institutional) in the context of performance-based remuneration of government employees.

Brazil's central institutions have made some efforts to streamline M&E standards that are results-based and that are not directly linked to the PPA. MP has provided guidance for executive branch managers to assist in M&E, and the Secretary for Public Management (Secretaria de Gestão Pública, or SEGEP) issued a performance evaluation manual to promote the use of performance management as a tool for driving improvements. For instance, in 2013, the MP recognised that evaluating performance and results is largely done upstream in the policy formulation process. In response, the Secretary for Public Management (Secretaria de Gestão Pública, or SEGEP) issued a manual to promote the use of performance management as a tool for driving continuous improvement in results. The manual aims to provide guidance to public sector management, public servants and employees of entities in the Federal Public Administration, among others, on how to operationalise performance evaluation (MP, 2013).[3]

Brazil's CoG entities could continue to promote the institutionalisation and standardization of M&E as a concept that is broader than performance-based budgeting. The CMAP initiative intends to serve this purpose. To further promote broader applications of M&E, guidance issued by CMAP (in accordance with article 6) or through other initiatives could better communicate the importance of conducting and using M&E to (i) better support government planning, (ii) to help ongoing management of government programmes and activities and (iii) to underpin accountability (World Bank, 2006). Amongst OECD member countries, monitoring progress of reforms is one of the top four priorities of the CoG. This role of the CoG means developing new mechanisms that emphasises outcomes rather than just tracking expenditures. Another key role of the CoG is in strategic planning and steering of the government programme in areas that extent beyond the budgeting process. Indeed, international good governance principles promote that such national steering and planning is evidence-based, integrating findings from M&E processes, foresight activities and stakeholder consultation (OECD, 2016a; 2014a).

The decentralised M&E system in Brazil also has implications for the evaluation of cross-cutting programs that serve national goals. CoGs require reliable evidence on performance across government that allows for some degree of comparability of results from manager and entity level evaluations. Regarding cross-cutting initiatives where multiple ministries or actors are involved, a central entity or lead ministry needs the capacity to co-ordinate and evaluate. In Brazil, lead or sectoral ministries may be responsible for oversight of particular cross-cutting programmes, as is done in other OECD member countries. However, until the establishment of CMAP, a single entity with the sole responsibility for monitoring or evaluating cross-cutting goals did not exist. The entities that comprise the CMAP – MP, MF, CGU and Casa Civil – are now mandated with the evaluation and assessment of cross-cutting policies, namely in the social area. If CMAP is effective in carrying out its mandate, it can provide a horizontal view on the performance of key, select, government-wide initiatives that was previously lacking. Such information if reliable and of quality could be used to inform decision-making at the CoG.

In view of cross-cutting initiatives, and interrelated policy goals such as those included in the Sustainable Development Goals (SDGs), Brazil could continue to develop its national, government-wide view of M&E, considering opportunities to develop guidance that goes beyond the PPA and builds on existing guidelines for institutional performance evaluation. A national view would bear in mind coherence between different approaches to M&E, the fluidity of information flows and the utility value of open data and information for policy makers related to cross-cutting initiatives, in particular. This government-wide view is particularly relevant in the coming years, as the government improves and creates national policies and programmes to achieve the SDGs, particularly SDG 14 on data gathering and monitoring (SDG 14).

What can TCU do to enhance its contributions to improved M&E system at the government-wide level? SAIs, like TCU, are assessing the effectiveness and efficiency of government wide evaluation systems. TCU can use its existing audits and frameworks, and orient future work, to support a more systematic, results-based M&E system across government. More specifically, TCU could more systematically support M&E across government by taking the following actions:

- TCU could conduct periodic evaluations of government-wide M&E mechanisms and policies, putting emphasis on the CoG's ability to foster more consistent, results-based management and M&E of cross-cutting initiatives; and
- TCU could assess the use of entity and programme results for decision-making across government.

TCU could conduct periodic evaluations of government-wide M&E policies and mechanisms, putting greater emphasis on the CoG's ability to foster more consistent, results-based management and M&E of cross-cutting initiatives.

In an OECD survey of ten SAIs, seven had assessed the following particular elements of the entire system: the mechanisms for ensuring reliable, quality, auditable financial and non-financial performance information; mechanisms for integrating government-wide monitoring and evaluation with strategic planning; alignment with international good practices; and alignment with key national indicators (OECD, 2016a). Given the historical linkages between the PPA and M&E in Brazil, much of TCU's work that touches upon M&E has necessarily done so in the context of evaluations and audits of budgetary processes and related budgetary policies and guidelines. For instance, the "Survey of monitoring and evaluation systems in the direct administration" aimed to characterize to what extent M&E practices are institutionalized. TCU analysed in detail the M&E of the Multi-Year Plan (the PPA) and the Identified Evaluation Systems in Sectoral Bodies (TCU, 2011).

TCU has also conducted audits related to the policy formulation stage and the MP as the central co-ordinator of M&E. In one example, TCU's "Audit of government evaluation maturity indexes" assessed the maturity index used for evaluation of government's programs in the direct administration of the Federal Executive (TCU, 2014b). TCU also contributes to more effective M&E in government at the entity level by "evaluating the evaluators." For instance, TCU undertook a regulatory governance review of Infrastructure Regulatory Agencies, and assessed the maturity of the decision making processes in the energy, communication and transport regulatory agencies. This review included verification of the independence of directors, management of conflict of interest and transparency in decision-making (TCU, 2015b). Another example of TCU evaluating the evaluators is its review of supervision policies of the Central Bank, and identifying priority areas in a range of areas, from governance to internal controls (TCU, 2015c).

These examples demonstrate that TCU has taken a systemic view on the functioning of M&E that goes beyond assessment of the M&E in the budget context and at the entity or programme level. This is consistent with TCU's explicit recognition of M&E as a key function of policy-making, demonstrated in TCU's *Framework to Assess Public Policies* (TCU, 2014a) and *the Framework on Centre of Government* (TCU, 2016a). The latter focuses on the role of central institutions in key functions. It provides key questions on the role of CoG in M&E for audit teams to consider. For instance, it asks—how is the role of monitoring of policy implementation and evaluation of government performance exercised, taking into account the coherence in the actions of government?—to verify (i) if there is a Central Government organ responsible for monitoring policy priorities of government, (ii) if monitoring is done in order to ensure consistency between actions from the government, and (iii) if monitoring efforts prioritize the commitments in the plan of the government (TCU, 2016a).

The principles reflected in TCU's existing Frameworks provide beneficial guidance for auditors, but TCU could make a greater emphasis in consistently and systematically applying them in its audits as criteria. Doing so will help to ensure that M&E is considered not only at the entity level, but also at the whole-of-government level. In addition, TCU could conduct periodic audits of cross-cutting M&E policies, focusing on the CMAP as its activities evolve to strengthen consistent government-wide M&E. Specifically, TCU could complement its existing frameworks with more criteria for directly assessing the responsibilities and capacity of the CoG in co-ordinating and overseeing M&E rollout across government, as well as to improve their own evaluation of cross-cutting programmes. Example questions below are inspired by the key themes that the UK's National Audit Office (2014) uncovered in its audits of the CoG. Such questions could help TCU to focus its audits on the CoG's role, capacity and effectiveness of its policies and mechanisms, including (NAO 2014):

- Does the centre have a clear vision for how government should operate and is it demonstrating the leadership required to achieve that?
- What are the roles and responsibilities of central entities in the M&E system in law, and how are they being fulfilled in practice?

- How well does the centre incentivise departments to act in ways that promote overall government effectiveness?
- How well does the centre incentivise departments to conduct rigorous and objective M&E?
- What constraints do central institutions have in providing effective co-ordination, guidance and oversight in M&E?
- Does a policy basis exist to incentivise coordination and communication across entities with regards to the results of M&E?
- To what extent, if at all, are M&E policies fragmented, overlapping or duplicated? To what degree, if at all, do they cause confusion or clarification for entities and programme managers about their responsibilities in M&E?

The questions above can inform research objectives and criteria to aid TCU in strengthening M&E across government by promoting consistency of M&E activities. Systematic application of such criteria can lead to more consistent results on performance across government. In addition, through a greater emphasis on government-wide M&E, TCU could help the CMAP to identify ways to foster more comparable results from entities that extend beyond performance-based budgeting, considering other applications of M&E. TCU could do this by honing new audits towards the role of the CoG in formulating M&E policies, and synthesising key findings from existing work to inform the CoG's understanding about areas for improvement to standardise and institutionalise M&E. TCU could also assess the CoG for its role in monitoring progress with reforms and ensuring departmental work plans reflect government-wide strategic priorities.

TCU could strengthen efforts to assess the extent and effectiveness of entities in using M&E results for decision making.

Effective M&E helps to ensure that at the central, entity and programme level, that decisions, trade-offs, policies and programmes are balanced and evidence-based (OECD, 2016a). It enables all actors to understand where gains can be made in efficiency, effectiveness and economy. This is particular important in times of fiscal consolidation. Moreover, central government entities, like those that make up CMAP, require reliable, objective and comparable information in order to monitor the implementation of government priorities. The emphasis that the CoG itself, or lead ministry of a cross-cutting initiative, places on gathering quality results will shape the M&E behaviour of entities and programme managers.

TCU's approach to assessing M&E as a key function of government has included analysis of the use of results. TCU's *Framework to Assess Public Policies* (TCU, 2014a) proposes that audit teams assess the extent to which "the monitoring system and evaluation of public policy is properly structured to produce information in order provide feedback to the decision-making processes in order to foster learning and improvement of actions to achieve results?" Supporting questions include the following:

- Is there is clear definition of communication flows of evaluative information to promote timely feedback under the public policy cycle?
- Is there sufficient, reliable and relevant data availability to support performance reporting policy?
- Does the M&E system policy have processes, procedures and sufficient resources (e.g. financial, people, and structures) to ensure that M&E activities provide reliable information, timely and necessary for decision making?

Further, in 2013, TCU conducted an audit of 27 Federal agencies to assess the maturity of M&E systems across government. The maturity index (iSA-Gov) quantified the level of institutionalisation of systems, looking at four elements: (1) demands for evaluation, (2) production of 'evaluative knowledge,' (results), (3) organizational learning capacity and (4) the use of 'evaluative knowledge' (results). Managers that responded to the survey considered themselves as having a high capacity to use results (TCU, 2013). While the iSA-Gov tool found that use of evaluative knowledge was, on average, "present, sufficient and satisfactory to meet the needs of the actors," other audits of TCU suggest room for improvement in this area – particularly in the use of performance information for budgeting, which is covered in more detail in chapter 3.

TCU could emphasis this aspect of M&E—the polices and mechanisms for using results from M&E inn decision making. On way TCU could do this is to build on its iSA-Gov tool to focus specifically on the use performance or evaluative information. GAO's body of work on "Managing for Results" and its "use of performance information index" could aid TCU in this effort. GAO developed this index to communicate the use of performance information of a random sample of mid-level and upper-level managers and supervisors at 24 federal Agencies, comparing results of survey waves in 2007 and 2013 (GAO, 2014). The set of survey questions that GAO used to develop the index are shown in Figure 5.1

Figure 5.1. **Questions from GAO's 2013 Managers Survey Used to Develop the 'Use of Performance Information Index'**

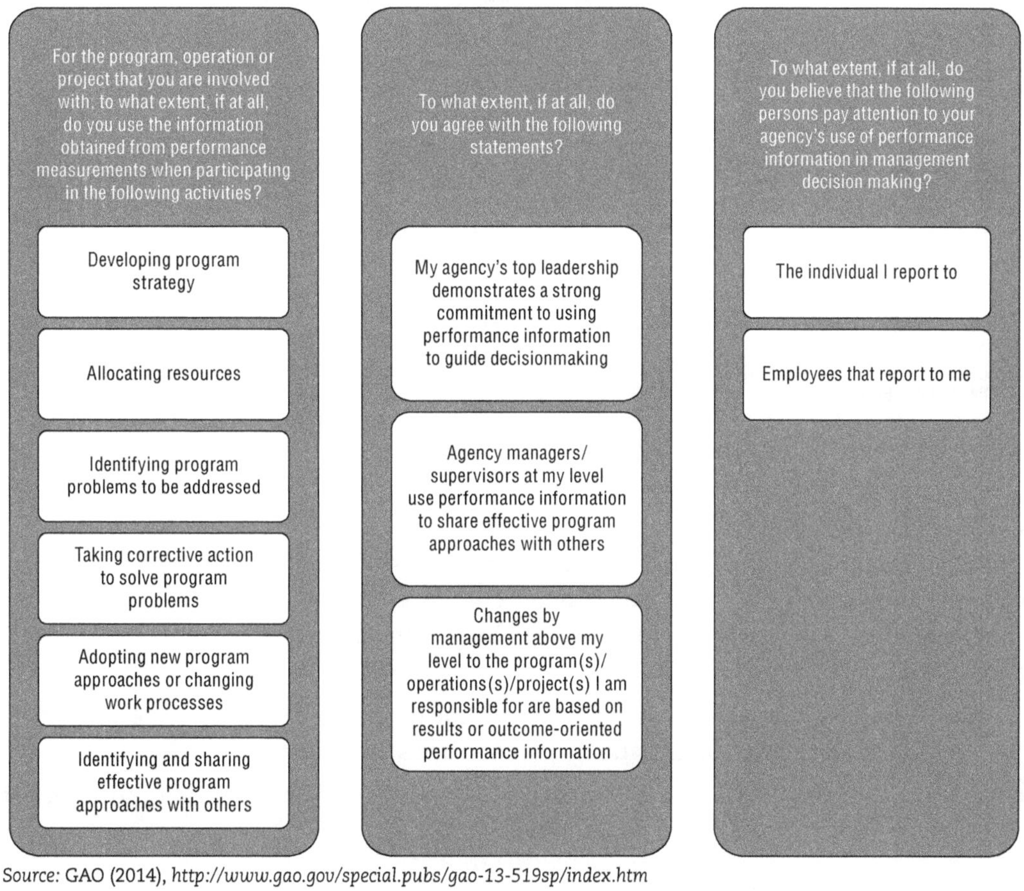

Source: GAO (2014), *http://www.gao.gov/special.pubs/gao-13-519sp/index.htm*

To better understand which factors influenced how an agency scored in the index, the 2013 survey questions were mapped against leading practices that can enhance or facilitate the use of performance information for management decision making. These leading practices were developed by GAO through prior work, including:

- Demonstrating management commitment;
- Aligning agency-wide goals, objectives and measures;
- Improving the usefulness of performance information;
- Developing the capacity to use performance information; and
- Communicating performance information frequently and efficiently.

Using its index, the GAO was able to comment on increases and reductions in use of performance information by entity and government-wide, offering a comparative perspective. TCU could replicate such an average on a new, more in-depth index that could be compared and reported on in conjunction with iSA-Gov findings. By generating an average for the whole-of-government, TCU can focus on elevating these findings to top decision makers or responsible bodies – for instance the MP in Brazil, or for the Congress meant to hold Executive to account. TCU could take such an index a step further, and generate an average of CoG entities' use of results, as shown in Figure 5.2 below.

Figure 5.2. **Federal Agencies' Average Scores on Use of Performance Information Index – 2007 and 2013**

Agency	2007 average score	2013 average score	Statistically significant increase or decrease between 2007 and 2013
Government-wide	3.46	3.41	▼
Office of Personnel Management	3.38	3.66	△
Department of Labor	3.37	3.58	△
Department of Veterans Affairs	3.71	3.49	▼
National Aeronautics and Space Administration	3.71	3.49	▼
Departent of Energy	3.52	3.34	▼
Nuclear Regulatory Commission	3.70	3.32	▼

Source: GAO (2014), *http://www.gao.gov/special.pubs/gao-13-519sp/index.htm*

Furthermore, to strengthen the focus of such an index on the CoG, TCU could consider integrating questions that are directed to the CoG's own awareness and use of information. TCU may be further inspired by the questions below from the U.K. NAO (NAO 2014):

- Does the centre have a comprehensive view of the cross-government picture, supported by reliable management information, to inform decision-making?
- Does the centre have adequate information to monitor the implementation of government priorities?

5.4. Auditing readiness, capacity and indicators for more effective M&E and results-based management

TCU could induce improvements in institutional and programme evaluations by auditing entities' readiness, capacity and indicators to manage for results.

International indicators suggest the Brazilian government has consistently demonstrated an ability to learn from its experiences through M&E (Bertelsmann Stiftung, 2016a). In particular, the Bertelsmann Stiftung's Transformation Index (BTI) gave the Brazilian government a score of at least 7 out of 10 in each of its past 6 assessments of "Steering Capability" (Bertelsmann Stiftung, 2016a). This element of the BTI includes an indicator for "Policy Learning," meaning the ability of government to learn and innovate through effective M&E, observation and knowledge exchange, as well as consultancy by experts and practitioners (Bertelsmann Stiftung, 2016b). The BTI reflects more than M&E, as it focuses on broader learning aspects of government. Nonetheless, the indicator can help to broadly illustrate the Brazilian government's recognition of and commitment to developing more effective M&E in the last decade.

While the BTI offers a general view that is positive, TCU's aforementioned 2014 "iSA-Gov" Maturity Index sheds light on the complexity and divergence in M&E across Brazil's federal administration. The Index quantified the level of institutionalisation of systems for monitoring and evaluating the performance and results of policies and programmes. The maturity level of the government programme evaluation systems, iSA-Gov, expressed public managers' perception of the adequacy of the mechanisms and instruments employed to demand, produce and use the available evaluative knowledge. On the one hand, managers in the 27 Ministries surveyed perceived having a high organizational learning capacity – higher than other elements of the study. On the other hand, managers identified being less developed in the production of evaluative knowledge, or results (TCU, 2014b). The report conveyed various findings about the maturity of M&E in selected Brazilian institutions, such as the maturity of the M&E system increased with budgets and that high turnover could affect the development of internal evaluation capacity.

The decentralised nature of M&E in Brazil is driven by self-evaluation, allowing individual entities to focus on their own priorities when conducting evaluations. In addition, ministries can create their own data systems and indicators. Yet, these activities require skills, time and resources, which can vary across entities and will therefore affect the M&E system as a whole. A lack of capacity can lead to a number of issues. For instance, as discussed later in this chapter, indicators are often not aligned with the policy or programme objectives, making it difficult for internal or external actors, including TCU, to assess. In addition, some government entities commission external parties to conduct evaluations. This practice may lead to more robust and reliable evaluations, it raises questions about the capacity within public entities to carry out evaluations.

Evidence shows that managers and entities struggle with certain stages of M&E more than others. TCU could aid executive branch entities in strengthening M&E by providing more evidence on the current "condition" of M&E across government and the capacity needs of those required to conduct M&E. Doing so will help to ensure that M&E is not seen as a compliance exercise. Indeed, if evaluation happens as a compliance-based exercise, or is geared towards broadening the programme budget in future years, it may not lead to meaningful improvements. In supporting entities to improve institutional and programme evaluations, TCU could consider the following recommendations:

- TCU could periodically conduct readiness assessments of selected entities to evaluate their effectiveness and maturity of M&E and their culture of results-based management; and
- TCU could strengthen reviews of entity and programme results, particularly indicators, for assessing their value for decision making and achieving medium to long-term goals.

TCU could periodically conduct readiness assessments of selected entities to evaluate their effectiveness and maturity of M&E and their culture of results-based management.

TCU's own findings highlight the need for increased understanding of what works in M&E in Brazilian government entities. Periodic reviews of the "readiness" of government entities to conduct M&E could help audited entities to establish a baseline for improving M&E activities. Assessing the readiness of an entity with regards to M&E is not just about evaluating policies, processes, procedures and structures, but it also involves understanding behaviours, incentives and the political economy within an entity. The following questions, some of which are elaborated on in subsequent sections, could provide a framework for conducting such assessments (adapted from Kusek et al., 2004):

- What are the pressures and incentives that are encouraging, or discouraging, M&E in the entity, and why?
- Who is the M&E advocate or champion within the entity, and what is his or her motivation for supporting it?
- Who are the owners of M&E within the entity and what are their incentives, or disincentives, for conducting robust M&E?
- How much information or data is enough for making informed decisions, without collecting too much?
- What is the anticipated reaction to negative information or findings from the M&E efforts?
- Where and what kind of capacity is there to support M&E in the entity?
- How will the M&E and its results link to broader goals and objectives, such as national goals?

TCU could also look to the GAO's "use of performance information index", discussed above, which delineates the findings by level of management group. TCU could apply this approach to the assessment of entity or managers' readiness for M&E, in order to pinpoint where needs are highest and thus where central agencies responsible for providing guidance should focus their attention. Canada's Office of the Auditor General (OAG) may offer additional insights for TCU in conducting such assessments. Specifically, the OAG conducted a series of audits that looked at whether government entities' evaluation units identified and responded to the various needs for effectiveness evaluations, and whether they had built the required capacity to respond to those needs. By including the Treasury Board Secretariat as a CoG entity in the scope of the audit, this evaluation also works to promote a culture of results-based management across government. The box below provides the criteria for analysis and the key findings of the audit (OAG, 2013 in OECD, 2016a).

Box 5.1. **The Auditor General of Canada**

From the period of 2004-2009, with a follow-up in 2013, the Office of the Auditor General in Canada (OAG) assessed the evaluation units of six government departments. Additionally, the audit assessed the oversight and support role of the Treasury Board of Canada Secretariat in monitoring and improving the evaluation function in government, particularly in regard to effectiveness evaluations (OAG, 2009). OAG used ten guiding expectations from various sources such as laws and policies as the criteria for their audit. The following audit criteria could guide TCU's own audit for effectiveness of evaluation units:

- 'We expected that departments could demonstrate that programme evaluation plans take appropriate account of needs for effectiveness evaluation.'
- 'We expected that departments could demonstrate that they have acted on programme evaluation plans to meet key needs.'
- 'We expected that departments could demonstrate that their effectiveness evaluations appropriately meet identified needs.'
- 'We expected that departments could demonstrate that they regularly identify and act on required improvements in meeting needs for effectiveness evaluation.'
- 'We expected that departments could demonstrate reasonable efforts to ensure sufficient qualified evaluation staff to meet key needs for effectiveness evaluation.'
- 'We expected departments could demonstrate that the amount and the time frame of funding for effectiveness evaluation meet key needs.'
- 'We expected that departments could demonstrate that evaluators have sufficient independence from programme managers and that their objectivity is not hindered.'
- 'We expected that departments could demonstrate that they regularly identify and act on required improvements to capacity to meet needs for effectiveness evaluation.'
- 'We expected that the Treasury Board of Canada Secretariat has the resources required for government-wide oversight of the programme evaluation function.'
- 'We expected that the Treasury Board of Canada Secretariat could support the practice of government-wide evaluation by identifying needed improvements and determining and carrying out actions required of the Secretariat to help ensure that departments and agencies have the tools they need to achieve the desired results.' (OAG, 2009).

The audit found that while the six departments examined followed systematic processes to plan their effectiveness evaluations, and completed most of the evaluations they had planned; their evaluations covered a low proportion of total programme expenses. Additionally, the audit found the departments in many cases had not gathered the performance information necessary to adequately assess effectiveness of evaluation (OECD, 2016a).

By including the Treasury Board Secretariat in the scope of the audit, this evaluation also works to promote a culture of risk based management across government. One of the listed objectives of the audit was to 'Determine whether the Treasury Board of Canada Secretariat's government-wide oversight of the programme evaluation function has regularly identified and addressed areas for improvement that ensure that departments have the capacity to meet needs for effectiveness evaluation' (OAG, 2009). Through ensuring the adequacy of this oversight function for effectiveness evaluation, the audit has a far greater reach than simply assessing the six departments. Enhancing the oversight function to provide a kind of sustained

Box 5.1. **The Auditor General of Canada** *(cont.)*

support of government entities will more systematically promote a culture of risk management than auditing and recommending entities individually. In this case, the Treasury Board did introduce initiatives to address the need for improvements in evaluation across government, however, it did not provide sustained support for effectiveness evaluation. Particularly, there was not enough progress on developing tools to assist departments with the long-standing problem of lack of sufficient data for evaluating programme effectiveness.

Source: OAG (Office of the Auditor General of Canada) (2013), Spring 2013 Report, Status Report on Evaluating the Effectiveness of Programs, accessed February 2017, *www.oag-bvg.gc.ca/internet/English/parl_oag_201304_01_e_38186.html*; OAG (2009), Fall 2009 Report, Chapter 1, Evaluating the Effectiveness of Programs, accessed February 2017, *www.oag-bvg.gc.ca/internet/English/parl_oag_200911_01_e_33202.html*; OECD (2016a), Supreme Audit Institution and Good Governance: Oversight, Insight and Foresight, OECD Publishers, Paris, *http://www.oecd.org/gov/ethics/supreme-audit-institutions-and-good-governance.htm*.

TCU could strengthen reviews of entity and programme results, particularly indicators, for assessing their value for decision making and achieving medium to long-term goals.

A key element of evaluating for improved performance in government is that evaluation enables reliable, measured performance-related information to be fed into decision-making processes (OECD, 2016). High quality or high-value performance information is a precursor to managing by results. TCU's work has embodied this principle and has sought to promote improved quality of performance information. Further, international principles require that "an effective system of oversight provides an assurance on the reliability and quality of disclosed information" (OECD, 2016a). As a key oversight body, TCU is responsible for providing this assurance. It is also reliant to a degree on the quality of performance information of auditees, as it impacts TCU's own ability to evaluate performance in executing its mandate.

In playing the role of evaluator itself, or auditor, as well as evaluator of evaluators, TCU has sought to promote higher quality performance information and data. It should continue to do so, given that its work has shown that public managers struggle most with actually producing evaluative knowledge, let alone high-quality knowledge that is valuable for decision-making. As discussed, this depends largely on the capacity and skills to measure impact and outcomes and not just inputs or outputs. It also requires an awareness of which tools are suitable to the purpose.

It can be useful, at the outset, to have a general framework with the core elements that constitute the foundation of M&E, whether applied to performance-budgeting and programme evaluation alike. One such general framework, as illustrated in igure 5.3, depicts *impacts* and *outcomes* (both intermediate and final) as the result of *activities* that convert *inputs* to *outputs* (Zewo, 2011). The definitions for each of elements can vary. For example, the Institute for Applied Economic Research presents a similar logic model, including an intermediate outcome, but the principles are similar. In addition, the importance of contextual factors, such as culture and institutional arrangements, is often stressed in theory and practice related to results-based M&E.

Selection of M&E tools. Creating a robust M&E function at a ministry or programme level requires a number of methodological decisions, including determining the type of evaluation to conduct and when. The choice of assessment types depends on what is being measured. Table 5.3 provides examples of ex ante and ex post evaluations that entities can employ depending on the purpose of the assessment.

Figure 5.3. **Logic Model - Building blocks of resulted-based M&E**

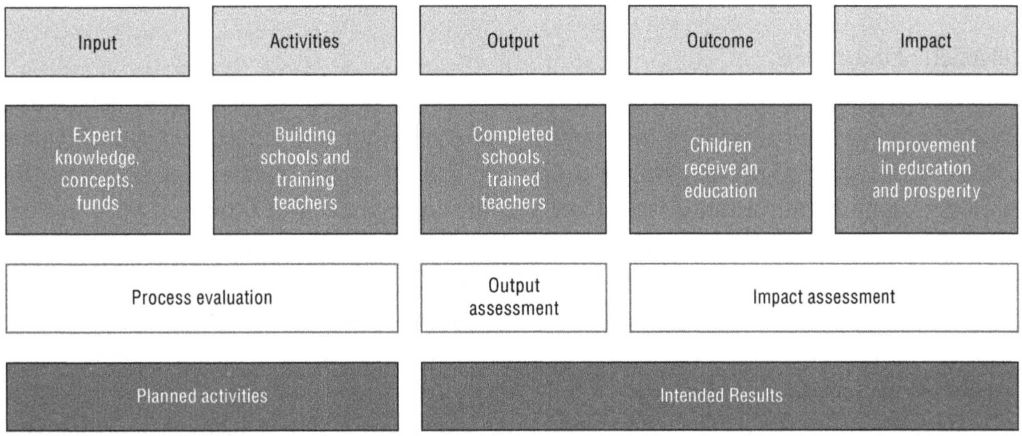

Source: Zewo Foundation (2011), Outcome and Impact Assessment in International Development: Short presentation of the Zewo guidelines for projects and programmes, *http://impact.zewo.ch/english/docs/Zewo_Wirkungsmessung_E_web.pdf*

Table 5.3. **Tools for ex ante and ex post evaluation**

EX ANTE	Description
Regulatory impact assessment	Assesses the impacts of future laws and regulations against a range of intended effects (economic, costs of regulation, impacts on inclusive growth related objectives are unevenly integrated).
Budget Impacts	Typical assessment of the cost of future programmes or policy measures. Often focuses on the strict public finance implications. This can include *ex ante* audit/authorization for programmes.
Modelling/Scenarios/Gaps analysis	A range of analytical techniques are used in the academia, think tanks or in the public sector to assess policy impacts.
Advisory committee	In-depth, consultative reports from authoritative bodies, such as Inquiry Commissions (Sweden), Productivity commission (Australia)
EX POST	**Description**
Performance (or VFM)	Targeted review, typically carried out by an internal or external audit institution, to assess whether objectives are being achieved, and/or with what levels of efficiency and effectiveness.
Programme evaluation	In-depth evaluation of a specific programme, by reference to original rationale, and effectiveness in achieving objectives, cost of delivery, alternative modalities and saving/ efficiency options.
Focused policy assessment	Short, sharp evaluation focused on one or more of the criteria used in programme evaluation. Often part of a spending review.
Spending review	Large-scale re-assessment of the disposition of resources within a sector of public expenditure by reference to new priorities and effectiveness in meeting objectives. Used to identify 'fiscal space.'

Source: OECD (2015), Session Notes, OECD's Public Governance Ministerial Meeting, 28 October 2015, *http://www.oecd.org/governance/ministerial/session-notes-helsinki.pdf*

In Brazil, executive branch entities are required to provide the MP with bimonthly and quarterly reports as part of the annual accounts process. These reports are primarily focused on assessments of compliance with fiscal rules, as well as deviations from planned expenditures. As such, they are not intended for discerning the impacts of individual programmes and policies throughout a given year.[4] The importance of accounts reporting for the budgetary process is discussed further in chapter 3. In the context of programme evaluation, TCU plays a critical role in strengthening M&E in Brazil by incentivising the use of a wider variety of evaluation tools for analysis. In other words, TCU can use its audit recommendations to encourage more robust results-based management and evaluation in entities that would otherwise be tempted to focus on compliance assessments.

Selection of indicators.

Once the methodological framework and tool or type of evaluation is selected, a variety of approaches exist for developing and selecting indicators, based on available data and existing information. In general, indicators should act as feedback mechanisms for managers, connecting activities to objectives, strategic goals and ultimately the entity's mission (Zewo, 2011). Indicators can vary in their policy application. For instance, the purpose of some indicators can be to monitor progress or goals (e.g. performance indicators), while others may serve to raise awareness, but are not useful for monitoring, such as certain composite indicators. This chapter focuses largely on indicators for measuring performance as part of results-based M&E.

Performance indicators can be quantitative or qualitative variables that offer a reliable way to measure progress or achievement of an outcome (Kusek, 2004). When developing performance indicators, managers should focus on the usefulness of the indicators for achieving outcomes. Indicators should be a simple and reliable means to measure achievement, reflecting the changes connected to a policy or programme, or helping to assess their performance. They specify what is to be measured along a scale, determining how expected results are measured and what data are collected. Using similar indicators over a period of time also provides consistent measurement over time (Sterck, M et al, 2006). The table below provides examples of indicators based on the results-based M&E logic model.

Table 5.4. **Types of performance measures**

	Types	Measures
Performance Measures	Input measures	What goes into the system? Which resources are used?
	Output measures	What products and services are delivered? What is the quality of these products and services?
	Outcomes measures	Intermediate: What are the direct consequences of the output?
		Final: What are the outcomes achieved that are significantly attributable to the output?
	Contextual measures	What are the contextual factors that influence the output (e.g. processes, antecedents and external developments)
Ratio Indicators	Efficiency	Cost / Output
	Productivity	Output / Input
	Effectiveness	Output / Outcome (intermediate or final)
	Cost-effectiveness	Input / Outcome (intermediate or final)

Source: Adapted from Sterck, M. and B. Scheers (2006), "Trends in Performance Budgeting in Seven OECD Countries", Public Performance and Management Review, 30(1), September, pp. 47-72, *https://www.jstor.org/stable/pdf/20447616.pdf.*

In the absence of indicators, it is impossible for governments to not only know what needs to be improved, but also what is working. However, too many indicators can lead to data saturation. Avoiding information overload is critical for the effectiveness of M&E and the use of indicators. Too much performance-related information can strain resources and create challenges in distinguishing the initiatives that work from those that do not, ultimately resulting in evaluation processes that are ineffective or costly. Moreover, excessive evaluation processes or indicators can lead to evaluations that managers see as an administrative burden. In turn, this can undermine a results-oriented culture that is conducive to producing reliable, timely and accessible evidence.

As discussed, indicators in Brazil are closely tied to the budgeting process and evaluations linked to the PPA. A 2015 audit by TCU noted indicators used in relation to M&E of PPA objectives are ineffective, and some objectives lack indicators and annual targets, among other issues (TCU, 2016b). Such challenges are not unique to Brazil. Many governments face challenges in developing performance information of sufficient quality, robustness and reliability to serve as a sound basis for informing resource-allocation decisions (OECD, 2016a). One challenge is that measuring change, whether linked to the budgetary process or for broader M&E of programme performance, involves not only decisions about *what* to measure, but also *how* to measure. Identification of selection of indicators is a key component of the latter. It is critical for managers at this level to understand what constitutes sound indicators that underscore quality performance information.

As noted by TCU's own work, managers can often struggle to produce quality performance information, since indicators and targets may be lacking altogether. Further, TCU's 2010 Performance Audit Manual elaborates on challenges managers may face in creating performance information, including inadequate or unreliable information systems as well as the difficulty in linking outcomes to specific policies or actions (TCU, 2010a). The manual offers general considerations for assessing the quality of indicators. Box 5.2 provides additional considerations and good practices, which TCU can focus on when assessing such elements in its audits (OECD, 2008).

TCU's work can reinforce and build on the guidance provided by the MP by focusing on key practices for ensuring that M&E results in high-quality, reliable performance information. Moreover, the MP's guidance as well as related laws do not require entities to consider the policy effects in the medium or long-term.[5] TCU's audits can aim to improve the quality of performance information, particularly indicators, so that information produced during M&E is reliable and useful for assessing intermediate and final outcomes and impacts. Looking ahead, the SDGs can provide TCU with indicators against which it can assess government results, where indicators are currently lacking. It is important that TCU take care not to fill the role that government must play in establishing indicators, as well as M&E. However, TCU could assess the reliability of indicators and data that the executive branch produces, and as noted, the formulation of the policies and processes aimed at facilitating the realisation of national goals and the SDGs. Doing so would be aligned with the 2017-2022 strategic plan of INTOSAI, which sets priorities for SAIs to monitor and evaluate the achievement of the SDGs in the 2030 agenda.

Box 5.2. **Good Practices for Developing Indicators**

In Brazil, the PPA provides high-level guidance on indicators. In addition, the MP has developed guidance to assist managers in thinking about developing indicators for measuring performance. Managers can consider the following concepts and practices for developing indicators.

- **Invest time in the process of choosing indicators and targets.** Reflect on all the options available to measure each result and refine targets and indicator sets over time as the programme, the understanding of partners, and the availability of information change.
- **Identify appropriate indicators at outcome level.** Ensure that the programme does not only monitor outputs and that there is sufficient emphasis on changes at outcome level.

Box 5.2. Good Practices for Developing Indicators *(cont.)*

- **Minimise perverse incentives.** Remember that "what gets measured gets done". Choosing to measure one indicator may mean that the programme de-prioritises other important actions and results. Routine measurement of certain indicators can have perverse results. For example, measuring the time taken to process applications for grants can make government employees process the applications faster, but at the cost of due diligence processes.
- **Use multiple indicators or "baskets" of indicators to measure results at higher-level outcome and impact levels.** A balanced set of indicators that measure different aspects and that may combine quantitative and qualitative measures is more likely to cancel out biases.
- **Use a mix of quantitative and qualitative methods to measure indicators. Quantitative indicators are often easier to collect and measure.** However, quantitative indicators often do not give the full picture, and not every change that is important can easily be expressed in numerical format. Qualitative indicators could be more appropriate in certain circumstances.
- **Ensure that indicators and targets reflect the needs and participation of various groups.** For instance, consider how to measure changes that are relevant to the poor and the vulnerable, especially by disaggregating data and checking for measurement biases for/against certain groups.
- **Avoid conflating indicators with targets.** Targets are the change(s) that the programme wishes to achieve. Indicators are pieces of information that are used to measure change and performance, and can thus indicate whether this target has been reached

Indicator and Target Measured Together	Indicator and Target Separated
Number of government managers trained in M&E increases by 500 in 2018	Indicator: Number of managers trained Baseline: 1,000 trained in 2017 Target: 1,500 trained in 2018
⊘	✓

- **Make indicators gender-sensitive.** Measure whether men and women are equally participating in the programme activities, and insist on sex- and age-disaggregated data whenever feasible.
- **Promote partnership, inclusion and ownership in setting and using indicators and targets.** Wherever possible, indicators and targets should be agreed jointly between the partner government and the international supporting organisations, and ideally with the participation of other local stakeholders and beneficiaries (this may include organisations that represent specific communities, such as women's organisations, religious leaders, disability rights groups, etc).
- **Choose indicators that can be measured.** When identifying indicators, consider whether this information is already available, and if not, how easy it will be to collect it given the context and the resources that are available.
- **Test indicators.** Test indicators to make sure they are valid and appropriate measures of the result you want to achieve.
- **Keep it simple.** Try to measure what is most important and do it as simply and cheaply as possible. Wherever possible, use information that is already available and that is routinely collected. Build on existing information systems, particularly those of national institutions.

Source: OECD (2008), *The OECD DAC Handbook on Security System Reform: Supporting Security and Justice*, OECD Publishing, Paris. *http://dx.doi.org/10.1787/9789264027862-en*

5.5. Strengthening cross-cutting government policies and programmes through improved data sharing, communication and coordination

TCU could assess the communication and coordination mechanisms, including interoperability of information and data systems, to improve M&E of cross-cutting government policies and programmes.

To aid in M&E, the Brazilian government has developed a plethora of national information and data management systems. For instance, in 2001, Brazil launched the Management and Planning Information System (Sistema de Informações Gerenciais e de Planejamento, SIGPLAN) to organise information and data for the government's annual evaluation report. Other systems currently exist that focus on specific issues and sectors, and are maintained by individual ministries. They include the Integrated Planning and Budget System (Sistema Integrado de Planejamento e Orçamento, SIOP), which replaced SIGPLAN, and the Ministry of Education's Integrated Monitoring, Execution and Control System (Sistema Integrado de Monitoramento, Execução e Controle, SIMEC). Other ministries, such as the Ministry of Health and the Ministry of Social and Agrarian Development, have their own indicators and mechanisms for monitoring performance of activities under their purview and within their relevant sectors.

In Brazil, M&E public policies and mechanisms vary not only by sector, but also by states at the subnational level. As discussed, the government may also contract out evaluation efforts to academics and M&E experts. Decentralised M&E allows for customisation and tailoring of individual approaches, indicators and other performance information to specific sectors and issues, but such variation can also pose challenges from a broader governance perspective. For example, decentralised performance information can be difficult to synthesise as inputs to government-wide achievement of outcomes. This can reflect a capacity or expertise issue, but it also can be a function of numerous systems designed for different purposes, indicators and of varying quality. For instance, the Ministry of Health has a Department of Monitoring and Evaluation that established its own key indicators to monitor programmes and measure the quality of Brazil's health sys-tems. The Ministry of Education, as noted, has a different framework with its own indicators. Moreover, the variety of data management systems within the Brazilian government has historically created challenges related to interoperability. For example, some systems for sectoral information and data (e.g. The Ministry of Health and the Ministry of Education) have mechanisms that are more sophisticated, detailed and accurate than others, which can exacerbate interoperability challenges (Vaitsman, 2013).

Mechanisms for communication and coordination are essential in a decentralised M&E system. As discussed, there is a policy element that drives coordination and alignment between M&E initiatives. In addition, a key issue for facilitating communication and information sharing are the systems individual entities create to manage results and data for assessing achievement towards goals. These individual systems vary in the way they manage data and as a result evaluation is not homogeneous across government, making evaluation of crosscutting initiatives and programmes difficult. As such, it is important to improve communication, compatibility and interoperability between these systems. Although there are a number of definitions for interoperability, this report contends interoperability is the ability of ICT systems to communicate, interpret and interchange data in a meaningful way through processes where independent or heterogeneous information systems or their components managed by different jurisdictions/administrations work together in predefined and agreed terms and specifications. Interoperability enhances effectiveness, efficiency and responsiveness in government and is thus an important component of decentralised M&E systems.

In Brazil, there is already an initiative to enhance interoperability in government. The ePing is a basic framework for electronic government interoperability standards. It is overseen by the Logistics and Information Technology Secretariat (SLTI) of the Ministry of Planning, Development and Management (*Ministério do Planejamento, Desenvolvimento e Gestão*, MP). The framework is originally intended for the Executive branch of the federal government, but does not restrict voluntary participation by other branches and levels of government. For federal agencies in the Brazilian Executive, however, adoption of standards and policies contained in the ePing is mandatory (SLTI/MP n° 92) (Government of Brazil, 2014).

The ePing's architecture covers the exchange of information between federal Executive branch agencies and their interactions with citizens, other levels of government and other branches of government. The interoperability framework includes architectural standards and guidelines to help integrate processes, applications, data, security, and networks. Implementation of ePing is gradual and decentralised. All of the federal government's Executive branch purchases and hiring related to the development of electronic government must be consistent with the ePing specifications and policies. Further, the focus of ePing will be only specifications that are relevant to ensure interconnectivity of systems, integration of data, access to electronic government service and content management.

In the past, TCU has evaluated the government electronic programme. The government electronic programme, which developed e-Ping, began in 2000 in order to increase the supply and improve the quality of public services and information provided through electronic means (TCU 2006). In 2006 then, TCU evaluated the government electronic programme with the audit scope defined as 'In what way have the Program actions contributed toward the provision of electronic public services directly to citizens?' Since 2006, however, there has not been another evaluation either on the government electronic programme or e-Ping specifically.

TCU has assessed digital governance from different angles. For example, at the beginning of the 2015-2017 External Control Plan (TCU, 2015d), TCU launched an audit to «evaluate the use of digital technologies in the provision of public services», or better known as «digital government audit» (TC 010.638 / 2016-4). TCU has audited the performance of Logistics and Information Technology Secretariat (SLTI) of the Ministry of Planning, Development and Management (*Ministério do Planejamento, Desenvolvimento e Gestão*, MP (STLI / MP) as the central overseer of IT. Its performance has been followed since 2007, when the first IT Governance Survey of the federal agencies was launched. The findings of each survey are presented in reports of the IT governance panorama at federal level, along with accompanying determinations and recommendations to the STLI / MP (TCU, 2014d; 2014c; 2012a; 2010b; 2008). In 2017, STLI / MP will present an individual year-end report, leaving potential for it to become part of the the annual accounts process and thus of TCU's year-end audit of the Consolidated Government Accounts.

Good governance principles emphasise the importance of mechanisms for transparency and openness in the flow of performance information, as well as the existence of fair and transparent systems for legislative and judicial review of the functioning of public administration (OECD 2016a). Moreover, adopting a government-wide strategy for public sector data based on these principles, among others, should be a priority to strengthen co-ordination, exploit synergies and create a shared view of open data within and across levels of government (OECD 2015a). In a recent survey, OECD found identified a number of SAIS that have activities to oversee mechanisms for transparency and the flow of performance information. For instance, in an OECD survey of 10 peer SAIs:

- 9 of 10 had looked at the existence of clear lines of reporting on outputs and performance outcomes from entities to authorities and to users/stakeholders (including citizens).
- 6 of 10 had looked at the accessibility and reliability of data systems for collecting, storing and using performance information, accessible for various levels of government.
- 8 of 10 SAIs had looked at mechanisms for effective information sharing and transparency: between levels of government; within entities; and across entities.

In alignment with peer SAIs and building on past efforts, TCU could further assess communication and co-ordination mechanisms with government-wide implications, and to strengthen M&E, the design of policies and the execution of programmes. One way TCU could do this is to assess the interoperability of data sharing systems. For instance, TCU could assess the progress and effectiveness of e-Ping across government to improve to cross cutting policy evaluation. Given interoperability of government has not been assessed since 2006 and progress of implementation of ePing has never been evaluated, TCU can begin an audit on this government programme. Alternatively, the agency in charge of coordinating e-government and e-Ping is the Logistics and Information Technology Secretariat (SLTI) of the Ministry of Planning, Budget and Management (TCU 2006). This agency is responsible for consolidating e-government standards, implementing the National e-government plan and disseminating e-government actions. Through auditing this agency specifically, it would also be possible to evaluate the progress of e-Ping.

Finally, because e-Ping is implemented in a decentralised fashion, TCU could assess compliance and implementation of e-Ping on an agency by agency basis. In addition, to advance the goal of improved co-ordination and sharing of data, TCU could select specific programs that have this goal in mind in order to provide targeted recommendations that affect multiple entities, sectors or levels of government (see Box 5.3 below for an example of such a project).

Box 5.3. **Transversal project on managing geospatial data at the federal, state, district and municipal levels**

The Ministry of Planning has co-ordinated, since its inception in 2008, a transversal project aimed at the National Spatial Data Infrastructure - INDE was established by Decree No. 6,666, of November 27, 2008, as the integrated set of technologies; Policies; Mechanisms and procedures for coordination and monitoring; Standards, and agreements necessary to facilitate and order the generation, storage, access, sharing, dissemination, and use of geospatial data of federal, state, district, and municipal origin.

Currently, INDE has been constituted as a management tool capable of supporting the monitoring and evaluation of public policies, above all, with the possibility of capturing its impact on the territory. It allows the processing of multisectoral information of different natures, thus enabling the extraction of more complete and accurate information, more quickly.

Box 5.3. **Transversal project on managing geospatial data at the federal, state, district and municipal levels** *(cont.)*

The platform aims to gather the geospatial data produced by government agencies in a single internet portal, allowing the rational use of geographic information and the dissemination of a culture of visualization of public policies in the territory. In this sense, INDE is born with the purpose of becoming the reference source of public and open geospatial data, capable of democratizing access to information, facilitating access by citizens, society and various public sector bodies.

Goals

1. Promote adequate planning in the generation, storage, access, sharing, dissemination and use of geospatial data;
2. To promote the use, in the production of the geospatial data by the public organs of the federal, state, district and municipal spheres, of the standards and norms approved by the National Commission of Cartography - CONCAR; and
3. Avoid duplication of actions and waste of resources in obtaining geospatial data, by disseminating the documentation (metadata) of the data available in the entities and in the public agencies of the federal, state, district and municipal levels.

Source: MP (Ministry of Planning, Development and Management) (2016d), *Infraestrutura Nacional de Dados Espaciais (INDE)*, [National Spatial Data Infrastructure] *http://www.planejamento.gov.br/assuntos/planejamento-e-investimentos/inde*

Notes

1. Noting Law 11,784, this report refers only to the performance evaluation of the entities of public administration, not to the evaluation of public servants.
2. Brazil's external auditor and Supreme Audit Institution (SAI), the Tribunal de Contas da União (TCU), and other international bodies including the OECD have promoted improved capacity for generating and using high quality results and performance information.
3. With reference to Law 11,784 of September 22, 2008 (Government of Brazil, 2008b), and Decree 7,133 of 19 March 2010 (Chamber of Deputies, 2010).
4. The website of the MP lists the bimonthly reports and reports issued every quarter, for each year since 2004. They are available here: *http://www.planejamento.gov.br/assuntos/orcamento/informacoes-orcamentarias/rel-de-avaliacao-fiscal-e-cumprimento-de-meta/relatorios-de-avaliacao-fiscal-e-cumprimento-de*
5. Relevant to Law 11,784, Chapter II (capitulo II), on evaluation of performance *http://www.planalto.gov.br/ccivil_03/_Ato2007-2010/2008/Lei/L11784.htm*; and to decreto nº 7.133, de 19 de março de 2010, which outlines the general criteria and procuedures to be followed for individual and institutional performance reviews and subsequent payment of bonuses, *http://www.planalto.gov.br/ccivil_03/_Ato2007-2010/2010/Decreto/D7133.htm*.

References

Bertelsmann Stiftung (2016a), Brazil: country report, Transformation Index 2016, *https://www.bti-project.org/fileadmin/files/BTI/Downloads/Reports/2016/pdf/BTI_2016_Brazil.pdf*

Bertelsmann Stiftung (2016b), Transformation Index of the Bertelsmann Stiftung 2016: Codebook for Country Assessments, *https://www.bti-project.org/fileadmin/files/BTI/Downloads/Zusaetzliche_Downloads/Codebuch_BTI_2016.pdf*

Chamber of Deputies of Brazil (2010), Decree number 7,133 of 19 March, 2010 (DECRETO Nº 7.133, DE 19 DE MARÇO DE 2010), *http://www2.camara.leg.br/legin/fed/decret/2010/decreto-7133-19-marco-2010-604126-normaatualizada-pe.pdf*

Government Accountability Office (GAO) (2014), Managing for Results: 2013 Federal Managers Survey on Organizational Performance and Management Issues (GAO-13-519SP, June 2013), an E-supplement to GAO-13-518, accessed February 2017, *http://www.gao.gov/special.pubs/gao-13-519sp/index.htm*

Government of Brazil (2014), SLTI/MP nº 92, *http://www.lex.com.br/legis_26329840_PORTARIA_N_92_DE_24_DE_DEZEMBRO_DE_2014.aspx*

Government of Brazil (2008a), Decree number 6.601, DECRETO Nº 6.601, DE 10 DE OUTUBRO DE 2008, accessed February 2017, *http://www.planalto.gov.br/ccivil_03/_Ato2007-2010/2008/Decreto/D6601.htm*

Government of Brazil (2008b), LEI Nº 11.784, DE 22 DE SETEMBRO DE 2008 (Law number 11.874 of 22 September 2008, *http://www.planalto.gov.br/ccivil_03/_ato2007-2010/2008/lei/l11784.htm*

Government of Brazil (2001), Law No 10.180, LEI No 10.180, DE 6 DE FEVEREIRO DE 2001, accessed February 2017, *http://www.planalto.gov.br/ccivil_03/leis/LEIS_2001/L10180.htm.*

IADB (Inter-American Development Bank) (2014), Governing to Deliver, Accessed September 2016, *https://publications.iadb.org/bitstream/handle/11319/6674/Governing-to-Deliver-Reinventing-the-Center-of-Government-in-Latin-America-and-the-Caribbean.pdf?sequence=1*

Institute for Applied Economic Research (IPEA) (2015), Planning and Evaluation of Public Policies, *http://www.ipea.gov.br/agencia/images/stories/PDFs/livros/livros/livro_ppa_vol_1_web.pdf*

Kusek, J., and Rist, R., 2004, 'Ten Steps to a Results-based Monitoring and Evaluation System', World Bank, Washington, D.C., accessed February 2017, *https://openknowledge.worldbank.org/bitstream/handle/10986/14926/296720PAPER0100steps.pdf*

MP (Ministry of Planning, Development and Management) (2016a), "Government institutes Committee to monitor and evaluate public policies", Ministry of Planning, Development and Management, accessed February 2017, *http://www.planejamento.gov.br/noticias/governo-institui-comite-para-monitorar-e-avaliar-politicas-publicas*

MP (2016b), "Interministerial Committee discusses public policies and evaluates effectiveness of actions", Ministry of Planning, Development and Management, accessed February 2017, *http://www.planejamento.gov.br/noticias/comite-interministerial-discute-politicas-publicas-e-avalia-efetividade-de-acoes.*

MP (2016c), National Press (Impresa Nacional), Ministry of Planning, Development and Management, (now *http://pesquisa.in.gov.br/imprensa/jsp/visualiza/index.jsp?data=08/04/2016&jornal=1&pagina=79&totalArquivos=204;*

MP (2016d), Infraestrutura Nacional de Dados Espaciais (INDE), [National Spatial Data Infrastructure] *http://www.planejamento.gov.br/assuntos/planejamento-e-investimentos/inde*

MP (2013), Manual de Orientação para a Gestão do Desempenho [Guidance Manual for Performance Management], Secretaria de Gestão Pública [Secretary for Public Management] *http://www.planejamento.gov.br/assuntos/gestao-publica/arquivos-e-publicacoes/manual_orientacao_para_gestao_desempenho.pdf/@@download/file/Manual_Orientacao_para_Gestao_Desempenho.pdf*

NAO (National Audit Office of the United Kingdom) (2014), 'The centre of government' HC 171, Session 2014-15, 19 June 2014, *https://www.nao.org.uk/wp-content/uploads/2014/06/The-centre-of-government.pdf*

OAG (Office of the Auditor General of Canada) (2013), Spring 2013 Report, Status Report on Evaluating the Effectiveness of Programs, accessed February 2017, *www.oag-bvg.gc.ca/internet/English/parl_oag_201304_01_e_38186.html.*

OAG (2009), Fall 2009 Report, Chapter 1, Evaluating the Effectiveness of Programs, accessed February 2017, *www.oag-bvg.gc.ca/internet/English/parl_oag_200911_01_e_33202.html*

OECD (2016a), Supreme Audit Institution and Good Governance: Oversight, Insight and Foresight, OECD Publishers, Paris, *http://www.oecd.org/gov/ethics/supreme-audit-institutions-and-good-governance.htm*

OECD (2015), Session Notes, OECD's Public Governance Ministerial Meeting, 28 October 2015, *http://www.oecd.org/governance/ministerial/session-notes-helsinki.pdf*

OECD (2015a), «Governments leading by example with public sector data», in *Data-Driven Innovation: Big Data for Growth and Well-Being*, OECD Publishing, Paris. *http://dx.doi.org/10.1787/9789264229358-14-en*

OECD (2014a) 'Centre Stage: Driving Better Policies from the Centre of Government' OECD Publishing, Paris, *https://www.oecd.org/gov/Centre-Stage-Report.pdf*

OECD (2008), *The OECD DAC Handbook on Security System Reform: Supporting Security and Justice*, OECD Publishing, Paris. *http://dx.doi.org/10.1787/9789264027862-en*

OECD (2002), Glossary of Key Terms in Evaluation and Results Based Management, OECD, Paris, accessed February 2017, *https://www.oecd.org/dac/evaluation/2754804.pdf*

Rede Brasileira (2016), accessed September 2016, *http://redebrasileirademea.ning.com.*

Rosenstein, B. (2015), Status of National Evaluation Policies. Global Mapping Report. 2nd Edition, Implemented by Parliamentarians Forum on Development Evaluation in South Asia jointly with EvalPartners, *http://www.iape.org.il/Upload/Members_Uploads/17_385652.pdf.*

Sterck, M. and B. Scheers (2006), "Trends in Performance Budgeting in Seven OECD Countries", Public Performance and Management Review, 30(1), September, pp. 47-72, *https://www.jstor.org/stable/pdf/20447616.pdf.*

TCU (2016a) Framework for Evaluation of the Centre of Government TCU Publishing, Brasilia, *http://portal.tcu.gov.br/lumis/portal/file/fileDownload.jsp?fileId=8A8182A25454C5A801545DC1433145ED*

TCU (2016b), TCU Judgement 033.142/2015-7 Survey Report, *http://bibspi.planejamento.gov.br/bitstream/handle/iditem/700/Acordao_TCU_948_2016.pdf?sequence=1*

TCU (2015a), Plano Estratégico do Tribunal de Contas da União para o período 2015-2021, [TCU Strategic Plan, 2015-2021], PORTARIA-TCU N° 141, DE 1° DE ABRIL DE 2015, Brasilia, *http://portal.tcu.gov.br/tcu/paginas/planejamento/2021/index.html.*

TCU (2015b), Agências reguladoras de infraestrutura: avaliação da governança da regulação, [operational audit. infrastructure regulatory agencies. evaluation of regulatory governance], TCU Judgement 240/2015 – Plenary, Performance Audit, TC 031.996/2013-2, *http://www.tcu.gov.br/Consultas/Juris/Docs/judoc/Acord/20150304/AC_0240_05_15_P.doc*

TCU (2015c), TCU Judgement 0548/2015, Acordo TC-020.137/2014-1 – Plenary, Performance Audit *http://www.tcu.gov.br/Consultas/Juris/Docs/judoc/Acord/20150320/AC_0548_09_15_P.doc*

TCU (2015d), External Control Plan of Brazil's Federal Court of Accounts (Plano de Contrôle Externo do Tribunal de Contas da União) April, 2015, Brasilia, *http://portal.tcu.gov.br/lumis/portal/file/fileDownload.jsp?fileId=8A8182A153234E0A01535D1006D60567.*

TCU (2014a), Framework to Assess Governance in Public Policies, TCU Publishing, Brasilia, *http://portal2.tcu.gov.br/portal/pls/portal/docs/2686056.PDF*

TCU (2014b), Evaluation of the Maturity Index used for evaluation of government's programs in the direct administration of the Federal Executive, TCU Judgement 1209/2014 – Plenary – Survey report *http://www.tcu.gov.br/Consultas/Juris/Docs/judoc/Acord/20140516/AC_1209_16_14_P.doc*

TCU (2014c), Relatório de levantamento. avaliação da governança de tecnologia da informação na administração pública federal [Evaluation of information technology governance in the federal public administration], Acordao 3117/2014, Processo TC 003.732/2014-2, *http://portal.tcu.gov.br/lumis/portal/file/fileDownload.jsp?fileId=8A8182A14D78C1F1014D794C57073235*

TCU (2014d) Diversos órgãos e entidades da Administração Pública Federal com vistas a avaliar a implementação dos controles de TI informados em resposta ao levantamento do perfil de governança de TI de 2012 [consolidation of audits carried out in various organs and entities of the Federal Public Administration with a view to evaluating the implementation of the IT controls informed in response to the survey of the 2012 IT governance profile] ACÓRDÃO N° 3051/2014, Processo n° TC 023.050/2013-6, *http://www.tcu.gov.br/Consultas/Juris/Docs/judoc/Acord/20141107/AC_3051_44_14_P.doc*

TCU (2013), Avaliação do perfil e do índice de maturidade dos sistemas de avaliação de programas governamentais dos órgãos da administração direta do poder executivo federal [Evaluation of profile and the maturity index of the evaluation of governmental programs of the organs direct administration of the federal executive power], Judgement TC 007.590/2013-0, Accessed February 2017, *http://portal.tcu.gov.br/lumis/portal/file/fileDownload.jsp?inline=1&fileId=8A8182A14D92792C014D92800B323307*

TCU (2012a), Avaliação da governança de tecnologia da informação na administração pública federal. oportunidades de melhoria [Evaluation of governance of IT in the Federal Public Administration: opportunities for improvement], Acórdão N°2585/2012, Processo n° TC 007.887/2012-4, *https://www.capes.gov.br/images/stories/download/editais/resultados/11102016_TCU_RelatorioFinal_2012.pdf*

TCU (2012b), Avaliar se a gestão e o uso da tecnologia da informação estão de acordo com a legislação e aderentes às boas práticas de governança de TI [Evaluation of whether the management and use of information technology is in accordance with legislation and adhering to good IT governance practices], Acórdão N° 1233/2012, Processo n° TC 011.772/2010-7, *http://www.ifam.edu.br/portal/images/file/0000029368-Acord+%C3%BAo%201233_2012_TCU-Plenario.pdf*

TCU (2011), Identified Evaluation Systems in Sectoral Bodies, TCU Judgment 2781/2011– Plenary – Survey Report, TC-032.287/2010-0, *http://www.tcu.gov.br/Consultas/Juris/Docs/judoc/Acord/20111031/AC_2781_43_11_P.doc*

TCU (2010a), Performance Audit Manual, TCU: Brazilian Court of Audit, Brasilia, *http://psc-intosai.org/data/files/21/60/D0/A0/81B07510C0EA0E65CA5818A8/tcu_performance_audit_manual.pdf*

TCU (2010b), levantamento destinado a avaliar governança de tecnologia da informação no âmbito da administração pública federal [Evaluation of information technology in the Federal Government], Acórdão N° 2308/2010, Processo TC 000.390/2010-0, *http://www.ticontrole.gov.br/lumis/portal/file/fileDownload.jsp?fileId=8A8182A24D7BC0B4014D8C4BF55573F5*

TCU (2008), Situation of Information Technology in Government, AcórdãoAC-1603-32/08-P, Processo 008.380/2007-1, *https://contas.tcu.gov.br/juris/SvlHighLight?key=41434f5244414f2d434f4d504c45544f2d3430323639&sort=RELEVANCIA&ordem=DESC&bases=ACORDAO-COMPLETO;&highlight=&posicaoDocumento=0&numDocumento=1&totalDocumentos=1*

TCU (2006), Evaluation of the Government's Electronic Programme [Acórdão N.° 1386/2006 – Plenário], accessed February 2017, *http://portal.tcu.gov.br/lumis/portal/file/fileDownload.jsp?inline=1&fileId=8A8182A14D92792C014D928268E24B27*

Vaitsman, J. et al (2013) Policy Analysis in Brazil, Policy Press at the University of Briston, Bristol, *http://dx.doi.org/10.1080/13876988.2015.1110962.*

Veja (2016), "Government scans social area to prevent fraud" (Governo faz varredura na área social para evitar fraudes), Veja, accessed online, January 2017, *http://veja.abril.com.br/economia/governo-faz-varredura-na-area-social-para-evitar-fraudes/*

World Bank (2006), Towards the Institutionalisation of Monitoring and Evaluation in Latin American and the Caribbean: Proceedings of a World Bank, Inter-American Development Bank Conference, Editors May E., et al., *http://documents.worldbank.org/curated/en/524591468225577264/pdf/362230ENGLISH010monitoring01PUBLIC1.pdf*

Zewo Foundation (2011), Outcome and Impact Assessment in International Development: Short presentation of the Zewo guidelines for projects and programmes, Stiftung Zewo, *http://impact.zewo.ch/english/docs/Zewo_Wirkungsmessung_E_web.pdf*

Glossary

Administrative burden The Index for Public Integrity considers administrative burden a measures of the extent of domestic bureaucratic regulations. The component is constructed based on the average numbers of procedures and time it takes to start a business and pay corporate taxes (IPI 2016).

Budgetary Governance "Budgetary governance" refers to the processes, laws, structures and institutions in place for ensuring that the budgeting system meets its objectives in an effective, sustainable and enduring manner (OECD, 2015)

Budget Circular A budget circular is a document/memorandum issued by the central budget authority to guide line ministries/agencies in the formulation of their initial budget proposals/budget estimates. A budget circular, for instance, may contain information or guidance on automatic productivity cuts, medium-term or annual expenditure ceilings, etc. (OECD 2015)

Budgetary Governance "Budgetary governance" refers to the processes, laws, structures and institutions in place for ensuring that the budgeting system meets its objectives in an effective, sustainable and enduring manner (OECD, 2015)

Carry over funds (*Restos a pagar*) Brazil is one of the only countries in Latin America which allows line ministries to carry over unused funds without thresholds for both operational and investment expenditure (OECD 2014)

Central Budget Authority "Central Budget Authority" refers to the ministry, institution or department of the executive (or combination of such bodies) that is or are responsible for the preparation of the annual public budget and its associated multi-annual processes.

Centre of Government The Centre of Government (CoG) is the administrative structure that serves the Executive (President or Prime Minister, and the Cabinet collectively). Often the Centre is made up of more than one unit, fulfilling different functions. For the purposes of this report, the CoG includes other core institutions at the "Centre" that directly support whole-of-government functioning, and usually exercise some oversight of ministries' activities (OECD, 2015).

Debt rules Debt rules limit the amount of government debt that can be accumulated and can be expressed in nominal terms as a debt-to-GDP ratio or as an explicit reduction of the debt-to-GDP ratio

Expenditure rules	Expenditure rules limit the amount of government spending and can be expressed in nominal or real terms as limits on spending levels or expenditure growth, or as an expenditure-to-GDP ratio
External audit of the consolidated year-end government report (CPR)	This report is a core element of the federal government's financial reporting framework, which aims to support fiscal sustainability, achieve cost-effective service delivery and enhance fiscal legitimacy. The PCPR contains information on: the federal government's financial performance; compliance with budgetary laws; non-financial information about service delivery; and information about key factors underlying financial and non-financial performance. The audit of the report is TCU's greatest means for assessing adherence to the budget (OECD 2013).
External Control Unit	External Control Units refer to the units that conduct ex post audit assignments.
Fiscal Rules	A permanent constraint on fiscal policy expressed in terms of a summary indicator of fiscal performance (Kopits and Symansky, 1998)
Good Governance	Public governance is the institutional arrangements and processes which develop, implement and deliver policies, programmes and services to benefit citizens and society. Good governance then is the optimisation of those processes and institutional arrangements to maximise benefits to society. It is the assurance that the mechanisms driving the policy cycle in formulation, implementation, and monitoring and evaluation are operating effectively, efficiently and economically and with integrity
Independent Fiscal Institution (IFI)	A unit typically referred to as fiscal councils, although the definition sometimes also includes Parliamentary Budget Offices. The role, structure and funding model of these bodies vary considerably across countries.
Long-term Fiscal Responsibility	The ability of governments to maintain public finances at a credible and serviceable position over the long run, in light of the prevailing mix of spending and revenue policies.
Medium-term expenditure framework (MTEF)	Medium-term expenditure fiscal frameworks (MTFFs) and expenditure frameworks (MTEFs) strengthen the ability to plan and enforce a sustainable fiscal path that forces stakeholders to deal with the medium-term perspective of budgeting and budgetary policies rather than adopt an exclusively year-by-year approach. MTEFs typically cover a period of three to four years.
Monitoring and Evaluation (M&E)	M&E is the systematic collection of evidence on the outcomes of policies and programmes in order to judge their relevance, performance and potential alternatives.[1] M&E a management tool for making informed choices about current and future policies and programmes. *Monitoring* can be seen as systematic, ongoing collection of data on specified indicators that provide management, and other stakeholders, with an idea on progress towards objectives. *Evaluation* is a systematic and objective assessment of an on-going or completed project, programme or policy, including its design, implementation and results.

Operational audit	Performance audit
Performance Budgeting	Various approaches which reflect governments' efforts to focus on the results achieved with the appropriations allocated.
Policy Coherence	Government-wide policy coherence is the quality of having unified and consistent public policies and programmes.
Priority spending	In accordance with the constitution of 1988, roughly 35% of the budget is 'priority spending,' which is set by the LDO and are exempt from cuts (OECD 2003)
Sound fiscal policy	"Sound fiscal policy" is one which avoids the build-up of large, unsustainable debts, and which uses favourable economic times to build up resilience and buffers against more difficult times, so that the needs of citizens and stakeholders can be addressed in an effective and enduring manner.
Sustainable Development Goals	The Sustainable Development Goals are a UN Initiative.The Sustainable Development Goals(SDGs), officially known as Transforming our world: the 2030 Agenda for Sustainable Development is a set of seventeen aspirational «Global Goals» with 169 targets between them
Three lines of assurance model of internal control	Three lines of assurance model for internal control consist of a line at the operational level, a second independent from delivery units, as well as an independent internal audit function (OECD 2013)

Note

1. Noting Law 11,784, this report refers only to the performance evaluation of the entities of public administration, not to the evaluation of public servants.

ORGANISATION FOR ECONOMIC CO-OPERATION AND DEVELOPMENT

The OECD is a unique forum where governments work together to address the economic, social and environmental challenges of globalisation. The OECD is also at the forefront of efforts to understand and to help governments respond to new developments and concerns, such as corporate governance, the information economy and the challenges of an ageing population. The Organisation provides a setting where governments can compare policy experiences, seek answers to common problems, identify good practice and work to co-ordinate domestic and international policies.

The OECD member countries are: Australia, Austria, Belgium, Canada, Chile, the Czech Republic, Denmark, Estonia, Finland, France, Germany, Greece, Hungary, Iceland, Ireland, Israel, Italy, Japan, Korea, Latvia, Luxembourg, Mexico, the Netherlands, New Zealand, Norway, Poland, Portugal, the Slovak Republic, Slovenia, Spain, Sweden, Switzerland, Turkey, the United Kingdom and the United States. The European Union takes part in the work of the OECD.

OECD Publishing disseminates widely the results of the Organisation's statistics gathering and research on economic, social and environmental issues, as well as the conventions, guidelines and standards agreed by its members.

OECD PUBLISHING, 2, rue André-Pascal, 75775 PARIS CEDEX16
(04 2017 08 1P) ISBN 978-92-64-27923-0 – 2017

www.ingramcontent.com/pod-product-compliance
Lightning Source LLC
Chambersburg PA
CBHW061216240926
51846CB00006B/1250
9789264279230